D0362420

The American History Series

SERIES EDITORS
John Hope Franklin, *Duke University*
Abraham S. Eisenstadt, *Brooklyn College*

Arthur S. Link
Princeton University
GENERAL EDITOR FOR HISTORY

Raymond A. Mohl

FLORIDA ATLANTIC UNIVERSITY

The New City

Urban America in the Industrial Age, 1860–1920

HARLAN DAVIDSON, INC.

ARLINGTON HEIGHTS, ILLINOIS 60004

Library of Congress Cataloging-in-Publication Data

Mohl, Raymond A.
  The new city.

  (The American history series)
  Bibliography: p.
  Includes index.
    1. Cities and towns—United States—History.
2. United States—Social conditions—1865–1918.
3. United States—Industries—History. 4. Municipal
government—United States—History. 5. City planning—
United States—History. I. Title. II. Series: American
history series (Harlan Davidson, Inc.)
HT123.M58   1985   307.7′64′0973   84-21417
ISBN 0-88295-830-5

Cover design: Roger Eggers. Cover illustration: Chicago Historical Society, Frank M. Hallenbeck photo, "Dearborn Street traffic jam, looking south from near Randolph, 1909."

Manufactured in the United States of America
91 90 89   3 4 5 6 7 EB

For Sandra

EDITORS' FOREWORD

Every generation writes its own history, for the reason that it sees the past in the foreshortened perspective of its own experience. This has certainly been true of the writing of American history. The practical aim of our historiography is to offer us a more certain sense of where we are going by helping us understand the road we took in getting where we are. If the substance and nature of our historical writing is changing, it is precisely because our own generation is redefining its direction, much as the generations that preceded us redefined theirs. We are seeking a newer direction, because we are facing new problems, changing our values and premises, and shaping new institutions to meet new needs. Thus, the vitality of the present inspires the vitality of our writing about our past. Today's scholars are hard at work reconsidering every major field of our history: its politics, diplomacy, economy, society, mores, values, sexuality, and status, ethnic, and race relations. No less significantly, our scholars are using newer modes of investigation to probe the ever-expanding domain of the American past.

Our aim, in this American History Series, is to offer the reader a survey of what scholars are saying about the central themes and issues of American history. To present these themes and issues, we have invited scholars who have made notable contributions to the respective fields in which they are writing. Each volume offers the reader a sufficient factual and narrative account for perceiving the larger dimensions of its particular subject. Addressing their respective themes, our authors have undertaken, moreover, to present the conclusions derived by the principal writers on these themes. Beyond that, the authors present their own conclusions about those aspects of their respective subjects that have been matters of difference and controversy.

In effect, they have written not only about where the subject stands in today's historiography but also about where they stand on their subject. Each volume closes with an extensive critical essay on the writings of the major authorities on its particular theme.

The books in this series are designed for use in both basic and advanced courses in American history. Such a series has a particular utility in times such as these, when the traditional format of our American history courses is being altered to accommodate a greater diversity of texts and reading materials. The series offers a number of distinct advantages. It extends and deepens the dimensions of course work in American history. In proceeding beyond the confines of the traditional textbook, it makes clear that the study of our past is, more than the student might otherwise infer, at once complex, sophisticated, and profound. It presents American history as a subject of continuing vitality and fresh investigation. The work of experts in their respective fields, it opens up to the student the rich findings of historical inquiry. It invites the student to join, in major fields of research, the many groups of scholars who are pondering anew the central themes and problems of our past. It challenges the student to participate actively in exploring American history and to collaborate in the creative and rigorous adventure of seeking out its wider reaches.

John Hope Franklin

Abraham S. Eisenstadt

ACKNOWLEDGMENTS

This book is based on twenty years of reading, research, writing, and teaching in American urban history. Bayrd Still's graduate courses at New York University first stimulated my interest in this field, and his enthusiasm for my work then and now has been a continual source of encouragement. The book owes much, as well, to the growing army of urban historians who have shaped this new and exciting field since the 1960s. Over the years, I have tested my ideas on students at Indiana University Northwest in Gary and at Florida Atlantic University in Boca Raton; I thank them for their interest and, I suppose, their patience. Fulbright lecturing assignments at Tel Aviv University in Israel and at the University of Western Australia forced me to sharpen my views about the American urban experience. For their insights and enthusiasm, I would like to thank my friends in Tel Aviv and Perth; they may find some familiar material in these pages. My editorial colleagues on the *Journal of Urban History*—Blaine A. Brownell, David R. Goldfield, and Bruce M. Stave—not only read portions of the manuscript but provided good cheer and good fellowship during the decade we have worked together. Our annual editorial gatherings at meetings of the American Historical Association and the Organization of American Historians have become open-ended urban history seminars to which we all look forward. Abraham Eisenstadt and John Hope Franklin, editors of the Harlan Davidson American History Series, not only took a chance on a neophyte textbook writer, but provided important critical readings of early drafts. Harlan Davidson never lost faith that I would ultimately deliver, and Maureen Trobec provided indispensable aid in transforming a raw manuscript into a published book. At Florida Atlantic University, Thelma Spangler and Betty Lofgren cheerfully provided exceptional typing services, while Laura Loeb proved expert at research, typing, word processing, and proofreading. The map was prepared by Ted Vitale of the Graphics Department at Florida Atlantic University. These acknowledgments would be incomplete without mention of my Xerox-820 microcomputer, which quickly became indispensable in the process of writing and revision.

Raymond A. Mohl
Boca Raton, Florida

CONTENTS

TABLES

MAP

Introduction

Twentieth-century Americans live in an urban age. In the mid-1980s, about 75 percent of the nation's population reside in places designated by the Census Bureau as *urban*. Some metropolitan areas have grown positively gargantuan in size— New York, for example, with 16 million people, or Los Angeles with almost 12 million. For better or worse, the city has become an undeniable fact of life for most contemporary Americans.

The process by which a group of small colonial settlements grew into a highly industrialized and urbanized nation is a chief theme in American history. Urban development was slow and gradual through most of the preindustrial period, but in the half century or so after the Civil War, the industrial city exploded onto the American scene. It was a new city— big, sprawling, crowded with newcomers, full of opportunity, and full of risk. The new city quickly came to dominate the economic and social landscape of the industrial age. The urban legacy of that era remains with us today. Abandoned factories, polluted environments, deteriorated housing, and rundown municipal facilities shape urban life in the old industrial regions today just as surely as economic opportunity and physical growth did in the late 19th century.

Recent decades have been characterized by the meteoric rise of the sunbelt cities of the South and Southwest. The other side of the coin, of course, is the decline and decay of the aging central cities of the industrial heartland. Since World War II, these older cities have been abandoned by business and industry seeking lower taxes and cheaper labor. The white middle class has fled the central city for the new suburban frontier, leaving behind an urban population that is increasingly poor, black, and Hispanic. As a result, the aging core cities have experienced racial conflict, economic decline, severe social problems, overburdened services, and serious budgetary crises. These problems have pushed many cities to the edge of bankruptcy.

The urban prospect was not always so gloomy. In the post–Civil War industrial era, Americans pinned their hopes for the future on the cities. At the time, city growth seemed to have no bounds. According to Adna F. Weber, an early social scientist and author of a pioneering book entitled, *The Growth of Cities in the Nineteenth Century* (1899), "the concentration of population in cities" was clearly "the most remarkable social phenomenon of the present century." Businessmen and industrialists sought urban locations for their factories and financial endeavors. Workers flocked to the cities from farms and villages, as well as from across the oceans—all sought economic opportunity and a better life. The lure of the city attracted those seeking culture, education, wealth, power, and opportunity of all sorts. "We cannot all live in cities," New York editor Horace Greeley noted in 1867, "yet nearly all seem determined to do so."

The trend noted by Greeley so shortly after the Civil War intensified in the following decades. The rise of the industrial city, perhaps more than any other feature of the national scene, characterized the social and economic development of the period. More often than not, however, the promise of the industrial city remained unfulfilled. The new city which lured the farmer and the immigrant became a cauldron of humanity struggling against heavy odds for a better life.

Pittsburgh, perhaps the ultimate industrial city, typified the condition of urban America in the late 19th century. In 1898 a British traveler in the United States, Charles Philips Trevelyan, graphically described this steel-producing city of about 320,000 people:

A cloud of smoke hangs over it by day. The glow of scores of furnaces light the river banks by night. It stands at the junction of two great rivers, the Monongahela which flows down in a turbid yellow stream, and the Allegheny which is blackish. . . . The industries have grown up uncontrolled because of the discovery of coal, gas, and iron. The city has collected hap-hazard to carry on the work. All nations are jumbled up here, the poor living in tenement dens or wooden shanties thrown up or dumped down with very little reference to roads or situation, whenever a new house is wanted. It is a most chaotic city, and as yet there is no public spirit or public consciousness to make the conditions healthy or decent.

Pittsburgh had other problems as well. The city government was corrupt, Trevelyan wrote. The streets were filthy and un-paved, the polluted air almost unbreathable, the downtown area incredibly congested, the streetcars not only packed but dangerous, the noise levels intolerable. Labor conflict wracked the city, as workers and capitalists struggled to protect their separate interests. The Pennsylvania steel city, Trevelyan concluded, represented "industrial greatness with all the worst industrial abuses on the grandest scale."

Pittsburgh was not the only American city suffering from these conditions. Trevelyan's description of the steel city could easily have been applied to most of the rampantly growing industrial cities of the age. The dynamic forces of modernizing change created the new industrial city in all its shame and glory. Industrial capitalism triggered economic and social change along a broad front of urban life—and not all of it was positive. Unbounded growth and almost unimaginable opportunity coexisted with deadly disease, grinding poverty, political corruption, and social disorder. Many of the economic, social, and political patterns which came to characterize such industrial cities as Pittsburgh persisted well into the 20th century.

This book traces the broad outlines of the urban transformation of the industrial era. It begins with a discussion of the dynamics of urban change—the impact of dramatic population shifts, the influence of new technology in transportation and building, the significant role of the factory, and the power of individual urban boosters, builders, and planners to shape the new city. The book's second section analyzes the changing patterns of urban government in the industrial era. It focuses particularly on the mid-19th century crisis in municipal government, the emergence of the political machine, and the rise of urban reformers who challenged the bosses. The final segment of the book addresses the important question of social order in the industrial city—how modernizing change undermined traditional society and how urban people responded to change and social disorder. The book ends with a short survey of 20th-century city development in the United States.

The book's present form represents one historian's perception of the important patterns of American urban history. Another historian might have shaped this material somewhat differently. Indeed, the variety and diversity of the American urban experience almost ensures debate among those interpreting the historical record. Despite the debate, most urban historians would agree to the essential proposition that the city has been a persistent, powerful, often shaping force in modern American history.

I.

The
Dynamics of
Urban Growth

ONE

Peopling the American City

People make cities, and urbanization depends in the first instance on population growth. Thus, an understanding of the American industrial city requires an examination of urban population patterns. Despite substantial urbanization in the preindustrial years, the proportion of urban dwellers in the total population of the United States barely reached 20 percent by 1860. Over the next 60 years, however, city populations skyrocketed. At the same time, an industrial revolution was dramatically transforming the United States. In these years, as

Table 1

Urbanization in the United States, 1860–1920

Date	Total U.S. Population (in thousands)	Total Urban Population (in thousands)	Percent Urban	Percent Increase in Total Population	Percent Increase in Urban Population	Number of Urban Places	Number of Cities over 100,000 Population
1860	31,444	6,217	19.8	—	—	392	9
1870	38,558	9,902	25.7	22.7	59.3	663	14
1880	50,156	14,130	28.2	30.1	42.7	939	20
1890	62,947	22,106	35.1	25.5	56.4	1,348	28
1900	75,995	30,160	39.7	20.7	36.4	1,737	38
1910	91,972	41,999	45.7	21.0	39.2	2,262	50
1920	105,711	54,158	51.2	14.9	29.0	2,722	68

Source: U.S. Bureau of the Census, *Historical Statistics of the United States, Colonial Times to 1970*. 2 vols. (Washington, D.C., 1975), Vol. 1, pp. 11–12.

historian Eric Lampard has noted, industrialism "put its stamp upon emerging urban society . . . and was itself stimulated and shaped by the related concentration of population."

Much of the story of urban population growth can be derived from official census statistics. According to the Census Bureau, the urban category includes incorporated towns or municipalities with 2,500 or more people, or unincorporated areas with at least 2,500 people per square mile. For analytical purposes, these definitions of an *urban place* leave much to be desired. Simple numbers often distort reality. Small towns as well as great cities are lumped together in the census statistics. Obviously, important differences exist between such places. The census does not explain the economic or social relationships between large central cities and nearby smaller towns and cities. Nor does it reveal the links between cities and surrounding rural areas. Nevertheless, the census definition does provide a quantitative standard for measuring urban population growth.

URBAN DEMOGRAPHIC PATTERNS

What do the census statistics reveal about the urbanization process in the United States? First, they show that the urban population grew much more rapidly than national population during the industrial era. As Table 1 demonstrates, total U.S. population tripled in size from about 31 million to over 105 million between 1860 and 1920. Simultaneously, the urban population leaped almost ninefold from around 6 million to more than 54 million people. During most of this period, the urban population was increasing more than twice as rapidly as total population. Because urban population rose faster than national population as a whole, the percentage of Americans living in urban places climbed persistently from a base of 19.8 percent in 1860. By 1920, the census statistics showed that for the first time more than 50 percent of the American people lived in cities and towns.

While the nation's population was being urbanized, the

Table 2

Percentage Urban by Region and State, 1860–1920

	1860	1890	1920
United States	19.8	35.1	51.2
Northeast	35.7	59.0	75.5
Maine	16.6	28.1	39.1
New Hampshire	22.1	39.3	56.4
Massachusetts	59.5	82.0	90.1
Vermont	2.0	15.4	31.2
Connecticut	26.5	50.9	67.8
Rhode Island	63.4	85.3	91.9
New York	39.3	65.1	82.7
New Jersey	32.7	62.6	79.9
Pennsylvania	30.8	48.6	65.0
North Central	13.9	33.1	52.2
Ohio	17.1	41.1	63.8
Indiana	8.6	26.9	50.6
Michigan	13.4	35.0	61.1
Illinois	14.4	44.9	67.9
Wisconsin	14.4	33.2	47.3
Minnesota	9.3	33.8	44.1
Iowa	8.9	21.2	36.4
Missouri	17.2	32.0	46.6
Kansas	9.3	18.9	34.8
Nebraska	—	27.5	31.2
South Dakota	—	8.3	16.0
North Dakota	—	5.6	13.6
South	9.6	16.3	28.1
Delaware	18.7	42.3	54.3
Maryland	33.9	47.6	59.9
District of Columbia	93.3	100.0	100.0
Virginia	9.5	17.1	29.2

Table 2

Percentage Urban by Region and State, 1860–1920

	1860	1890	1920
South (Continued)			
West Virginia	5.3	10.6	25.2
North Carolina	2.5	7.2	19.1
South Carolina	7.0	10.1	17.5
Georgia	7.1	14.0	25.1
Florida	4.3	19.7	36.6
Kentucky	10.5	19.2	26.2
Tennessee	4.2	13.5	26.1
Alabama	5.1	10.0	21.7
Mississippi	2.7	5.4	13.4
Louisiana	26.1	25.4	34.9
Arkansas	.9	6.5	16.6
Oklahoma	—	3.5	26.5
Texas	4.5	15.7	32.4
West	16.0	37.0	51.8
Montana	—	27.3	31.3
Idaho	—	—	27.5
Wyoming	—	33.3	29.4
Colorado	14.7	45.0	48.2
Utah	20.0	35.5	48.1
Nevada	—	17.0	19.5
New Mexico	5.3	6.3	18.1
Arizona	—	9.1	36.2
Washington	—	35.8	54.8
Oregon	5.8	27.7	49.8
California	20.8	48.6	67.9

Source: U.S. Bureau of the Census, *Historical Statistics of the United States, Colonial Times to 1970.* 2 vols. (Washington, D.C., 1975), Vol. 1, pp. 22–37.

number of urban places grew steadily as well. In 1860, the Census Bureau reported only 392 urban places in the United States. By 1920, however, the number of places designated as urban had risen sevenfold to 2,722. Large cities with populations of over 100,000 sprouted at about the same rapid pace. Nine American cities surpassed the 100,000 plateau by 1860, but by the end of the industrial era the number of such large cities had reached 68 (see Table 1). However, the number of urbanites living in smaller cities and towns kept pace with those residing in larger urban centers. In 1920, about half of America's 54 million urban dwellers lived in cities of over 100,000 people, and about half in towns and cities of less than that size. Thus, American urban growth in the industrial era was spread about evenly between large and small cities.

The northeastern section of the country was consistently the most heavily urbanized region throughout the industrial era. As noted in Table 2, more than 75 percent of the population of the New England and Middle Atlantic states lived in urban areas by 1920, compared to 51.2 percent for the nation as a whole. By contrast, the South persistently lagged behind in the race to build an urbanized society. By the end of the industrial era, only about 28 percent of southerners were urban dwellers. For most of the period, the percentage of southern urbanites was substantially less than that. The Midwest and the Far West stood just slightly above the national urban average by 1920.

In some states, urbanism had become pervasive by the early 20th century. In Massachusetts and Rhode Island, for instance, more than 90 percent of the people lived in urban places in 1920 (see Table 2). In New York and New Jersey, the proportion of urban dwellers hovered around 80 percent of total population. Ohio, Michigan, and Illinois led the urban parade in the Midwest, each state surpassing national and regional averages. In the West, only California and Washington had a majority of urban dwellers by 1920. In the South, urbanism was significant only in Delaware and Maryland, two border states with a substantial industrial base. Thus, the urban population was unevenly distributed across the nation. Much of the nation remained heavily rural. The urban population was concentrated in a few states, and often in only a few cities or metropolitan districts in the urbanized states.

THE INDUSTRIAL HEARTLAND

For the most part, those states with large urban populations were also the most heavily industrialized states. Indeed, as geographer David Ward has suggested in *Cities and Immigrants* (1971), it is possible to define an economic core region as a manufacturing belt which gradually expanded during the industrial period of the late 19th century. By 1910, this industrial core area stretched from Massachusetts and Maryland on the east to Illinois, southern Wisconsin, and eastern Missouri on the west (see Map 1).

Throughout the industrial era, the economic core region contained not only most of the nation's manufacturing, but most of the largest American cities as well. These included older seaport cities such as New York, Philadelphia, Boston, and Baltimore founded in the colonial period, as well as midwestern lake and river cities established in the early 19th century. In 1860, 20 of the nation's 25 largest cities, and 9 of the 10 largest, were located in the industrial core region (see Table 3). Even as late as 1920, after considerable urban development in the West and on the Pacific coast, the industrial core held 16 of the 25 largest cities, and again 9 of the 10 largest. The cities of the Northeast-Midwest manufacturing belt anchored the industrial revolution in the United States.

Some of the industrial core cities experienced staggering growth rates during this period. New York City, for instance, retained its urban leadership status, rising from about 800,000 in 1860 to more than 5.5 million by 1920. With its great size, New York served as a national metropolis—an unrivaled center for business, finance, manufacturing, and transportation, as well as for communications and culture.

Among Midwestern cities, Chicago grew at an astonishing

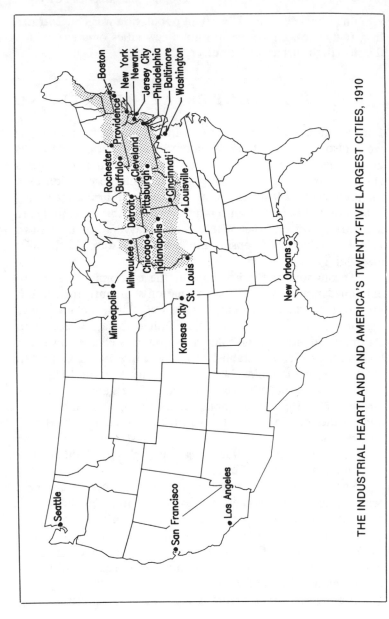

THE INDUSTRIAL HEARTLAND AND AMERICA'S TWENTY-FIVE LARGEST CITIES, 1910

Source: Adapted from David Ward, *Cities and Immigrants: A Geography of Change in Nineteenth-Century America* (New York: Oxford University Press, 1971), pp. 42–43.

Table 3

Rank Population of 25 Largest Cities

	1860			1890			1920	
Rank	City	Population	Rank	City	Population	Rank	City	Population
1	New York	813,669	1	New York	1,515,301	1	New York	5,620,048
2	Philadelphia	565,529	2	Chicago	1,099,850	2	Chicago	2,701,705
3	Brooklyn	266,661	3	Philadelphia	1,046,964	3	Philadelphia	1,823,779
4	Baltimore	212,418	4	Brooklyn	806,343	4	Detroit	993,678
5	Boston	177,840	5	St. Louis	451,770	5	Cleveland	796,841
6	New Orleans	168,675	6	Boston	448,477	6	St. Louis	772,897
7	Cincinnati	161,044	7	Baltimore	434,439	7	Boston	748,060
8	St. Louis	160,773	8	San Francisco	298,997	8	Baltimore	733,826
9	Chicago	109,260	9	Cincinnati	296,908	9	Pittsburgh	588,343
10	Buffalo	81,129	10	Cleveland	261,353	10	Los Angeles	576,673
11	Newark	71,941	11	Buffalo	255,664	11	Buffalo	506,775
12	Louisville	68,033	12	New Orleans	242,039	12	San Francisco	506,676
13	Albany	62,367	13	Pittsburgh	238,617	13	Milwaukee	457,147
14	Washington	61,122	14	Washington	230,392	14	Washington	437,571
15	San Francisco	56,802	15	Detroit	205,876	15	Newark	414,524
16	Providence	50,566	16	Milwaukee	204,468	16	Cincinnati	401,247
17	Pittsburgh	49,221	17	Newark	181,830	17	New Orleans	387,219
18	Rochester	48,204	18	Minneapolis	164,738	18	Minneapolis	380,582
19	Detroit	45,519	19	Jersey City	163,003	19	Kansas City	324,410
20	Milwaukee	45,246	20	Louisville	161,129	20	Seattle	315,312
21	Cleveland	43,417	21	Omaha	140,452	21	Indianapolis	314,194
22	Charleston	40,522	22	Rochester	133,896	22	Jersey City	298,103
23	New Haven	39,267	23	St. Paul	133,156	23	Rochester	295,750
24	Troy	39,235	24	Kansas City	132,716	24	Portland	258,288
25	Richmond	37,910	25	Providence	132,146	25	Denver	256,491

Source: U.S. Bureau of the Census, *Fourteenth Census of the United States: 1920*, Vol. 1, *Population* (Washington, D.C., 1921), pp. 80–81.

rate. With a little over 100,000 people in 1860, Chicago at least doubled its population during each of the next three decades. Chicago's meteoric rise came despite the great Chicago fire of 1871, the most destructive fire in American history. It destroyed more than three square miles of the city and left 100,000 people homeless. But the fire was only a temporary setback. Chicagoans quickly rebuilt the burned-out city, which resumed its forward progress toward urban dominance in the Midwest. By 1920, with a population of 2.7 million, the metropolis on Lake Michigan ranked second only to New York in size and economic importance.

Western cities grew rapidly, as well, demonstrating that the westward movement was not simply a migration of frontiersmen, cattlemen, and farmers. The explosive growth of Los Angeles typified western urbanization. A small settlement of 5,700 in 1870, Los Angeles doubled in size during the 1870s, jumped fivefold in the 1880s, doubled in the 1890s, and rolled up another fivefold increase between 1900 and 1920. By the end of the industrial period, Los Angeles boosters had capitalized on climate, tourism, land promotion, and good transportation, creating a thriving metropolis of more than half a million people.

Urbanization characterized the entire industrial era. But more than any other decade of the period, the 1880s witnessed a virtual urban explosion. Total U.S. urban population increased by 56.4 percent during that decade. Some of the older eastern and midwestern commercial and manufacturing cities grew at about the same rate, as well. However, some remarkable population increases were registered elsewhere. Chicago, Detroit, and Milwaukee each doubled in size during the 1880s; this was a notable increase for already sizable cities. Dozens of smaller cities—including Akron, Youngstown, Trenton, Passaic, Kansas City, Minneapolis, St. Paul, Topeka, Des Moines, Denver, Salt Lake City, Jacksonville, Memphis, Dallas, and numerous others—doubled, tripled, or quadrupled their populations. A decade of relative prosperity, substantial industrialization, and rural depopulation, the 1880s experienced unparalleled urban growth.

The pace of urbanization slowed somewhat in succeeding

decades. Nevertheless, a few cities registered meteoric rises in the early 20th century. Detroit more than doubled in size to 993,000 between 1910 and 1920. During the same decade, increases ranging between 135 percent and 440 percent occurred in Pontiac and Flint, Michigan, and in Akron, Tulsa, Gary, and Miami. Generally, these were new cities rising from a small population base, or cities that owed their development to an emerging industry such as automobiles, rubber, oil, steel, or tourism. Essentially, the great surge of urbanization had begun to taper off by the early 20th century.

THE METROPOLITAN DISTRICT

By the 20th century, some new population movements had become discernible. Beyond the city limits, numerous heavily populated suburbs had sprouted. Separate political units with their own governments, these suburbs were linked to the economic and social life of the central cities. To measure this central city-suburban linkage, the Census Bureau in 1910 began reporting population information on metropolitan districts.

A metropolitan district, according to the census statisticians, included central cities of at least 200,000 people, plus the urbanized areas within 10 miles of the cities' boundaries. Between 1900 and 1920, a rising percentage of metropolitan district population resided in the suburban rings surrounding the central cities. The rate of suburban population increase during these decades generally surpassed central city growth, often substantially so. The emerging suburban pattern foreshadowed the more intensified suburban dispersal in the automobile-oriented city of the post–1920 period.

FERTILITY AND MORTALITY

The great growth of the American urban population in the industrial era was affected by changing rates of fertility and mortality. Demographers have noted that both birth rates and death rates declined during the industrial period. Actually, birth rates in the United States had been dropping since about 1800, but the most substantial declines occurred after the middle of the 19th century. The birth rate in 1860, as measured by the number of live births per 1,000 population, stood at 44.3. By 1900 the rate had fallen to 32.3, and by 1920 it had declined still further to 27.7. However, rural birth rates always exceeded urban birth rates. The great explosion in the urban population did not result from a rising birth rate among urban dwellers.

A second demographic trend—a decline in mortality rates—had a somewhat more positive relationship to urban population growth, especially after 1900. In Massachusetts, for instance, the crude death rate (as measured by the number of deaths per 1,000 population) stood at 27.8 in 1789, fluctuated between 18 and 22 until 1900, and then plunged rapidly to 12.5 by 1925. These dramatic declines in mortality resulted from developments in modern science and medicine in the late 19th century. Most important, improved water supplies drastically reduced death rates from typhoid, cholera, and other epidemic diseases. As with birth rates, however, death rates were always lower in rural areas than urban. The demographic evidence, therefore, suggests that neither natural increase nor declining mortality can fully account for the explosive gains in the American urban population during the industrial era. Actually, the fertility and mortality trends in the United States after 1860 accentuated rural population growth rather than urban.

FARM TO CITY

It seems clear, then, that in the industrial era American cities gained population almost entirely through net migration. Urban populations grew because more new people arrived to make the cities their home than left the cities for other places. Net migration to the cities resulted from two great population movements—first, rural movement to the cities in the United States, and second, intensified European immigration to America. Essentially, the rapid urban growth of the period resulted from a tremendous release of rural population. Most of the new urbanites came from the American farm and peasant villages of the old world.

Internal migration resulted from millions of individual decisions about life, work, and economic opportunity. The higher birth rates of rural areas, as well as lower mortality rates, created a surplus of rural population. Agricultural mechanization displaced farm workers and hired hands in large numbers. Many small farmers went under during the periodic depressions of the late 19th century, while others could not afford the costs of mechanization. Lower agricultural prices and the hardships of farm living in the days before tractors and electricity drove rural dwellers into the cities in search of jobs and a better life. Many farmers' sons and daughters were lured from the farm by the bright lights of the city. For younger people, the cities possessed cultural and educational attractions, along with a more active social and recreational life. Much of the urban population increase, then, stemmed from the mass exodus of rural Americans. As Table 4 indicates, these internal migrants contributed substantially to big-city populations.

The city rather than the rural frontier supplied the safety valve for the nation's surplus and economically discontented population. Frederick Jackson Turner and other early historians of the American West emphasized the significance of the frontier in American history. They argued, with little supporting evidence, that the great expanse of cheap western land drained off unhappy or unemployed urban workers, thus preventing the working-class violence and revolution often experienced in European cities. But as one scholar demonstrated: "At least twenty farmers moved to town for each industrial laborer who moved to the land, and ten sons of farmers went to the city for each one who became the owner of a new farm." Rural America had a surplus of population, as well as declining economic opportunities. For the farmers and their sons and daughters, the

Table 4

Composition of Population in Selected Cities, 1860–1920*

1860 City	Percent Out-of-State Migrants	Percent Black	Percent Foreign Born	1890 City	Percent Out-of-State Migrants	Percent Black	Percent Foreign Born	1920 City	Percent Out-of-State Migrants	Percent Black	Percent Foreign Born
New York	6.3	1.5	47.6	New York	8.9	1.6	42.2	New York	8.0	2.7	36.1
Philadelphia	8.4	3.9	28.9	Chicago	19.3	1.3	41.0	Chicago	18.3	4.1	29.9
Brooklyn		1.6	39.2	Philadelphia	10.4	3.8	25.7	Philadelphia	13.8	7.4	22.0
Baltimore	6.4	13.1	24.7	Brooklyn	9.7	1.3	32.5	Detroit	25.3	4.1	29.3
Boston	15.5	1.3	35.9	St. Louis	20.7	5.9	25.4	Cleveland	17.7	4.3	30.1
New Orleans	10.8	14.3	38.3	Boston	14.2	1.8	35.3	St. Louis	25.0	9.0	13.4
Cincinnati	13.4	2.3	45.7	Baltimore	10.2	15.4	15.9	Boston	11.0	2.2	32.4
St. Louis	17.0	2.1	59.8	San Francisco	19.5	.6	42.1	Baltimore	15.6	14.8	11.6
Chicago	24.3	.9	50.0	Cincinnati	13.4	3.9	24.1	Pittsburgh	12.6	6.4	20.5
Buffalo		1.0	46.4	Cleveland	11.7	1.1	37.2	Los Angeles	57.8	2.7	21.2
Newark		1.8	37.0	Buffalo	6.4	.4	35.0	Buffalo	9.0	.9	24.0
Louisville		10.0	33.7	New Orleans	9.7	26.6	14.2	San Francisco	24.1	.6	29.4
Albany		1.0	34.7	Pittsburgh	8.3	3.3	30.7	Milwaukee	10.7	1.3	24.1
Washington		18.0	17.6	Washington	47.3	32.8	8.2	Washington	55.8	25.1	6.7
San Francisco		2.1	50.1	Detroit	11.6	1.7	39.7	Newark	16.7	4.1	28.4
Providence		3.0	24.8	Milwaukee	8.5	.2	38.9	Cincinnati	22.8	7.5	10.7
Pittsburgh		2.3	36.7	Newark	12.7	2.3	30.6	New Orleans	12.4	26.1	7.1
Rochester		.9	39.2	Minneapolis	32.5	.8	36.8	Minneapolis	27.6	.9	23.2
Detroit		3.1	46.8	Jersey City	23.8	1.3	32.7	Kansas City	45.5	9.5	8.5
Milwaukee		.2	50.5	Louisville	14.4	17.8	14.6	Seattle	49.7	.9	25.7
Cleveland		1.8	44.8	Omaha	54.0	3.3	25.0	Indianapolis	29.2	11.0	5.4
Charleston		42.3	15.6	Rochester	5.8	.4	29.7	Jersey City	21.0	2.7	25.6
New Haven		3.8	27.1	St. Paul	26.8	1.1	39.9	Rochester	7.5	.8	24.1
Troy		1.6	34.3	Kansas City	51.5	10.3	15.7	Portland	50.4	.5	19.3
Richmond		37.7	13.1	Providence	19.9	3.0	30.6	Denver	53.3	2.5	14.9

* This table presents statistics for the 25 largest cities in 1860, 1890, and 1920. The Census Bureau collected out-of-state migration statistics for only 8 cities in 1860.

Sources: U.S. Bureau of the Census, *Population of the United States in 1860; Compiled from the Original Returns of the Eighth Census* (Washington, 1864), pp. xxxi–xxxii, 2–590, 608–15; U.S. Bureau of the Census, *Report on Population of the United States at the Eleventh Census: 1890* (Washington, 1895), Vol. 1, pp. cxxvi, cxxix, 451–85; U.S. Bureau of the Census, *Fourteenth Census of the United States: 1920,* Vol. 2, *Population* (Washington, 1922), pp. 661–65; U.S. Bureau of the Census, *Negroes in the United States, 1920–32* (Washington, 1935), pp. 54–55.

growing cities served as safety valves. As the patterns of internal migration suggest, the city became the new frontier of the industrial era.

BLACK MIGRATION

The new urban frontier had a special magnetism for one group of native-born migrants. Rural southern blacks began moving to northern industrial cities soon after the end of the Civil War. The movement gradually intensified in the late 19th century. Between 1900 and 1920, some 750,000 blacks made the northward trek (see Table 5). Actually, the great black migration from the South was larger following 1920. Nevertheless, the black exodus from the rural South represented a significant demographic movement in the industrial era. The movement was especially strong during and after World War I, when the labor needs of American industry and simultaneous cotton crop fail-

Table 5

Black Migration from the South 1870–1970

1870–1880	68,000
1880–1890	88,000
1890–1900	185,000
1900–1910	194,000
1910–1920	555,000
1920–1930	903,000
1930–1940	480,000
1940–1950	1,581,000
1950–1960	1,458,000
1960–1970	1,400,000

Sources: Reynolds Farley, "The Urbanization of Negroes in the United States," *Journal of Social History,* 1 (Spring 1968), p. 251; George Groh, *The Black Migration: The Journey to Urban America* (New York, 1972), p. 48.

ures and agricultural unemployment stimulated black migration. Discrimination, lynching, and white terrorism helped drive blacks out of the South, but it seems clear that the promise of economic opportunity in northern factories provided the essential pull attracting black sharecroppers and tenant farmers.

The great majority of the black migrants headed for the industrial cities of the Northeast and Midwest. By 1920 almost 85 percent of the blacks residing outside of the South lived in urban centers. New York, Philadelphia, and Chicago developed the largest black communities before 1920, each substantially surpassing 100,000. By the 1920s, however, newly popular destinations were the cities of the industrial heartland—Detroit, Cleveland, Cincinnati, Pittsburgh, St. Louis, and Kansas City—as well as numerous smaller factory towns, such as Youngstown, Gary, Toledo, Newark, and Buffalo. For the rural southern blacks, the industrial city became the "promised land."

FOREIGN IMMIGRATION

While millions of white and black rural Americans sought economic opportunity in the cities, so also did unprecedented numbers of rural people from Europe. Between 1820 and 1920, about 34 million immigrants converged on the United States, mostly from Europe but also from Asia, Canada, Mexico, and other parts of the Western Hemisphere. Not all of the immigrants remained in America. Many came temporarily to make their fortune by working in American mines, mills, and factories, hoping eventually to return to their homelands. Perhaps as many as 8 million immigrants returned to the old country after living and working in "the land of opportunity." Thus as Table 6 illustrates, net immigration during the 100-year period amounted to about 26.8 million.

The immigrants came in several great waves. The first mass movement across the Atlantic occurred in the mid-19th century. This early immigration brought Irish, German, British, and

Table 6

Net Immigration to the United States 1820–1920

1821–1830	123,000
1831–1840	493,000
1841–1850	1,420,000
1851–1860	2,593,000
1861–1870	2,102,000
1871–1880	2,622,000
1881–1890	4,966,000
1891–1900	3,711,000
1901–1910	6,294,000
1911–1920	2,484,000

Source: Conrad Taeuber and Irene B. Taeuber, *The Changing Population of the United States* (New York, 1958), p. 294; Stephan Thernstrom, ed., *Harvard Encyclopedia of American Ethnic Groups* (Cambridge, Mass., 1980), p. 476.

Scandinavian newcomers from northern and western Europe. By the 1880s and 1890s, a second great wave of immigration—a "new immigration"—was developing. The immigrant ships carried increasing proportions of southern and eastern Europeans—Poles, Russians, Italians, Greeks, Hungarians, Armenians, Turks, East European Jews, and various Slavic peoples. The new immigrants came in even larger numbers than their predecessors. This foreign influx was swelled by immigrants from China and Japan, by French-Canadians who migrated to New England factory towns, and by Mexicans who settled in California, the Southwest, and such Midwestern cities as Chicago, Minneapolis, and Detroit.

The new immigration surpassed all previous population movements. For example, net immigration totaled almost 6.3 million between 1900 and 1910 and in 1907 alone more than 1.3 million immigrants entered the United States. As economist Richard A. Easterlin has noted, "the magnitude of immigration to America is unmatched in the history of mankind."

Most of the immigrants had been rural peasants, farmers, and villagers in the old country. In America they became city people, drawn by the magnet of economic opportunity. Indeed, the timing of immigrant arrival in the post–Civil War years dictated urban settlement. Most immigrants came with little money, and few could afford to set up as farmers. Higher rural birth rates and farm mechanization created a surplus of rural population rather than labor shortages. The nation's great manpower and labor needs were in the cities.

In a very real sense, shifting urban economic opportunities in the cities controlled the immigrant flow. Rates of immigrant arrival corresponded closely to the cycles of prosperity and depression in the United States. European immigration intensified during periods of prosperity, but tapered off during the periodic depressions of the late 19th century. Thus, the degree of prosperity or depression often determined the timing of immigrant arrival, while the geographic distribution of employment dictated their concentration in American cities.

Both the older and the newer immigrants made the American city their destination. Census statistics show high proportions of urban residents among the earlier Irish and German immigrants, as well as among the later newcomers from Italy, Poland, Russia, Austria, and Hungary. As late as 1920, for example, 87 percent of all Irish immigrants lived in cities. Similarly high percentages of urban dwellers prevailed for other immigrant groups—89 percent for those from the Russian Empire, 84 percent for Italians and Poles, 80 percent for Hungarians, 75 percent for Austrians, Britons, and Canadians, 69 percent for Yugoslavs, and 67 percent for Germans. In 1900 about two thirds of the nation's immigrant population resided in cities; by 1920 the proportion had increased to three fourths. The concentration of immigrant newcomers in the industrializing cities remained a persistent chracteristic of the age.

The foreign-born presence was especially pervasive in the larger eastern and midwestern cities. In 1860 immigrants comprised 40 percent or more of the populations of New York, Cincinnati, St. Louis, Chicago, Buffalo, San Francisco, Detroit,

Milwaukee, and Cleveland (see Table 4). These percentages gradually went down over the next 60 years, even as aggregate immigration increased. This pattern reflected the impact of native rural migration on the cities and the rising proportion of urbanites whose parents were immigrants. Actually, addition of the American-born children of the immigrants to the foreign-born totals provides a better measure of the size and influence of the immigrant communities. By 1910 immigrants and their American-born children comprised more than 70 percent of the population of New York, Chicago, Boston, Cleveland, Detroit, Buffalo, and Milwaukee. In numerous other cities—San Francisco, Newark, Pittsburgh, St. Louis, Philadelphia, and Cincinnati, for instance—the percentage of foreign stock ranged between 50 and 70 percent of total population. Thus, because they were so highly urbanized, the immigrants contributed substantially to the growth of American cities in the industrial era.

POPULATION TURNOVER

One final aspect of the changing urban demography deserves attention. As many observers of the United States have noted, Americans have always been a restless and footloose people. Industrial workers, particularly, were constantly "on the wing." During a working lifetime, recent historians have suggested, a typical worker might have had as many as 30 different jobs and lived in a dozen different towns or cities. Mobility research, especially the work of historians Stephan Thernstrom and Peter Knights on Boston, has revealed the extraordinary volatility of urban populations in the 19th and early 20th centuries. Between 1880 and 1890, for instance, the population of Boston rose from 363,000 to 448,000—a total gain of about 85,000. Some 20,000 of this total increase resulted from natural increase, leaving 65,000 attributable to in-migration. However, these net migration statistics are quite misleading and reveal little of the great fluidity and turnover of the Boston population. Incredibly, as Thernstrom and Knights have demonstrated, almost 800,000 people moved into and out of Boston between 1880 and 1890 to produce the net increase of 65,000. Hundreds of thousands of native-born and foreign newcomers moved into Boston during the decade, stayed for a time, and then moved on.

High rates of population turnover were not unique to Boston. Indeed, most other large American cities had higher rates of in-migration and out-migration than Boston. Thus, historians have suggested that the population turnover pattern which prevailed in Boston typified most of America's rapidly growing industrial cities. While the cities grew, they also served as a sort of population pump—sucking people in and spitting them out in extraordinary numbers on a regular basis.

All of these demographic changes—European immigration, internal migration, and population turnover—contributed to the peopling and the reshaping of the modern American city. The presence of such large numbers of rural newcomers, unaccustomed to city ways and industrial labor, altered the fabric of urban life. Above all, the shifting demography of the industrial city initiated a continuous cycle of social change.

TWO

Streetcars,
Skyscrapers,
and Urban Space

As new population poured into the cities, visible changes became evident in urban spatial patterns. The new technology of the industrial era initiated changes in the internal structure of American cities. In particular, innovations in urban transportation and building construction altered the spatial arrangement of people and economic activities. A new urban spatial order emerged—one characterized by changing patterns of city expansion, land usage, social organization, and political conflict.

THE WALKING CITY

Historians have characterized the preindustrial city of the early 19th century as the pedestrian or walking city. Business and commerical enterprises clustered in central areas, usually near the waterfront. Business people and workers, shoppers and shopkeepers, all got to their destinations by foot; only the wealthy could afford a horse and carriage. Without mass transit, the physical expansion of the city was limited to walking distances—usually the distance one could walk within half an hour, or about two miles. Even as late as the 1850s, the built-up portions of large cities such as Philadelphia, Boston, and New York rarely spread beyond two miles from the city center.

As a result, the walking city developed a characteristic internal structure. It was compact and congested, as more and more people squeezed into limited urban space. In some immigrant wards in New York City, population density surpassed 170 people per acre by 1840. Densities of 100 or more per acre were common in parts of Philadelphia by 1850. With some exceptions, most employment was centralized in the downtown and waterfront areas. And because they relied on foot power, urban workers lived close to their workplaces in the city center.

Limited housing options in the walking city brought a degree of social integration. Blacks, immigrants, and native-born whites clustered in houses and tenements near the waterfront. Wealthy business people and professionals also lived in the city center, usually in fashionable neighborhoods close to their places of business. Thus, short distances separated rich and poor, native and immigrant, white and black. Moreover, land usage had not been functionally specialized; residential, commercial, industrial, transportation, and storage facilities shared limited space in the confined city center. As historian Joseph

Arnold has noted, this pattern of mixed land usage in the preindustrial city "produced an offensive stew of factories, furnaces, and warehouses jumbled across a tangle of streets, alleys, canals, and railroads." Despite the appearance of regularity conveyed by the gridiron street layout, the walking cities of the preindustrial era grew haphazardly and without much planning.

Several significant forces combined to reorder the spatial patterns of American cities in the late 19th century. The growing importance of manufacturing intensified competition for desirable urban land near waterfronts and railroad terminals in central locations. Great urban population increases placed new demands on the housing market. Real estate development and speculation on the urban periphery, along with the appeal and attraction of suburban living, stimulated the physical expansion of the walking city. Most important, however, in reshaping central city space were new innovations in urban mass transit.

URBAN MASS TRANSIT

Urban transportation technology developed slowly in the early 19th century, but a succession of new innovations tumbled off the drawing boards of inventors and engineers in the last quarter of the century. Innovation began in the 1830s, with the introduction of the horse-drawn omnibus in most of the larger cities. Carrying 12 to 20 passengers and drawn by one or two horses, the omnibus traveled over a fixed route and charged a fixed fare. The popularity of this early form of mass transit spread quickly.

By the 1850s, omnibus service had become a regular feature of urban life in New York, Boston, Brooklyn, Philadelphia, Washington, Baltimore, Pittsburgh, Chicago, and New Orleans. In 1853, for example, about 700 New York omnibuses carried more than 120,000 passengers a day. Most of the omnibuses were operated by small, independent businessmen. Rivalries were intense, as omnibus operators competed for riders on the most heavily traveled streets, while less lucrative routes were poorly served. Mass transit was not yet thought of as a public service; rather, private profit for the operater stimulated the expansion of omnibus service in most cities.

By mid-century, the omnibus had begun altering urban spatial patterns. It permitted a longer journey to work for those who could afford the daily fare, ranging between 6 and 12 cents in most cities. The wealthy business and professional classes gradually began to move from their prestigious but aging neighborhoods in the city center to the urban periphery and outlying suburbs.

Even at this early date, the less developed areas outside the urban core had an appeal to those who could afford to escape the increasingly crowded, congested, and unhealthy city. On the introduction of omnibus service in Baltimore in 1844, the *Baltimore Sun* described the impact of the new transit innovation: "In addition to the general convenience, they have tended greatly to enhance the value of property in the outskirts of the City, enabling persons to reside at a distance from their places of business in more healthy locations, without the loss of time and fatigue of walking." However, for unskilled urban workers, whose wages rarely surpassed a dollar a day during the mid-19th century, the omnibus had less impact. Unable to afford the daily omnibus fare, city workers continued to live close to their workplaces. The city remained a walking city for the worker and the mass of the urban population.

A second urban transportation innovation emerged simultaneously with the omnibus—the steam-powered commuter railroad. As the railroads developed in the 1830s and 1840s, they often provided local commuter service as well as long-distance freight and passenger service. This commuter service began in Boston in the 1830s and then spread to other cities in the 1840s and 1850s. By mid-century, about 20 percent of Boston's business people used commuter railroads for the 10 to 15 mile daily journey to work. In New York City, the New York and Harlem Railroad ran commuter trains from the urban core to the suburban village of Harlem in northern Manhattan; by 1859 the Harlem Railroad was selling some 3.5 million passenger tickets annually. In the same year, the Philadelphia, Germantown and Norristown Railroad ran 40 commuter trains a day between Philadelphia and Germantown.

In the Midwest, beginning in 1855 the Chicago and North Western Railroad extended commuter trains from Chicago to Evanston, Wilmette, Winnetka, Glencoe, Highland Park, Lake Forest, and other growing suburbs north of the city. As one Chicago area newspaper noted in 1857: "An accommodation [commuter] train . . . affords business men an excellent opportunity to avail themselves of the beautiful quiet of a country residence without shortening the number of hours usually devoted to their daily avocations."

Like the omnibus, the commuter railroad served a wealthy clientele. Daily fares ranged from 15 to 25 cents, an amount that effectively excluded the working classes and the poor. Thus, the impact of the commuter railroad was relatively moderate at first, encouraging some of the well-to-do to abandon the city as a residence in favor of the more pleasant surroundings of the urban periphery. Nevertheless, the suburban trains served ever larger numbers of commuters as the metropolitan areas grew in population. By 1888, the *Chicago Tribune* could report that "there seems to be no sign of a let-up in the development of the territory reached by the suburban trains of the Illinois Central." The commuter trains, along with the omnibus lines, established a decentralizing pattern—one accelerated by new transit innovations in the 1850s and after.

The development of the street or horse railway represented the most significant technological advance in urban transit in the mid-19th century. Beginning in the 1850s, some omnibus operators and new street railway companies began laying iron rails in city streets to facilitate urban travel. Generally drawn by two horses, these new omnibuses on rails carried more passengers, moved through city streets more rapidly (about six to eight miles per hour), and provided a smoother and more comfortable ride. The use of rails also established fixed transit routes along the most heavily traveled streets, adding a measure of certainty and predictability to the daily lives of urban residents.

But there were added costs for the operators. Urban transit increasingly became a big business requiring heavy capital investment. Smaller and independent transit operators were gradually forced out of business by increasing costs, or bought out by aggressive entrepreneurs who created large citywide systems. Since government franchises were required to lay rails on city streets, transit companies often became actively involved in urban politics. By the late 19th century, urban transit came to be defined as a necessary public service, but involvement in the political arena had its costs in the form of bribery, fraud, and corruption.

Contemporaries hailed the horsecar system as a revolutionary improvement over the omnibus. The new innovation spread rapidly throughout urban America. By the mid-1880s, some 525 horsecar lines were operating in 300 American cities. Between the 1850s and about 1890, as urban geographer David Ward has noted, "horsedrawn streetcars were the most important form of local transportation in American cities."

The horsecar system had a more significant impact on urban spatial development than earlier transit innovations. Horsecar fares were lower—about five cents per ride. Urban politicians generally sought to keep fares low through their control over transit franchises. Thus, the luxury of riding to work rather than walking was no longer limited to the wealthy and business classes. Now middle-class urbanites, white-collar workers, perhaps even some skilled tradesmen could join the outward movement of population. As one Philadelphian observed in 1859, the streetcar was "producing a complete revolution" in urban life by encouraging the "spread of the city over a vast space, with all the advantages of compactness and also the advantages of pure air, gardens, and rural pleasure."

As horsecar lines radiated outward as much as five miles or more from the urban center, new residential development sprang up along and near the transit arteries. Many transit companies were actively involved in real estate speculation and subdivision development in outlying areas. The availability of horsecar service to workplaces in the urban core hastened suburban lot sales and house building. Suburban development, in turn, increased both the outward movement of population and the profits of the companies. Thus, at the very time when American industrial cities were experiencing explosive population growth, the horsecar lines permitted a dispersal of population to outlying city wards and new suburban towns. Indeed, it was the pressure of rising population that stimulated new technological innovation in transportation and many other fields.

But the days of the horse were numbered. Through technological innovation, mechanically powered vehicles soon replaced the horsecar. In the 1870s, for instance, a number of cities experimented with the cable car. Introduced in San Francisco in 1873 by Andrew S. Hallidie, a wire manufacturer from Scotland, the cable car was put into motion by clamping onto a moving underground wire cable. A stationary steam engine provided the power to keep the cable moving, while the cable car operator could attach or detach the car from the cable by the use of a grip extending below the street's surface through a slot between the tracks. The cable car was superior to the horsecar as a means of urban transportation, especially in hilly cities such as San Francisco and Pittsburgh where horses often had difficulty traversing steep grades. The cable car was also faster, easily attaining speeds of 10 miles per hour. Larger cars meant more passengers, and the ride was smoother and more comfortable than that provided by the horsecar.

By the mid-1890s, some 626 miles of cable car track had been put into operation in over 20 American cities. Chicago, with 86 miles of track in 1894, had the largest cable car system of any city. By that time, however, several disadvantages had become apparent. Heavy construction and installation costs burdened most cable car systems. In 1893 in New York City, for example, the Metropolitan Traction Company completed a cable car line from lower Manhattan to 59th Street at a cost of $1 million per mile, or about 20 times the cost of horsecar track. Other problems included broken cables, frequent breakdowns, high maintenance costs, hazardous conditions at curves and intersections, and the necessity to operate at a uniform speed regardless of traffic conditions. The limits of cable car technology stimulated the search for new alternatives in urban transit.

The most important transit innovation of the late 19th century came with the electrification of the street railways. In 1888 Frank Sprague, a young engineer who had worked with Thomas Edison, successfully converted the horsecar system of Richmond, Virginia, to electricity. Drawing electrical current from overhead wires, the new streetcars—or trolleys, as they were called—proved vastly superior to horsecars and even the cable car system. Average speeds of 10 to 12 miles per hour made possible an even longer journey to work for residents of the urban periphery and the new suburbs. As electric trolley systems were built, densely settled areas in cities such as Boston and Chicago sprawled 10 and more miles from the urban core.

Electrified transit caught on quickly in the 1890s. City after city abandoned the horsecar and the cable system in short order. By 1902, when the federal government surveyed city transportation, 97 percent of urban transit mileage had been electrified. In that year, more than 2 billion urban passengers were carried on 22,000 miles of trolly car track. In Pittsburgh alone, between 1890 and 1902 electric streetcar mileage increased from 13 to 470, passengers from 46.3 million to 168.6 million, and rides per inhabitant from 108 to 263. The electric streetcar, according to transportation scholar, George W. Hilton, "was one of the most rapidly accepted innovations in the history of technology."

Electrification stimulated two other mass transit innovations. Like horsecars and cable cars, the electric trolley had to compete with pedestrians and with other vehicles for space in city streets. Frequent traffic jams in congested downtown areas slowed the streetcars considerably. In the most populous cities, engineers sought to avoid street-level congestion by building rapid transit systems both above and below ground. Soon after Sprague's successful experiment with electrification in Richmond, elevated lines were constructed in Brooklyn, Boston, Philadelphia, Kansas City, and Chicago. In New York City, a steam-powered elevated system built in 1869 was converted to electricity, while newly built elevateds extended out into the suburbs.

Electricity also permitted the establishment of subway systems, beginning with Boston in 1897, followed by New York in 1904, and Philadelphia in 1908. Some of these systems were quite extensive. New York City, for instance, built about 100 miles of subways between 1900 and 1920. Subway building in the early 20th century brought to an end more than a half century of technological innovation in urban mass transit. In 1908, the year the Philadelphia subway was completed, Henry Ford brought out his first Model T automobile. Mass production of automobiles at a relatively moderate price soon began to influence urban transportation patterns. By 1920 more than 8 million automobiles were registered in the United States, along with over 1 million trucks and buses. As they were for the horsecar in the 1890s, the days of the electric streetcar were numbered. The future belonged to the automobile.

Many commuter rail lines also converted to electric power after 1890. New interurban trains linked central cities with distant suburbs far beyond the reach of the streetcar systems. In Los Angeles, for instance, a wealthy transit operator and land developer named Henry E. Huntington built two extensive interurban railway systems—the Pacific Electric Railway and the Los Angeles Railway. By 1911, the two companies had 975 miles of interurban track—a commuter rail network which stretched all across the Los Angeles metropolitan area. As were the streetcar companies, many interurban operators were involved in land speculation and development, thus shaping the growth of the urban periphery. Nationwide, by 1920 some 40,000 miles of electric interurban track carried long-distance commuters, while permitting speedy and efficient travel between cities. By the mid-20s, however, many interurbans had become bankrupt. Like the streetcar, the electric interurban train fell victim to the automobile.

A NEW GEOGRAPHY
OF URBAN SPACE

It would be difficult to overestimate the significance and the impact of the urban mass transit innovations of the late 19th century. The horsecar and the electric trolley brought numerous spatial and structural changes to the American industrial city. The streetcar intensified the patterns first initiated by the omnibus and the commuter railroad. The streetcar, one scholar noted, "acted as an inexorable force in molding American cities." It caused dramatic changes in population distribution, economic location, and the uses of urban space. Technological advances in urban transportation, in short, ended the era of the walking city.

The new transit facilities permitted the physical expansion of the city. The horsecar and the electric trolley, with their five cent fares, encouraged middle-class people, white-collar workers, and skilled artisans to join the wealthy and the professionals in the trek to the urban fringe. As the streetcar lines radiated from the urban core, outlying city wards experienced rapid population growth. New suburbs sprouted beyond city limits. A vast population movement to the periphery took place over the last part of the 19th century and the early years of the 20th. The residential suburb, with its single-family homes and other amenities, seemed an attractive alternative to the crowded, noisy, unhealthy living conditions of the industrial city.

Urban growth and annexation patterns reflected the new spatial order of the industrial city. As urban populations spread out, cities began to annex the newly developing suburbs. One of the largest 19th century annexations took place in 1854, when the city of Philadelphia consolidated with Philadelphia County. As a result Philadelphia expanded its area from 2 to 130 square miles. Between 1868 and 1873, the streetcar suburbs of Roxbury, Dorchester, and West Roxbury were added to Boston, adding over 20 square miles to the city. Annexations in 1868 and 1873 added 75,000 people to Pittsburgh's population and increased the city's size from 2 to 27 square miles. In 1889 Chicago annexed 133 square miles of suburban territory, including the communities of Hyde Park, Kenwood, Woodlawn, South Chicago, and Pullman. This annexation added over 200,000 people to the city's population. In 1898 New York City grew from 44 to 299 square miles when Manhattan was consolidated with Brooklyn, Queens, Staten Island, and the Bronx. During 30 years of suburban annexation between 1890 and 1920, Los Angeles grew from 29 to 364 square miles.

The annexation process was the same almost everywhere. Cities in the Northeast and Midwest expanded mostly in the years before 1900, while southern and western cities grew in size primarily after 1900 (see Table 7). The timing of annexation movements was generally related to a city's age, its population growth, and its level of economic development. Integral to suburban development and the annexation process throughout urban America, however, was the streetcar—the technological link between the central cities and the expanding suburban frontier.

As the urban population sprawled outward, other spatial and structural changes were taking place in the industrial city. The walking city of the early 19th century had been characterized by a mixture of land uses and a residential pattern in which small distances separated people of different economic classes and ethnic groups. New mass transit facilities contributed to a spatial rearrangement of these patterns in the urban core. The streetcar encouraged the wealthy and the middle class to abandon the central district of the city as a place of residence. Simultaneously, the urban working class, immigrants, and the poor began occupying vacated housing in the urban core. In this process, large homes built for the middle and upper classes were subdivided into small apartments or transformed into boarding houses for the less well off. Rising urban population made housing competition intense, thus driving up rents and population densities.

New methods of urban transit had other long-range results. The physical growth and expansion of the city promoted social fragmentation and differentiation, as people sorted themselves out by class, ethnicity, and race. The working class and the poor concentrated in the urban center. Patterns of social life and residence increasingly became segregated by race and ethnic group. Black ghettos emerged for the first time in the largest cities; this development was intensified by the black migration to the North after 1890. Similarly, immigrants tended to cluster in neighborhoods with their fellow countrymen. It was rare that one ethnic

Table 7

Size of Selected Cities in Square Miles 1860–1920

City	1860	1890	1920
Atlanta	—	9	27
Baltimore	13	30	79
Birmingham	—	3	49
Boston	5	39	44
Chicago	17	178	199
Cincinnati	7	25	71
Cleveland	9	28	57
Dallas	—	9	23
Denver	—	17	59
Detroit	13	28	80
Houston	9	9	39
Kansas City	4	13	60
Los Angeles	29	29	364
Memphis	2	4	25
Minneapolis	5	53	53
New Orleans	162	196	196
New York	22	44	299
Oakland	5	11	53
Omaha	6	25	38
Philadelphia	130	130	130
Pittsburgh	2	27	42
Portland	2	6	66
Providence	5	15	18
Richmond	2	5	24
St. Louis	14	61	61
St. Paul	5	52	52
Salt Lake City	—	8	52
Seattle	11	13	68

Source: R. D. McKenzie, *The Metropolitan Community* (New York, 1933), pp. 336–39.

group comprised more than 40 percent of any particular neighborhood, but the presence of ethnic institutions such as churches, clubs, saloons, coffee houses, restaurants, and groceries served as a magnet drawing immigrants to one urban neighborhood or another.

People sorted themselves out in the new streetcar suburbs, too. As Sam Bass Warner demonstrated in his now-classic book, *Streetcar Suburbs: The Process of Growth in Boston, 1870–1900* (1962), the new suburbanites tended to live in income-graded communities—that is, they lived in neighborhoods with others of a similar economic status and they built houses of a style and cost much like those of their neighbors. The inner city was usually segregated by race and ethnicity, while the suburbs radiating out from the center divided along economic class lines. The existence of tree-shaded homes in the suburbs, Warner wrote, persuaded the urban working class "that should they earn enough money they too could possess the comforts and symbols of success." Urban workers dreamed of home ownership and a suburban lifestyle for their families, but only economic success could make that dream come true. Thus, the new spatial order of the industrial city promoted a deep-seated social segmentation based on class, race, and ethnicity.

As people sorted themselves out in the city and the suburbs, social and political life became fragmented. In the walking city, as historian Samuel P. Hays has noted, human relationships had been based on personal, face-to-face contacts. Expanding rapidly and filled with newcomers who remained highly mobile in their new locations, the American industrial city came to be characterized by looser and more impersonal human relationships. Social fragmentation also affected life in the streetcar suburbs. The new suburbanites were united in their desire to escape the evils of the city, but they did not always create cohesive new communities with shared values and visions. And, as Warner has pointed out, the imposition of the gridiron street pattern on the suburbs tended to create a weak and formless community life—a pattern shared by the automobile suburbs of the 20th century.

These social and structural changes in urban life demonstrated the impact of both decentralizing and centralizing forces. The outward spread of population and its differentiation clearly reflected decentralization. New communities, subcultures, and neighborhoods based on class, ethnicity, and race developed around common physical space, cultural traditions, group interests, and local institutions. Ultimately, city politics provided the forum where these conflicting groups and interests competed for a share of power and decision making.

Centripetal pressures were at work in the industrial city, as well, but the impact of such forces was felt at different levels of urban existence. This pattern was more apparent in the business sector. Financial, industrial, and marketing operations were increasingly concentrated physically in the downtown commercial center and centralized functionally in the emerging giant corporations. Urban politics also reflected the interests of these centralizing forces, as the business class sought to influence or control municipal government. In the largest sense, new mass transit technology revolutionized the social and political life of the industrial city, as well as its spatial and residential patterns.

THE CENTRAL BUSINESS DISTRICT

Technological innovation in urban transit initiated a significant redistribution of urban population and residence to the suburbs. Similarly important changes were taking place in central city geography. During the industrial era, most American cities first developed a central business district (CBD). The CBD resulted from the convergence of several dynamic forces in the last three decades of the 19th century. Rapid economic growth, for instance, increased the commercial and manufacturing activities that took place in the city. The emergence of large industrial corporations in this period was accompanied by the growth of a managerial bureaucracy—a white-collar work force centralized in new downtown office buildings. The availability of a multitude of standardized manufactured products contributed to the development of a consumer-oriented society, which in turn stimulated extensive and specialized retail activities in central urban locations. And, of course, the streetcar drew population away from the urban core, leaving behind few with sufficient power or wealth to challenge the emerging spatial order of the central business district.

As these various forces worked their inexorable influence on the industrial city, a startling transformation of the urban core took place. Central city space became exceedingly desirable for business, commercial, and retail purposes. Land values in the central city shot up astronomically. In downtown Chicago, as land economist Homer Hoyt demonstrated, lots averaging $500 a front foot in 1877 had risen to $4,000 a front foot in 1891. Some particularly desirable locations sold for as much as $18,000 per front foot in the 1890s. As a result of changing land values, older residential buildings in the CBD, occupied primarily by low-income workers, immigrants, and blacks, were leveled to make way for more profitable business uses.

By the late 19th century, most industrial cities experienced building booms in the emerging CBD. New banks, hotels, department stores, office buildings, and even skyscrapers went up in short order. In Pittsburgh, for instance, some 428 buildings were constructed in the CBD between 1888 and 1893. Construction slowed temporarily during the depression of 1893, but soon picked up again. Another 356 buildings were added to the Pittsburgh CBD between 1894 and 1906. The building boom in downtown Pittsburgh typified the experience of industrial cities across the nation.

Not only were most residential buildings displaced by business and commercial structures in the emerging CBD, but land uses became differentiated and specialized for the first time. As the industrial role of the city grew in importance, waterfront and railroad terminal facilities expanded over substantial areas of centrally located urban space. Designed to facilitate the movement of both passengers and freight, dozens of new central city rail terminals were built as the national railroad network was completed. Indeed, the railroad terminal became a symbol of urban progress and prestige. Cities sought to out do one another in the architectural opulence and grandeur of their railroad stations. More than just symbols, however, urban railroad facilities served crucial economic functions.

Along with the expansion of transportation facilities, separate warehouse and storage districts developed close to railroad terminals and harbor facilities. Numerous industries, especially light manufacturing that did not require much horizontal space, also located nearby because of easy access to docks and rail terminals. Thus, as central city space became too valuable and too expensive for low-income residences, much of the urban territory on the fringes of the CBD was gobbled up by expanding transportation, manufacturing, and storage uses.

In addition, clearly defined portions of the urban core were given over to other economic functions. Most large American cities became regional financial, administrative, and commercial centers. They served surrounding rural and agricultural hinterlands as well as their own urban populations. The new multistory office buildings of the CBD housed banks and insurance companies, the agencies of state and city governments, and the white-collar bureaucracies of the corporations. Distinct sections of the CBD emerged as hotel, theater, and entertainment districts. Eventually, urban specialization was completed, as "red light" districts offering prostitution, gambling, and other illegal entertainment sprouted on the fringes of the urban core.

Downtown shopping districts also grew up in the CBD. Specialized retail stores catering to middle-class and wealthy consumers concentrated in centrally located areas near streetcar lines. The role of the CBD as a shopping district was strengthened by the department store—a new urban institution that rose to prominence during the industrial era. Among the early department stores, some dating as early as the 1850s and 1860s, were A. T. Stewart's and Macy's in New York, Filene's in Boston, Wanamaker's in Philadelphia, Rich's in Atlanta,

Marshall Field's in Chicago, and the Emporium in San Francisco. Each of the great department stores sold a wide range of merchandise. Using advertising, promotion, and mass sales techniques, they appealed to a large urban consumer market, especially women. These giant consumer palaces, whose patrons came by streetcar from the suburbs and the urban periphery, enhanced the downtown shopping districts as a central focus of city life.

A transformation of the urban core, then, accompanied the industrialization of urban America. Business, administrative, commercial, cultural, and entertainment functions were centralized. This process reached its height in Chicago's highly concentrated central business district, called the Loop because it was encircled by an elevated transit line. "Within an area of less than a square mile," one Chicago booster wrote in 1910, "there are found the railway terminals and business offices, the big retail stores, the wholesale and jobbing businesses, the financial center, the main offices of the chief firms of the city, a considerable proportion of the medical and dental professions, the legal profession, the city and county governments, the post office, the courts, the leading social and political clubs, the hotels, theaters, Art Institute, principal libraries, labor headquarters, and a great number of lesser factors of city life." The streetcar paved the way for the deconcentration of residential population and permitted the centralization of the urban labor force. The new corporate-industrial economy demanded greater amounts of urban space. The CBD was the ultimate result of this changing geography of the industrial city.

New spatial patterns were observable on the urban periphery, as well. Several historians have noted that the modern industrial city became divided functionally between zones of work and residence. The spatial reorganization of the central city gradually pushed low-income and working-class residential areas toward the urban fringe. Most cities also experienced some industrial development on the urban periphery, especially in those industries requiring extensive horizontal space. High land costs eventually forced such industries to seek cheaper factory sites outside the urban core—a pattern typical in such industries as steel, stockyards and meatpacking, food processing, and, by the 20th century, automobiles.

In addition, as the streetcar lines radiated outward from the CBD, secondary business districts grew up at important intersections on the urban fringe. Land values along street car routes rose rapidly. In Baltimore, for instance, land in one urban fringe area sold for $450 per acre in 1866. After the introduction of horsecar service in 1872, the same land sold for $16,000 per acre. Lots along the horsecar and streetcar routes were especially desirable for commercial, retail, and multifamily residential uses. The interstices between the radiating arms of the streetcar lines filled in only slowly and not completely until the automobile freed urbanites from the dictatorship of mass transit. Thus, the radial pattern of urban development prevailed until the end of the industrial era.

THE SKYSCRAPER

New building technology altered the use of urban space. The growing demand for central city land stimulated technological innovations that permitted cities to grow upward as well as outward. In 1888, a real estate columnist for the *Chicago Tribune* remarked on the new building pattern: "In real estate calculations Chicago has thus far had but three directions, north, south, and west, but there are indications now that a fourth is to be added, and that it is to cut a larger figure in the coming decade than all the others. This new direction is zenithward. Since water hems in the business centre on three sides and a nexus of railroads on the south, Chicago must grow upward."

By the early 20th century, the skyscraper had come to dominate the urban skyline in many large cities. Until the 1880s, the massive weight of brick and masonry construction limited building heights to between 5 and 10 stories. Use of a structural steel framework, with light masonry walls and plate-glass windows, freed architects to build upward to the sky. The invention of the electric elevator provided an efficient means of carrying passengers to the higher reaches of the new skyscrapers.

Although most large cities eventually had some tall buildings, skyscraper construction was concentrated in Chicago and New York City during the industrial era. By the 1870s, the erection of tall office buildings started the transformation of New York from a horizontal to a vertical city. Two of these buildings—the Western Union Building, designed by George B. Post, and the New York Tribune Building, by Richard M. Hunt —reached the unprecedented heights of 230 and 260 feet respectively. However, these and other tall buildings in New York's central business district in the immediate post–Civil War era utilized traditional masonry construction.

It was in Chicago, rather than New York, that architects and builders first adopted the internal steel skeleton and light masonry curtain walls for tall office buildings. Using these revolutionary construction techniques, Chicago architect and engineer, William LeBaron Jenney, built the Home Insurance Building, a functional 10-story structure completed in 1885. Clearly a departure from the New York buildings, the Home Insurance Building has been called by architectural historian Carl W. Condit "the first true skyscraper, the first complete answer to the problem of large-scale urban construction." Jenney's innovative achievement touched off a wave of late 19th-century skyscraper construction in Chicago in the new architectural style—a style that emphasized efficiency and economy and has come to be called the "Chicago school of architecture." As architectural historian Sigfried Giedion pointed out in his classic study, *Space, Time, and Architecture* (1949), in the 1880s and 1890s such Chicago architects as Louis Sullivan and Daniel H. Burnham "covered the whole business district with a new architecture" and "changed the entire face of a great modern city."

But if Chicago leaped ahead in the construction of functionally efficient skyscrapers in the late 19th century, all shrank before New York's early 20th-century architectural wonder—the Woolworth Building. Designed by architect Cass Gilbert and completed in 1913, the Woolworth Building soared to 55 stories. Some 760 feet in height, it was the tallest building in the world and remained so for almost two decades before being surpassed first by the Chrysler Building (1929) and then the Empire State Building (1931), both also in New York City. Built by Frank W. Woolworth, founder of a chain of over 600 five-and-dime stores, the Woolworth Building featured a Gothic design that stressed the vertical lines of the structure and gave it the appearance of soaring into the sky. With its towers and piers, its pointed arches, its elaborate ornamentation, and its extravagant style, the Woolworth Building resembled the Gothic cathedrals of medieval Europe. Indeed, Cass Gilbert's creation became a sort of secular cathedral—an architectural symbol of the commercial spirit and a huge billboard advertising the Woolworth stores.

The skyscraper also found its way into the realistic fiction of the late 19th century, where it symbolized the modern and technological character of the urban landscape. Skyscraper imagery dominated Henry Blake Fuller's novel, *The Cliff-Dwellers* (1893), which opened with a dramatic description of high-rise Chicago in the 1890s:

Between the former site of old Fort Dearborn and the present site of our newest Board of Trade there lies a restricted yet tumultuous territory through which, during the course of the last fifty years, the rushing streams of commerce have worn many a deep and rugged chasm. These great canyons . . . cross each other with a sort of systematic regularity. . . . Each of these canyons is closed in by a long frontage of towering cliffs, and these soaring walls of brick and limestone and granite rise higher and higher with each succeeding year, according as the work of erosion at their bases goes onward—the work of that seething flood of carts, carriages, omnibuses, cabs, cars, messengers, shoppers, clerks, and capitalists, which surges with increasing violence for every passing day.

Towering cliffs and canyons seething with traffic and business life—these were the images conveyed in Fuller's fiction. The skyscraper symbolized the new business and corporate domination of the modern city.

Yet, the skyscraper was more than a symbol. Whether it took the form of the functionalism of the Chicago school or the Gothic towers of the Woolworth Building, the new skyscraper architecture represented a realistic response to the changing geography of the American city. As soon as a new building technology became available, the race to the sky began.

APARTMENTS AND TENEMENTS

In only a few decades, the skyscraper startlingly altered the urban skyline. Less dramatic but no less significant was another transformation in the use of urban space—a new residential architecture. Traditional brownstone row houses continued to be popular in sections of New York City, and brick row houses predominated in Philadephia and Baltimore. But single-family dwellings could not meet the rising demands on the urban housing market. Only a more efficient use of urban residential space could accommodate burgeoning city populations. As often happens, demand stimulated innovation. Thus, architects and builders provided two new types of residential building—the apartment house for the rich and the middle class, and the tenement house for the workers, the immigrants, and the poor. While skyscrapers piled offices on top of one another, apartments and tenements stacked up people's homes on centrally located urban real estate.

The rising cost of centrally located urban space made the single-family home almost obsolete in many large industrial cities of the Northeast and the Midwest. Multifamily dwellings for the middle class and the well-to-do, which were unheard of in 1860, became the predominant form of urban residence for such groups by the end of the 19th century. Architectural historians trace the first American apartment house to the five-story Stuyvesant Apartment House built on 18th Street in New York City in 1869. Designed by architect Richard M. Hunt and financed by wealthy socialite Rutherford Stuyvesant, the first apartment house was modeled on the so-called French Flats common in European cities, especially Paris. It was built exclusively for affluent tenants. They had private dwelling space, but none of the burdens of upkeep and maintenance that accompanied homeownership. "The modern flat," one 19th century Chicago writer noted, "is the palace of those who wish to be relieved of house owning and its cares."

The Stuyvesant, according to housing expert James Ford in *Slums and Housing* (1936), "marked a distinct and important step in advance in the design of multiple dwellings and was far reaching in its ultimate influence." The luxury apartment idea caught on quickly—in 1878 the *New York Times* described it as "a domiciliary revolution." Similar buildings soon went up in fashionable residential areas of Manhattan. One such building, the celebrated Dakota on West 72nd Street, although built in 1884, remains to this day an exclusive address of the rich and famous.

Apartment living also became common for the urban middle class. As the *New York Times* noted in 1878, "when the well-to-do and the rich consented to occupy flats, and liked them, the . . . not rich felt that they could afford to occupy them and like them also. Hence, flats became popular." In Boston, apartment construction proliferated in the Back Bay section of the city, as well as in Brookline, Cambridge, and other streetcar suburbs. According to one architectural historian, "miles of new middle-class apartment houses . . . marched out of Boston in every direction." These middle-class apartments were especially popular in that they possessed most of the facilities formerly only available to the rich—luxuries such as electricity, elevators, telephones, central heating, plumbing innovations, and so on.

Boston architects and builders also developed a variation of the standard apartment house—the triple-decker. A three-story building with a single apartment on each floor, the triple-decker represented a new form of multifamily architecture particularly common in Boston and some other New England cities like Worcester. Some triple-deckers were built of brick and stone and quite elegant. Most had cheap wood-frame construction and served the city's working classes. Some 16,000 triple-deckers were built in Boston between 1870 and 1920.

Chicago also experienced a boom in middle-class apartment construction in the late 19th century. In 1883 alone, according to land economist Homer Hoyt, some 1,142 apartment buildings went up, signaling the appearance of "flat fever" in the midwest metropolis. By 1888, however, the *Chicago Tribune* was lamenting the oversupply of apartments in the city: "When this style of building first came into vogue in Chicago it met the needs of a large proportion of the population and was a highly profitable investment. The consequence was a great rush to build them, and now hundreds of them go begging." Some of these new apartment buildings sprouted along Chicago's Gold Coast—the fashionable residential neighborhood of the rich along the city's north shore. Most were built in the central city on the fringes of the business district and strung out along the streetcar lines radiating from the CBD.

The apartment house was more than just a place to live. It also represented a significant business investment on the part of the builder and owner. Luxurious apartments such as the Dakota were well constructed and attractive, with the builder making profits through high rents rather than cheap construction. Apartment buildings for middle-income and working-class families, however, were often shabbily built and thrown up quickly to take advantage of great urban housing demands. As one architectural scholar has suggested: "In a majority of cases in the past the apartment building has been the instrument of speculators, who were interested in it primarily as a means of exploiting land values and only incidentally as a means of providing good living facilities for its occupants."

Nevertheless, the apartment house boom of the industrial era resulted in rather far-reaching changes in urban life and residence. The shift from single-family homes to apartment houses brought a significant transformation of the built environment—one which remains to the present day. In the streetcar city, vertical space became acceptable and even necessary for residential as well as business and commercial purposes.

The urban tenement house also came of age during the industrial era. The first tenement house of record was erected on Water Street in New York City in 1833—a four-story building designed for "many tenants." Others quickly followed in New York and other cities experiencing explosive population growth, especially of poor and unskilled newcomers. In New York City, as Roy Lubove has demonstrated in *The Progressives and the Slums* (1962), some 18,000 shabby tenements had sprouted by 1867. By the end of the 19th century, the inner residential zones of many large cities were covered over with tenement buildings.

The typical form emerged in New York. Here the standard lot of 25 by 100 feet encouraged the construction of deep but narrow buildings covering all but 10 feet at the back of the lot. Usually four to six stories in height and with four separate apartments on each floor, these tenements had none of the conveniences such as elevators and indoor plumbing incorporated in apartment house design; outdoor privies usually filled up the back end of tenement house lots. Because tenement buildings were built on adjacent lots with adjoining walls, interior rooms had no windows until the Tenement Reform Law of 1879. This law imposed minimum requirements of light and air for every room, thus encouraging construction of the so-called dumbbell tenements with their narrow airshafts between buildings. Cheaply built, badly overcrowded, and lacking even the most minimal of facilities, tenement buildings quickly deteriorated. The dumbbell tenement, Lewis Mumford wrote in *Sticks and Stones* (1924), "raised bad housing into an art." By 1901, when new tenement reform legislation outlawed the dumbbell tenement, New York City had some 82,000 "old law" tenement buildings.

Like the skyscraper, the tenement house came to have symbolic functions in some of the realistic fiction of the late 19th century. In *Maggie: A Girl of the Streets* (1893), Stephen Crane depicted the slum inhabitants of New York's Bowery and Tenderloin districts. One particular tenement, a "careening building" in a "dark region,' is described in gruesome detail. Filled with dust, clutter, fighting children, and screaming women, "the building quivered and creaked from the weight of humanity stamping about in its bowels.''

Similarly, in *Yekl: A Tale of the New York Ghetto* (1896), Abraham Cahan wrote about the Jewish immigrants in New York's Lower East Side. Walking the tenement streets, Cahan's protagonist Jake ''had to pick and nudge his way through dense swarms of bedraggled half-naked humanity; past garbage barrels rearing their overflowing contents in sickening piles, and lining the streets in malicious suggestion of rows of trees; underneath tiers and tiers of fire escapes, barricaded and festooned with mattresses, pillows, and featherbeds not yet gathered in for the night. The pent-in sultry atmosphere was laden with nausea and pierced with a discordant and, as it were, plaintive buzz. Supper had been despatched in a hurry, and the teeming populations of the cyclopic tenement houses were out in full force.'' The fiction of Crane and Cahan dramatized the plight of the immigrant poor in the tenement house districts.

In 1900, portions of the Jewish Tenth Ward in the Lower East Side reached density levels of 900 persons per acre, or about 500,000 per square mile. As historian Kenneth T. Jackson has noted, the Lower East Side at the turn of the century had ''the highest recorded density of population in world history.'' The Lower East Side, of course, had been built over with five and six story tenement houses, making such a concentration of population possible.

Although few cities had a tenement problem to match New York's, every big industrial city developed inner districts of shabby and deteriorating multifamily dwellings. In Boston, for instance, districts of badly built triple-deckers turned into lower-class slums. Thus, while the wealthy and the middle class were adjusting to the vertical residential space of the apartment house, the lower class found their vertical niche in the new spatial order of the city, as well. For immigrants and blacks, for unskilled workers and the urban poor, the architectural innovation with the greatest impact on their lives was the tenement house.

The industrial era, then, was characterized by new technologies that revolutionized urban life and the uses of urban space. Other technological achievements of the era simply strengthened the dynamic forces underlying the new spatial configuration. New engineering techniques, for instance, permitted the spanning of rivers with suspension bridges, thus pulling new peripheral territory into the urban orbit. The magnificent Brooklyn Bridge, designed by engineer John A. Roebling and completed in 1883, not only linked Manhattan Island with Brooklyn, but symbolized the indomitable and expansive spirit of the industrial era. Similarly, the invention of the telephone in 1876 by Alexander Graham Bell eliminated the necessity for the face-to-face contacts of the preindustrial period and brought a communications revolution to urban America. The typewriter, patented by a Wisconsin printer in 1868, soon made its appearance in every skyscraper office building, bringing a new degree of efficiency to the paperwork of the corporate-industrial economy. The invention and widespread adoption of the cash register in the 1880s brought a similar sort of efficiency to the department stores and retail shops of the emerging central business districts.

But the technological innovations with the greatest impact in creating the new spatial order of urban America were those in transportation and building. Streetcars and subways, skyscrapers and tenements changed the texture of urban life and permanently altered the built environment of the American city. Together these innovations in transit and construction dealt the death blow to the preindustrial walking city and ushered in the era of the modern metropolis.

THREE

The Factory and the City

By the late 19th century, most of the necessary preconditions for the rise of the large industrial city had been satisfied. The United States entered a period of sustained industrial growth after the Civil War. During these years, the United States had the fastest growing economy of any nation in the world. These were also the years of intense urbanization. Obviously, important inter-relationships linked the city and the factory. Indeed, "the multiplication of factories, product output, and markets since 1860," urban geographer Allan Pred has written, "is virtually synonymous with city development." The dynamic forces of industrialization and urbanization nurtured and sustained each other. The factory and the city grew up together in the 19th century, strengthening and stimulating each other in the process.

INDUSTRIALIZATION

A number of closely intertwined ingredients combined to prepare the United States for an industrial revolution, each interacting with others and pushing the process along. For instance, the native-born and foreign newcomers flocking to the cities for jobs furnished a pool of cheap and easily exploitable labor. The concentration of people in cities and metropolitan areas also created a substantial and compactly situated internal market for manufactured products, consumer goods, and services. At work in this process, as well, was what economists call the multiplier effect. As Pred puts it: "New local demands created both by the factories themselves and by the purchasing power of their labor force . . . call into being a host of new business, service, trade, construction, transportation, professional, and miscellaneous white-collar jobs." The continual growth of the urban population, and of total population as well, meant a constantly expanding market. This, in turn, stimulated greater and greater production, more services, more jobs, more demands.

Technology no less than population growth stimulated industrial development. Inventiveness has often been singled out as one of the distinctive aspects of the American character. This pattern surely prevailed throughout the industrial era. Hundreds and thousands of trained engineers and backyard tinkerers applied their skills in the creation of new machines and new processes. Economic historians have demonstrated a close link between the city and invention during the industrial era. Urbanization encouraged inventiveness, which in turn generated continuous economic growth. By 1910, more than 1 million patents had been registered at the U.S. Patent Office, nine-tenths of them in the years after 1870.

Invention and innovation affected virtually every productive process and every industry. Technology created new industries in such fields as steel, oil refining, farm machinery, locomotives, food canning, machine tools, electrical equipment, cigarettes, rubber, and automobiles. Technology also provided new sources of energy such as steam, oil, and electricity needed to replace older and less-efficient forms of power. Clearly, innovative industrial technology revolutionized the productive process.

Technology also contributed to the completion of the rail transportation network linking producers to their markets. The railroads had a tremendous impact on American economic growth. Industries such as iron and steel, industrial machinery, and coal received a great stimulus from the railroads. Similarly, the railroads created jobs, hundreds of thousands of them, ranging from unskilled laborers to highly skilled engineers and managers. Railroad employment rose from 80,000 in 1860 to over 2.2 million in 1920. A striking increase in railroad mileage, from 31,000 miles in 1860 to 297,000 miles in 1920, reflected the completion of an integrated railroad network. By 1890, smaller rail lines in the East, Midwest, and South had been consolidated into large railroad empires. Simultaneously, several transcontinental lines pushed across the West to the Pacific coast. Given the vast scale of their investment, operations, and organization, the railroads became the nation's first big business. The railroad network linked far-flung cities in a national market, making possible the startling industrial and urban growth of the late 19th century.

The opening up of the market triggered a vast transformation of the American business structure. A wave of consolidations permanently altered American industry by the end of the 19th century. The centralizing pattern was reflected both in the increasing size of individual firms and in the creation of a few large firms in the major industries. It involved both horizontal consolidation (the merger of firms in the same business) and vertical integration (acquiring control of all aspects of production from raw materials through sales and marketing).

The chief instrument for this transformation of American industry was the corporation—an innovative form of business organization that carried the capitalist drive for profits to new and dizzying heights. The growth of large corporations stimulated an organizational and managerial revolution. The corporate structure became bureaucratic and departmentalized. Business decision making was increasingly confined to the hierarchical structure of the corporation and taken over by a professional managerial class. Business historian Alfred D. Chandler has argued that the corporation emerged as "the major innovation in the American economy between the 1880s and the turn of the century."

The new urban market stimulated the corporate and managerial revolution. However, the role of government in underwriting the industrial surge of the late 19th century should not be overlooked. Government at all levels conceived of economic growth as beneficial and desirable and thus sought to encourage industrial development. In the early 19th century, this encouragement tended to take the form of direct investment in canals and railroads. In the industrial era, the more typical pattern of government support for industry involved easing access to natural resources, providing tax exemptions or tax reductions, or supplying subsidies such as the land grants to the transcontinental railroads. More pervasive was the creation by governments and courts of an unregulated, laissez-faire economic climate. The big new corporations flourished without much governmental interference. Legislation such as the Sherman Antitrust Act designed to curb the monopoly power of large corporations had little effect. Even the regulatory agencies, such as the Interstate Commerce Commission, were often dominated by businessmen and hence were ineffective. In the industrial era, prevailing views held that government should not hinder the businessman's ability to make goods or profits.

THE NEW FACTORY SYSTEM

By the last half of the 19th century, the basic ingredients of an industrial revolution had been brought together. American cities became massive centers for industrial production and related economic enterprise. Previous modes of production—the domestic handicraft system and the small shop pattern—gave way to the new factory system and mass production in virtually every industry. New technology and new machinery revolutionized the process of production by increasing the output, standardizing the product, and reducing costs and the need for skilled labor. With the rise of industrialism, the factory became a characteristic and ever-present urban institution—one that dominated the lives of urban workers and cast its shadow and often its pollution over the urban landscape.

Ultimately, the new factory system became a model of scientific efficiency. Scientific factory management, pioneered by an engineer named Frederick W. Taylor, spread widely by the end of the century. Scientific management brought a new level of organization and structure to factory work. Factory managers rearranged and integrated various aspects of production on the shop floor. They introduced a greater degree of specialization and imposed a more rigorous work discipline on the labor force.

New factory machinery hastened the transformation of work and production. In the shoe industry, for example, the invention of the sewing machine in the 1850s destroyed the traditional artisanal shop pattern of the preindustrial era. Within a decade, shoemakers had become machine tenders, each worker performing one of three dozen or more subdivided tasks in the making of a single pair of shoes. In the clothing industry, jobs formerly completed by a single tailor were subdivided into a dozen or more specialized occupations. Some industries specialized earlier and faster than others, but division of labor soon became, as Harry Braverman suggested in *Labor and Monopoly Capitalism* (1974), "the fundamental principle of industrial organization."

The emphasis on division of labor and specialization of tasks was carried to an extreme in the meat packing industry. According to Sigfried Giedion in *Mechanization Takes Command* (1948), the modern assembly line had its origins in the 1860s in the packing houses of Cincinnati—widely known as "Porkopolis" in the mid-19th century. The early assembly (or rather, disassembly) line consisted of an overhead conveyor system that moved hog carcasses to work stations along the packing-house floor, permitting specialization in the slaughtering process. By the 1880s, the center of the meat packing industry had shifted to Chicago and the division of slaughterhouse labor was intensified.

In his anticapitalist novel, *The Jungle* (1906), Upton Sinclair described in fascinating detail the moving production line in the Chicago slaughterhouses. Moving out of livestock pens and through chutes into the factory, hogs were jerked up by a chain attached to a hind leg and their throats slit. One by one, Sinclair wrote, "a long line of hogs, with squeals and life-blood ebbing away," sailed down the room on an overhead conveyor belt, splashed through a vat of boiling water, and passed through a scraping machine. Then, the carcasses were hoisted again and "sent upon another trolley ride, this time passing between two lines of men, each doing a certain single thing to the carcass as it came to him."

Now, Sinclair wrote, the division of labor in slaughterhouse work really began in earnest, as men performed their minute and repetitive tasks:

One scraped the outside of a leg; another scraped the inside of the same leg. One with a swift stroke cut the throat; another with two swift strokes severed the head, which fell to the floor and vanished through a hole. Another made a slit down the body; a second opened the body wider; a third with a saw cut the breastbone; a fourth loosened the entrails; a fifth pulled them out—and they also slid through a hole in the floor. There were men to scrape each side and men to scrape the back; there were men to clean the carcass inside, to trim it and wash it. Looking down this room, one saw, creeping slowly, a line of dangling hogs a hundred yards in length; and for every yard there was a man, working as if a demon were after him. At the end of this hog's progress every inch of the carcass had been gone over several times, and then it was rolled into the chilling room.

After 24 hours in the chilling room, the hogs were split, cut, chopped, sliced, pickled, salted, sorted, wrapped, packed, sealed, labeled, and sent on their final journey to the consumer.

The whole slaughterhouse process, Sinclair noted with more than a bit of amazement, was "pork-making by machinery, pork-making by applied mathematics." Thus, scientific management and the drive for efficient factory production encouraged an evermore minute division of labor. In such industries as meat packing and, later, automobiles, the large-scale moving assembly line was the ultimate result of scientific management—the hallmark of the new factory system.

Bigness also characterized the emerging factory system. The factories of the preindustrial era had been small by modern standards. Even as late as 1870, few factories employed more than 500 workers. But as the manufacturing sector expanded rapidly after 1880, factory size grew apace. For instance, the Cambria Iron Works employed about 1,000 workers at its Johnstown, Pennsylvania, plant in 1860. However, Cambria Steel had 4,200 workers in 1880, almost 10,000 in 1900, and 20,000 in 1910.

Huge factories employing many thousands of workers became common across the urban landscape. General Electric employed 15,000 workers at its Schenectady plant in 1910. The Pullman Car Company and International Harvester, both in Chicago, Goodyear Tire and Rubber in Akron, U.S. Steel in Gary, and the Ford Motor Company in Highland Park each had over 15,000 workers by the midteens. By 1920, suggesting the direction of the nation's economic growth, both the Ford and Goodyear plants employed more than 33,000 workers. In 1924, Ford's new River Rouge plant employed over 68,000 auto workers, making it the largest factory in the world. By the 1920s, Detroit's huge new automobile factories had come to symbolize the massive industrial strength of the United States. One direct relationship between the factory and the city, it should be clear, lay in the increasing numbers of industrial workers attracted to life and labor in urban America.

The largest American cities developed highly diversified economies during the industrial era. This pattern prevailed in the big urban centers in the Northeast and the Midwest. In Chicago, for instance, the six largest industries in 1900, in order of importance, were slaughtering and meatpacking, metal products and machine tools, men's clothing, iron and steel, agricultural implements, and railroad cars. In the same year, the leading industries of New York City included men's and women's clothing, printing and publishing, tobacco products, and slaughtering. In St. Louis, leading manufactures included tobacco products, meatpacking, brewing, metal products and boots and shoes. With their numerous factories and huge industrial labor forces, the big manufacturing cities became, as urban historian Sam Bass Warner noted in his innovative study, *The Urban Wilderness* (1972), giant "engines of private enterprise." Generally, the larger the city, the more diversified its industrial economy.

But not all cities followed the diversified pattern of the giant metropolises. Often drawing on local technology, nearby resources, or the production of an agricultural hinterland, many smaller cities specialized in certain kinds of manufacturing— rubber in Akron, glass in Toledo, cash registers in Dayton, electrical products in Schenectady, fur hats in Danbury, brassware in Waterbury, silverware and jewelry in Providence, collars and cuffs in Troy, leather gloves in Gloversville, brewing in Milwaukee, flour milling in Minneapolis, farm machinery in Racine, meat packing in Kansas City and Omaha, cotton goods in Fall River and New Bedford, shoes in Lynn, Haverhill, and Brockton, steel in Youngstown, Johnstown, Birmingham, and Gary. Many of these cities also became regional marketing and financial centers, for industrial activity of any kind generally stimulated subsidiary industries and business operations.

THE URBAN MARKET AND CITY BUILDING

The emergence of a mass consumers' market stimulated urban business people and manufacturers to mechanize production of thousands of consumer items. As a result, the cities became centers for wholesaling and retailing, as well as for manufacturing and industry. Department stores and chain stores selling standardized products clustered in downtown shopping districts. A new emphasis on advertising promoted consumer values and helped to create a consumer market. The urban marketing function reached its height in Chicago, from which the mail-order catalogs of Montgomery Ward and Sears, Roebuck reached into homes in every part of the nation. Actually, the industrial era was characterized by a rising proportion of American workers in transportation, finance, marketing, and service occupations. The new consumer society required armies of workers to move, distribute, advertise, finance, sell, and service mass-produced goods. Thus, the growth of the industrial city was closely tied to the growth of the mass market and consumerism.

Clearly, the industrial and economic growth of the era focused on the American city. Although distinctly different processes, urbanization and industrialization were closely intertwined and often interdependent. Technology supplied a common thread, for both the big city and the new factory were made possible by new forms of transportation, new machines, new sources of power, and new industrial processes. Similarly, the growth of an urban market stimulated industrial production, which in turn attracted more workers to the city, thus speeding the urbanization process, enlarging the urban market, spurring further production, and so on. As Chandler has suggested, "without the rapidly growing urban market there would have been little need and little opportunity for the coming of big business in American industry." The factory and the city grew to maturity together during the industrial era.

The city building process itself suggests another connection, another dimension of the inseparable tie between urbanization and industrial growth. Rapid urban population increases and the consequent physical expansion of American cities created unprecedented building and construction demands. The cities of the industrial age experienced incredible building booms in houses and apartments, factories and warehouses, office build-ings and department stores, government buildings and skyscrapers. The physical growth of the city required expansion of public services and the creation of entirely new facilities—streets, bridges, docks, parks, sewer systems, subways and elevateds, and public utilities such as electricity, natural gas, and water supply.

These urban construction projects created a major market for producers of iron, steel, and other metals, as well as stone, brick, concrete, asphalt, glass, lumber, and electrical equipment. Urban construction and physical development, financed both by public and private capital, put hundreds of thousands of people to work in cities across the nation, stimulating the consumer market in the process. One such construction project—the 35-mile New York City subway system completed in 1904—employed 10,000 men for almost four years and required 73,000 tons of steel and cast iron and 551,000 yards of concrete. Every city had its big building projects. As economic historian Edward C. Kirkland argued in *Industry Comes of Age: Business, Labor, and Public Policy, 1860–1897* (1961), the city building process during the industrial era served as a "generative factor" in the growth of the American economy.

SATELLITE CITIES

Industrial development promoted urban expansion in another way, as well. As urban space became less available and more costly in the industrial city, many industries sought less expensive undeveloped land on the urban periphery. In addition, property taxes were lower outside the central cities and various municipal regulations could be avoided. As a result, as Jon C. Teaford has noted in *City and Suburb* (1979), "many manufacturers withdrew from the heart of the city and sought to create suburban industrial enclaves protected by pliant, made-to-order municipal governments" that would keep taxes low and impose few onerous regulations. The centrifugal pattern was especially common in industries which required large amounts of horizontal space such as steel, meat packing, and automobiles. The railroads also used vast expanses of urban territory for storage and loading facilities, repair yards, and the like.

Thus, the growth of great cities was accompanied by the development of outlying industrial suburbs. Contemporary journalist Graham R. Taylor labeled them *satellite cities*. Typical was Pullman, Illinois, a factory and residential town eight miles south of Chicago built in 1880 by George W. Pullman, a manufacturer of railroad sleeping cars. Pullman became famous, first as a planned industrial community, and then as the center of a violent and bloody strike in 1894. But Pullman is also significant for what it reveals about the process of urban growth and expansion. Built in a wild and deserted area, Pullman was annexed to Chicago within a decade, having become part of an expanding industrial district on Chicago's south side.

A similar pattern of satellite city urbanization can be found elsewhere. First established in 1871, Birmingham, Alabama, soon became the boomtown of the new South. The city's iron and steel mills were located in a ring of industrial communities outside the city limits, but many were annexed to the city in 1910. The steel industry of Pittsburgh gradually spread beyond the city boundaries and up the banks of the Allegheny and Monongahela rivers, spurring the growth of such cities as McKeesport, Homestead, and Allegheny; Allegheny was eventually annexed by Pittsburgh in 1907, although McKeesport and Homestead retained their independence. Detroit's auto industry fueled the growth of nearby factory towns such as Hamtramck, Highland Park, Dearborn, and Pontiac. Near Los Angeles, the newly developing oil industry grew in El Segundo and Long Beach, while metal manufacturing provided the impetus for the growth of Torrance. In northwest Indiana, the steel city of Gary emerged after its founding in 1906 as an important satellite city of Chicago. By 1915, when Graham Taylor published his book, *Satellite Cities,* the factory had become a suburban as well as an urban institution.

The suburban movement of industry, then, constituted an important stimulus to the urbanization process. Satellite towns grew up on the outskirts of large cities, filling in empty land with factories and the inevitable housing developments that followed. Although many industrial suburbs retained their political independence, more often they were incorporated into the larger central city through annexation. For each large city, this process of industrial expansion was replicated many times as urbanization relentlessly pushed the periphery outward.

TIME AND THE CAPITALIST ETHIC

Thus, the American industrial city emerged in the late 19th century as the locus of several separate economic functions: a center of production and distribution, the location of financial and corporate decision-making, and a workplace for office and retail clerks, construction laborers, and factory workers. The underlying dynamic, of course, was American capitalism, which held that the values of individualism, competition, consumerism, and economic growth were uniformly positive and beneficial. As historian Oscar Handlin has written, the modern city "housed a pack of people seeking after gain." In the industrial era, the pursuit of profit prevailed, although relatively few enjoyed its rewards.

Buttressed by capitalism, consumerism, the corporation, and the factory, the American economy surged ahead. Urbanization and industrialization together pushed the United States into a period of highly sustained economic expansion. As a result, by the end of the 19th century, the value of American manufactures surpassed the combined industrial output of Britain, France, and Germany, the world's industrial leaders in 1860.

Industrialism and the new factory system substantially transformed ways of living and working in the modern American city. For example, industrialization brought a new conception of time. The streetcar schedule, the factory whistle, the time clock, the railroad timetable, even the school bell—all were integrally related to the new capitalistic order. Typically, in his new factory town in Illinois, George Pullman erected a huge Victorian bell tower in 1880, a constant reminder to the workers of the discipline demanded by the new factory system. "In scores of 19th and early 20th-century mill towns," historian Daniel T. Rodgers asserted in *The Work Ethic in Industrial America, 1850-1920* (1978), "no feature stood out more prominently than the great, looming bell towers of the factories. . . . In their great clock faces and clanging bells, the towers broadcast the mechanization of work and time."

Time comprised an important aspect of Frederick W. Taylor's ideas about scientific factory management. Taylor conducted various time-motion studies, using a stopwatch to determine scientifically the time necessary for separate factory operations, then demanding that workers produce according to these standards. When the moving assembly line was introduced in meat packing plants, automobile factories, and other industries, factory workers became the servants of a dictator named time, for the moving production line slowed down for no one.

The new consciousness of time and its importance pervaded American industrial society. When the New York City subway opened in 1904, the *New York Times* editorialized that "in modern city life distance is measured in time"—the point being that with speedier urban transit, less time would be wasted in the journey to work. "The dictatorship of the clock and the schedule became absolute," Handlin has written, and the lives of men and women, and children too, became subjected to the new demands of a time-oriented corporate-industrial society.

The growth of the modern industrial city, then, was accompanied by and indeed inseparable from the rise of the new factory system. The city and the factory together marched across the land, putting an indelible mark on modern American society. The mark was not always positive. The noted urbanologist Lewis Mumford has observed that industrialism supplied "the main creative force of the nineteenth century," but that it also "produced the most degraded urban environment the world had yet seen.'' Some would argue that Mumford overstated the case against the industrial city. But uncontrolled urban growth and industrial "progress" did have environmental and social costs. Whatever the costs, the factory became a dominant urban institution and a typical workplace for city people. Like the skyscrapers watching over the new central business districts, the modern factories springing up all over the urban landscape came to symbolize the new age of big business and industry.

FOUR

Boosters, Builders, and Planners

The new city was the product of many dynamic forces that buffeted American society during the industrial years. The industrial revolution and the factory gradually moved the city from a commercial economic base to one centered on manufacturing. Demographic change, especially European immigration and native rural migration, supplied the cities with growing populations of workers and consumers. Technological innovation in urban transit and urban architecture gave the city a new spatial order. To a great degree, therefore, the American industrial city grew as a result of the action and interaction of powerful and impersonal forces—forces that determined the economic structure and physical configurations of urban America.

Yet, the impact of such impersonal forces as industrialization, immigration, and technology should not blind us to the very real and important role of the individual in American urban history. Human choice, individual decision-making, and personal achievement had a great deal to do with the direction of American urbanization and its ultimate results. In some ways, the larger dynamic forces were really comprised of thousands and millions of individual actions and decisions. Each immigrant who came to America, each farmer who moved to the city, each southern black who migrated to the industrial North made a personal choice. Manufacturers and workers, inventors and architects all made individual decisions about where to locate a factory, where to work, where to live, what to invent, or how to build. Sam Bass Warner has demonstrated that in the Boston streetcar suburbs of Roxbury, West Roxbury, and Dorchester, some 23,000 new houses were put up by 9,000 private builders between 1870 and 1900, all personal and individual decisions. Although often constrained by law or by cultural and social values, individual choice and decision making has had a significant and shaping impact on the American city. The individual's role is nowhere better illustrated than in the work of the builders and boosters who promoted city development, and the city planners, landscape designers, and architects who envisioned and created striking new urban designs.

THE CITY BOOSTER

Nineteenth-century American cities, especially those newly established in the raw and unsettled western regions, often owed their origins to individual entrepreneurs, promoters, and speculators. Even before the American Revolution, land speculation had become deeply embedded in the American tradition. Townsite speculation—a particularly intense form of land speculation

—characterized much of the urban development of the Midwest, the great plains, and the Pacific Coast regions. Traditional land speculators profited by selling large tracts to settlers and farmers. By contrast, a townsite speculator needed only a small amount of choice land to set up in business.

The ubiquitous townsite speculator marched across the western frontier, laying out potential metropolises at every likely location, and some that were not so likely. In Kansas, for instance, townsite speculators platted or mapped out the plans of nearly 5,000 towns, but by the 1960s, only 617 remained in existence. As these statistics suggest, most townsite speculations never progressed beyond the planning stage. Yet, some of these instant cities succeeded beyond the expectations of even the most optimistic urban entrepreneur. What generally distinguished success from failure was a combination of luck, timing, and individual initiative.

American history is full of such urban success stories. Some of our largest cities grew from tiny townsite speculations. Chicago, for example, grew rapidly after the arrival on the scene in 1835 of real estate speculator William B. Ogden. Purchasing large tracts of Chicago land, Ogden successfully promoted the city over several decades and realized tremendous profits. This typical 19th-century urban booster served as Chicago's first mayor, organized hospitals, schools, and banks, built bridges and streets, promoted canals and railroads, and developed the city's early water supply, sewage, and park systems. He boosted numerous railroad schemes, helping to make Chicago the rail center of the Midwest. Especially important was his promotion of the Union Pacific Company, a transcontinental line which eventually linked Chicago with the West Coast and of which Ogden became president in 1862. It was commonly suggested at the time and with only slight exaggeration, that "Ogden had built and owned Chicago."

Individual promotion worked urban wonders elsewhere, too. In the late 1850s, gold fever attracted men to the Pike's Peak region of Colorado. One of those drawn to the area was William Larimer, a Pennsylvanian who had engaged unsuccessfully in townsite speculation in Nebraska and Kansas. Larimer arrived on the Cherry Creek in 1858, where the townsite of Auraria had already been laid out. Undaunted, Larimer staked a claim across the creek and set up a rival townsite called Denver. Soon the two nascent communities merged and Larimer became the most effective booster of the new town of Denver. "I am Denver City," Larimer wrote in 1859—a judgment with which most of the town's early residents would have agreed. Larimer pushed for territorial government, built a hotel, and helped organize a newspaper, various business establishments, and other urban amenities. Equally important, he was influential in bringing transportation arteries into Denver, first a stage line and then railroads. According to Daniel Boorstin, author of *The Americans: The National Experience* (1965), Larimer's career as an urban booster "proved the extraordinary ability of the American businessmen of these upstart cities to fuse themselves and their destiny with that of the community."

In 1861, Denver boosterism received new impetus with the arrival of William Gilpin as the first governor of the Colorado Territory. A native Pennsylvanian like Larimer, Gilpin had had a long career as a land speculator and town promoter in Missouri and Oregon. From the 1860s to his death in 1894, Gilpin speculated in Denver real estate, promoted the city's development, lured railroads to Denver, wrote many promotional books and articles, and lectured widely on the prospects of the American West. An enthusiastic booster, Gilpin promoted Denver as the world's future great metropolis—"the crossroads of the world." While this prediction remained unfulfilled, the promotional efforts of Gilpin and Larimer did have some effect. By 1880, with a population surpassing 35,000, Denver had become the largest city in the vast region stretching between Kansas City and San Francisco.

It was a pattern replicated many times over. Tacoma, Washington, was originated by a townsite speculator named Morton M. McCarver. Drawing on his experience in previous speculative projects in Iowa and California, McCarver laid out a town on the eastern shore of Puget Sound and successfully promoted his settlement as the western terminus of the Northern Pacific Railroad, one of the transcontinental lines. Businessman Henry W. Corbett invested his money in the city of Portland, Oregon, where he organized several banks, speculated in real estate, built a hotel and transit system, and established a newspaper. Further south, railroad builder F. M. Smith turned Oakland into a huge real estate speculation, while building and controlling most of the city's transit facilities.

In San Diego, the city's earliest booster was William Heath Davis, who laid out the town's grid system, speculated in land, established a newspaper, and promoted the town by building a wharf, hotels, and numerous stores. When Davis ran out of money, the booster role was assumed by another businessman, Alonzo Erastus Horton, who in the 1860s and 1870s engineered an extensive publicity campaign to promote and sell his town. By the end of the 19th century a third San Diego booster, sugar magnate John D. Spreckels, began pumping large amounts of money into urban promotion and improvement. In Salt Lake City, Brigham Young and the Mormons combined religious fervor with urban development—a boosterism which produced a city with more than 45,000 people in 1890. And so it went throughout the Trans-Mississippi West and the Pacific Coast region. Townsite speculators and urban boosters laid out towns by the hundreds and the thousands, promoting these small planned communities and sometimes guiding them to a future of urban greatness.

The role of railroads cannot be separated from the urban boosterism of the late 19th century. Indeed, the coming of a rail line could make a town spectacularly successful. By the same token, towns bypassed by railroads were often doomed to certain failure, or at least slow growth. Thus, townsite speculation really became dependent on railroad development.

In some ways, railroad men themselves became city builders. In Tacoma, the Northern Pacific Railroad organized a subsidiary, the Tacoma Land Company, which guided the future development of the city. Ignored by the Northern Pacific, Seattle developed slowly until selected by railroad magnate

James J. Hill as the western terminus of the Great Northern Railway, another transcontinental line. The Kansas Pacific Railroad spurred the growth of Denver; the Atchison, Topeka and Santa Fe Railroad underlay the late 19th-century surge of Los Angeles; Reno, Nevada began as a land speculation of the Central Pacific Railroad. In the Southwest, the Texas and Pacific Railroad accelerated the late 19th-century growth of Dallas and Fort Worth, while the Santa Fe, through its subsidiary New Mexico Town Company, boosted the development of Albuquerque. In Arizona, both Tucson and Phoenix owed their survival and growth to the presence of the Southern Pacific Railroad.

According to planning historian John W. Reps, author of the monumental *Cities of the American West* (1979), the railroads were indisputably the chief reason for the rapid urban development of the American West in the late 19th century. The great transcontinental railroad men—James J. Hill, Edward H. Harriman, Henry Villard, Collis P. Huntington, Cyrus K. Holliday, Grenville M. Dodge, and others—were city builders as well as railroad magnates. The railroad men were no less urban boosters and developers than the townsite speculators. Often they were one and the same.

Not all of the great urban promotions occurred in the West. By the late 19th century, a new frontier was opening up in Florida. As in the West, town and city promotion accompanied and sometimes even preceded agricultural development. Florida's chief urban builder was Henry M. Flagler, a partner in John D. Rockefeller's Standard Oil Company. In the 1880s, having made a fortune in oil, Flagler settled in northern Florida and built luxury hotels in St. Augustine. He bought the Florida East Coast Railroad, which he began extending southward along the Florida coast, first to Daytona, then to West Palm Beach in 1894 and Miami in 1896. A tiny village when the railroad arrived, Miami grew rapidly as a result of Flagler's investments and promotion.

In Miami, Flagler built a huge tourist hotel; laid out streets; and built a rail terminal, an electric plant, a sewage system, and a water works. He helped establish public schools and churches, giving land and contributing toward construction costs. He donated land at the town's center for municipal buildings, built docks and wharfs, and dredged the Miami River and a harbor to accommodate oceangoing ships. In addition, in 1896 he established the city's first newspaper, the *Miami Metropolis*—a somewhat pretentious title for a paper in a village of 260 people, but one which suggested big things for the future. At the same time, Flagler was reaping great profits from his Miami land speculations. By 1913, when Flagler died, Miami had become a thriving town of 11,000 people—a town, moreover, destined for future urban greatness. But until Flagler touched the place with his railroad and his millions, Miami had few prospects.

Throughout the late 19th century, then, the planting and promotion of new cities in the South and West was largely the result of individual initiative, drive and profit-seeking. Urban land speculation was limited in the already established cities of the East and Midwest. But the unsettled regions of the western frontier and isolated areas such as south Florida offered unparalleled opportunities for the townsite speculator and the urban developer. Although the dynamic forces of industrialism and change dominated the era, the role of individual action and decision making was not altogether lost. A booster tradition emerged—one promising quick profits but also giving free play to the ambitions of those with an eye out for the main chance.

FREDERICK LAW OLMSTED

While city builders and city boosters promoted their urban development schemes across the nation, another urban tradition was emerging—city planning. Underlying the planning tradition was the belief that urban land uses could be determined scientifically and rationally. However, the very notion of planning contradicted deeply held ideas about private property, rugged individualism, and capitalist competition.

From the beginning of British colonization in America, land was conceived of as a private resource. This concept remained powerful throughout the industrial era. City landowners sought to use their land in the most profitable ways, without much regard for public convenience or human welfare or aesthetics. The ubiquitous rectilinear or "gridiron" street pattern of most American cities reflected the entrepreneurial values of American city builders and big property owners. The gridiron brought a monotonous sameness to American cities, but it was the most efficient and profitable method of dividing up urban land for business purposes and for speculation. Thus, the development of a planning tradition ran against the dominant ideology of the industrial era. That such a tradition emerged at all was due largely to the influence of a few talented and creative individuals who left an indelible mark on the American city.

Frederick Law Olmsted was such a man. A giant of a figure in American urban history, Olmsted made a science of landscape architecture, park development, and urban planning. Born in 1822 in Hartford, Connecticut, Olmsted passed through a succession of careers before finally finding his niche as an urban park maker. He began as a scientific farmer, spent several years as a travel writer in England and in the American South, and in the 1850s embarked on an unsuccessful publishing venture. In 1857, out of work and in debt, Olmsted took a job as superintendent of the labor force that was building New York City's huge Central Park. Soon after, Olmsted joined with Calvert Vaux, an English landscape architect, in submitting a plan in the city-sponsored competition to redesign the park.

The Olmsted-Vaux plan was chosen, and Olmsted himself was put in charge of the park-building project. With the exception of the Civil War years, when he worked with the U.S. Sanitary Commission and as manager of a California mining company, Olmsted spent the rest of his life as a designer and builder of urban parks and other planning projects—parkways, boulevards, riverfronts, suburban developments, and the grounds of railroad stations, public buildings, beaches, playgrounds, fairs, cemeteries, college campuses, private homes, even the U.S. Capitol. Along with a few other early planners, Frederick Law Olmsted was instrumental in establishing the idea and the importance of city planning in America.

Olmsted was a man with an appreciation of urban civilization and a vision of the urban future. In an address in 1870 to the American Social Science Association entitled "Public Parks and the Enlargement of Towns," Olmsted laid out his views about the potentials and the problems of cities. Olmsted identified cities with progress and civilization; they were not only economic centers but the home of learning, art, and culture. And they were destined to grow larger in the future: "Towns which of late have been increasing rapidly on account of their commercial advantages are likely to be still more attractive to population in the future [and] . . . there will in consequence soon be larger towns than any the world has yet known."

City living, however, was accompanied by loss of the old-time, small-town values and sense of community, as well as by the emergence of new social tensions and antagonisms. Olmsted envisioned the large urban park as a natural landscape—a combination of green open spaces and forested areas that would bring rural beauty to the modern city. Such parks would not only provide recreation for urban residents, but because of the marked contrast to the surrounding city they could restore lost happiness and create a psychological sense of freedom. Moreover, parks competed with grog shops and other social evils, thus bringing a sort of moral uplift to urban life. As historian Thomas Bender has suggested in *Toward an Urban Vision* (1975), Olmsted "understood and explained to urban Americans the possibilities of using the natural landscape creatively in an urban civilization."

New York City's Central Park, of course, remains one of Olmsted's greatest contributions. Some two and one-half miles long and one-half mile wide, Central Park is today situated in the center of Manhattan, a great green oasis surrounded by the vertical towers of the city. At the time it was laid out, however, Central Park was located far to the north of the heavily populated residential sections of the city. The park, in other words, was built for the future. In *Frederick Law Olmsted and the American Environmental Tradition* (1972), Olmsted scholar Albert Fein has noted: "The fact that the park was planned in anticipation of future open-space needs is but one reason why

Central Park deserves to be considered the beginning of modern city planning.'' The park had miles of pedestrian paths and bridle trails, sunken transverse roads to accommodate crosstown city traffic, ingeniously separated interior spaces, and a variety of recreational uses. By 1870, according to Olmsted, on days of peak usage as many as 100,000 or more city residents enjoyed the numerous facilities and rural splendors of Central Park.

The success of the Central Park project brought Olmsted a national reputation as a park planner, as well as a national clientele. City after city commissioned Olmsted to plan parks, parkways, and park systems. The large parks that Olmsted designed tended to be located on the urban periphery, where undeveloped land was available. Olmsted generally sought to link these periphery parks with the central city by use of tree-lined parkways or linear riverside parks. Typical of his overall landscape design was the large park system he created for Boston in the 1880s and 1890s. Several large parks on the outskirts of the city were connected by a series of linear watercourse parks and the Commonwealth Avenue parkway to the Public Garden and the Boston Common in the center of the city. Also part of the system were the parks built along the banks of the Charles River, which in turn linked up with beaches and parks laid out around the harbor. As Olmsted's biographer, Laura Wood Roper, has noted: "It was a grand concept, the most sweeping Olmsted had devised."

Olmsted's genius for urban park building found expression not just in New York and Boston, but in more than 20 other large American cities. He put his distinctive stamp on park systems in Brooklyn, Buffalo, Rochester, Detroit, Louisville, Milwaukee, Hartford, Bridgeport, and Wilmington, as well as Montreal in Canada, among others. In Chicago he supervised the conversion of the 1893 World's Fair site into a permanent lakefront park system. In Washington, D.C., he designed the grounds of the United States Capitol. This creative and talented planner also designed the campuses of Stanford University and the University of California at Berkeley, along with numerous suburban developments such as that at Riverside, Illinois.

While Olmsted is best remembered for Central Park in New York, he also had a monumental influence on city planning and urban design in the industrial era. His park designs inspired other landscape architects, notably Horace W. S. Cleveland, who designed marvelous park systems in Minneapolis and Omaha in the 1880s, and George E. Kessler, who built an extensive park and boulevard system in Kansas City and smaller park systems in Cincinnati and Indianapolis in the 1890s. The urban park systems designed by Olmsted and his followers in the late 19th century became a permanent part of the built environment of America's cities—a legacy of individual inspiration and achievement.

DANIEL H. BURNHAM

If Frederick Law Olmsted helped shape the post–Civil War American city, Chicagoan Daniel H. Burnham played a similarly decisive role during the decades spanning the turn of the 20th century. Born in 1846 in upstate New York, Burnham grew up in mid-century Chicago, dabbled unsuccessfully in a variety of jobs, and finally settled on architecture in the mid-1870s. With his partner, John Wellborn Root, Burnham soon established himself as one of the leading practitioners of the emerging Chicago school of architecture.

Jenney's Home Insurance Building may have been the first steel skeleton skyscraper, but the firm of Burnham and Root quickly dominated this new building style. Their tall office buildings, with the clean and efficient lines typical of the Chicago school of architecture, soon dominated the city's central business district. The firm also peppered Chicago with hundreds of private homes, apartment houses, hotels, office buildings, department stores, warehouses, churches, schools, and other structures. Achieving a national reputation, Burnham designed buildings in virtually every major American city, including the Flatiron Building (1903) in New York City—perhaps his most famous and distinctive structure. But Burnham's significance for American urban history lies not so much with his architectural achievements, important though they were, as with his contribution to the developing movement for city planning.

Most planning historians trace the impetus for modern urban planning to the Chicago World's Fair of 1893. Designed to commemorate the 400th anniversary of Columbus's discovery of America, the Chicago Fair was an extravagant and exuberant testimonial to American achievement and progress—"a celebration of America's coming of age," historian David F. Burg has noted, "a grand rite of passage." As Chicago's leading architect, Daniel Burnham was the natural choice as the fair's chief planner and "director of works." Burnham supervised a team of architects and landscape experts, including Olmsted, pushed and cajoled a massive construction crew, conquered a host of logistical and building problems, and succeeded in completing the fair in time for opening in the spring of 1893.

During the summer months, more than 21 million visitors were treated to a dazzling display of American technology and talent. But the central and lasting achievement of the so-called White City lay in its unified planning and the predominantly neoclassical architecture of its main buildings. It stimulated a new sense of the aesthetic possibilities of the city, spurring a city beautiful movement across the land. The fair, according to Burnham biographer Thomas S. Hines, "provided for Burnham and his fellow planners and architects a laboratory for testing ideas and turning dreams into realities." Moreover, Hines wrote, "the challenge of organizing and building the exposition inspired and equipped Burnham ultimately to become one of modern America's first great city planners." Burnham later described the fair as a sort of watershed in American history, one which taught the great lesson of unified and comprehensive city planning.

Burnham himself spent much of the rest of his life spreading the planning message. His 1901–1902 plan for the nation's capital typified the city beautiful movement of the progressive era. Heading a commission for the planning of Washington,

D.C., Burnham revived and enlarged the original 1791 plan of Pierre L'Enfant. Burnham had been impressed by the classical styles and imperial splendor of Paris and Rome. His Washington plan called for removal of a railroad depot on the west front of the Capitol building and laying out a great mall between the Capitol and the Washington Monument. It also accentuated the city's diagonal boulevards and envisioned the creation of vast promenades and open vistas befitting the capital of a great nation. This aesthetic planning for Washington, Burnham argued, should be accompanied by a uniform neoclassical architectural style for the government buildings, galleries, museums, and memorials which lined the great mall. Gradually implemented over several decades, Burnham's Washington plan drove home the value of comprehensive city planning. Like the Chicago World's Fair, the monumental Washington plan awakened and nurtured the belief that urban life could be orderly and efficient, that cities could be beautiful and inspiring.

Capturing the attention of civic leaders in other cities, Burnham's grandiose Washington plan gave new impetus to urban planning. Over the next decade, in plans for Cleveland, San Francisco, and Chicago, Burnham made distinguished contributions to the new planning movement. Burnham's 1903 plan for Cleveland, for instance, drew inspiration from both the Chicago World's Fair and the Washington model. The Cleveland plan called for a magnificent new civic center, grouping a number of uniformly designed government and cultural buildings around the vast open spaces of a mall.

In San Francisco in 1905, Burnham designed a truly comprehensive city plan. It envisioned a civic center of neoclassical design, a landscaped park and boulevard system, subways to relieve traffic congestion, and a totally new street layout that included a circular drive around the outskirts of the city and diagonals cut across the gridiron. The destructive 1906 earthquake and fire leveled much of the city and made reconstruction along the lines suggested by Burnham possible. Nevertheless, for a combination of political and business reasons, San Francisco adopted very little of the Burnham plan, a plan which Hines described as "the most famous ghost of the City Beautiful Movement."

Fittingly, Burnham's greatest success as an urban planner came in his native city of Chicago. His 1909 plan for Chicago represented comprehensive city planning on the grandest scale. Developed over several years with the support of the Chicago Commercial Club, a powerful civic and business group, Burnham's plan sought to make Chicago practical and efficient as well as beautiful. Burnham called for extensive lakefront development, a monumental civic center, the widening of major streets, diagonal and circular boulevards to ease traffic circulation, the beautification of the Chicago River, the relocation of railroad tracks and terminals, and an extensive system of parks, beaches, harbors, and recreational spaces. Burnham even anticipated the regional planning of the 1920s by incorporating the city's suburbs in a scheme for the redevelopment of the entire Chicago region.

Unlike San Francisco, where the Burnham plan was shelved, Chicago was gradually redesigned over the next 20 years along the basic lines set forth by Burnham. Thus, while Frederick Law Olmsted led the late 19th-century movement for urban parks and park systems, Daniel Burnham dreamed on an even larger scale of entirely new kinds of physical and spatial arrangements in American cities. Burnham spread the idea that comprehensive urban planning would create both the "city beautiful" and the "city efficient."

Olmsted and Burnham made significant and lasting contributions to the emerging urban society in the United States. As their lives and achievements suggest, the rise of industrialism and mass society did not entirely erase the role of the individual as a shaper of the city. The social forces of the industrial era were powerful agents of change. Nevertheless, builders and boosters—such as Ogden, Larimer, and Flagler—and planners and dreamers—such as Olmsted and Burnham—achieved perhaps even more than they intended or imagined.

II.

Urban Government and Politics

FIVE

City Bosses and Machine Politics

The 19th-century growth of the big city posed unprecedented problems for urban government. In the colonial era, municipal government closely resembled what the colonists had known in England. Particularly important was the municipality's role as regulator of the urban market place. The American Revolution, however, with its ideology of personal liberty, freed Americans from the economic restraints of the British mercantilist system. As a result, municipal regulation of the urban economy quickly withered and died. At the same time, the rampant free market ideology of the postrevolutionary period hampered the development of effective municipal government. The perceived lesson of the American Revolution was that powerful government threatened popular liberty. Consequently, governments were slow to assume new powers or provide new services in the exploding 19th-century cities.

These conditions were intensified by the democratization of urban politics and the decentralization of city government in the early 19th century. With the rise of universal male suffrage in the 1820s and other democratizing political changes, mayors served limited terms and lost executive authority. City councils became larger and more representative, but their powers were diluted by decentralization and state intervention. Cities lacked home rule; state legislatures controlled city charters and often limited the powers of city governments. City officials often seemed paralyzed, failing to use what powers they possessed until prompted into action by emergency or crisis. Urban government everywhere became weak and fragmented. By mid-century, a great vacuum had grown at the center of municipal decision making. Typically, *Harper's Weekly* noted in 1857 that New York City had become "a huge semi-barbarous metropolis . . . not well-governed and not ill-governed, but simply not governed at all."

The structural and constitutional weakness of urban government encouraged the emergence of political machines and bosses after the 1850s. As historian Edward K. Spann suggested, in *The New Metropolis: New York City, 1840–1857* (1981), "the fragmentation of authority in politics and government was an invitation for a strong leader with sufficient talent and ruthlessness to seize power." In city after city, it was exactly this fragmented political life that brought the bosses to power.

Urban government was transformed in a variety of ways during the industrial era. One significant new pattern was the rise of the urban political machine. Building on the votes of the urban masses, the machine obtained a tenacious grip on municipal government in the new city. Periodically, reformers swept into office on a wave of revulsion against the machine and the excesses of boss politics. Yet, the bosses were just as regularly voted back into power. Over the long span of modern American history, machine politics has demonstrated a surprising strength and resiliency. Indeed, the boss and the machine buttressed a political system which fit remarkably well with the business and entrepreneurial values of the industrial era.

CHANGING HISTORICAL INTERPRETATIONS

Only recently have historians begun to sort out the political dynamics of the industrial era. Traditional interpretations emphasized the evils of the boss system and the laudable ideals of the municipal reformers. The literature of the late 19th century is filled with complaints about the corruption of city government. As early as 1867, for instance, *New York Times* editor George Jones wrote that the government of New York City was "worse than a failure. . . . It is corrupt, inefficient, wasteful and scandalous. The people are overburdened with taxation and there is nothing to show for it. Millions are wasted and nothing is done. The streets are not cleaned; the public health is not cared for; waste and extravagance characterize every department; and although more money is spent than anywhere else in the world for the purpose of government, the government actually procured by it is the worst in the world." Twenty years later, in his famous book *The American Commonwealth* (1888), a visiting Englishman named James Bryce criticized urban government as "one of the conspicuous failures of the United States."

This sort of criticism of machine-dominated city government continued through the 1890s and into the 20th century. One popular book, *The Twentieth Century City* (1898), written by Protestant leader and publicist Josiah Strong, described the American city as "a menace to state and nation" because it was incapable of self-government: "The maladministration of municipal affairs in our large cities has long since become a national scandal, and the opening up of its rottenness has made municipal democracy a stench in the nostrils of the civilized world.''

Washington Gladden, a popular religious reformer, issued a similar judgment in *Social Facts and Forces* (1897): "The civic corporation in America, in a vast number of cases, is an instrument employed not primarily for the promotion of the public welfare, but for plundering citizens and enriching officials.'' "A horror of great darkness rests now upon our cities,'' Gladden sadly concluded. Lincoln Steffens, the renowned muckraking journalist of the progressive era, blasted both corrupt municipal government and the apathetic citizens who made it possible in his book, *The Shame of the Cities* (1904). Viewing the city from the reform perspective, these writers and scores of others condemned the urban boss and the political machine.

In a sense, early historians of this era became moral critics. They viewed the political machine much the way the reformers themselves did. On the simplest level, it appeared to be a struggle between the masses and the classes—between the workers, immigrants, and lower-class groups on the one hand and the middle-class, professional, and business groups on the other. Historians traditionally argued that immigrants and workers were easily led by corrupt machine politicians. The urban masses provided essential support for the city machines, selling their votes to the bosses or putting them in office in return for patronage jobs and other favors. By contrast, the reform interpretation held, middle-class urbanites and professionals supported efforts to root out corruption and restore morality to urban life. It was, according to this analysis, a struggle pitting the forces of good against evil.

This reformist interpretation continued to dominate the writing of urban political history until fairly recently. In reexamining the available evidence, however, recent historians have begun sketching the outlines of a new and quite different interpretation. Rather than simply condemning bosses and machines as reprehensible and corrupt, these historians have tried to understand their functions and the sources of their support. The results of this historical revisionism have been interesting, to say the least.

The new interpretations of urban machine politics have followed several separate but nevertheless interrelated lines of analysis. For instance, a new emphasis has been placed on the so-called latent functions of the political machine—a term utilized by sociologist Robert K. Merton in his influential book, *Social Theory and Social Structure* (2d ed., 1957). According to Merton, the bosses and the machines were able to "satisfy the needs of diverse subgroups in the larger community," needs not adequately satisfied through legally approved or culturally acceptable channels. Earlier historians puzzled over the electoral success and longevity of the urban machines. Given the reform bias of these historians, it was easy to dismiss such political success as the result of bribery, corruption, and vote fraud. But, as Merton and other scholars have made quite clear, the urban machines did not have to steal elections. Rather, they had consistently strong political support in immigrant and working-class neighborhoods during the industrial era. Why? In an age when official municipal welfare and social services were weakly developed or administered in a bureaucratic or tight-fisted manner, the bosses and the machines provided very real and important services in the urban neighborhoods.

Essentially, the city machines were political parties organized on the local level. They nominated candidates and got out the vote as political parties had been doing since the founding of the nation. To reach the voters effectively, the local political organizations extended down to the ward, the precinct, and even the block level. The precinct captains and the election district leaders comprised the heart of the political machine. They knew their neighbors and their problems. They offered a humanizing contact with a government increasingly perceived as distant and bureaucratic.

The machine's local leaders provided jobs, entertainment, legal assistance, food and welfare, help of all kinds. They aided immigrant arrivals at the docks, workers who had lost their jobs, people in trouble with the police, and families burned out by fires (fires were "considered great vote-getters," one Tammany politician in New York City noted). They attended baptisms and funerals, gave presents at weddings, and socialized with people in saloons, clubs, and coffeehouses. They asked only for votes in return. They were rarely disappointed by their constituents.

The latent functions provided by the machine, then, help to explain big-city voting patterns in the industrial era. As historian John M. Allswang has noted in his book, *Bosses, Machines, and Urban Voters* (1977): "The machine has existed because of the very large numbers of dependent or semidependent people who have been found in the modern American city, and because it has been better able to respond quickly and directly to their needs."

Recent historical research has also demonstrated that strong links existed between machine politicians and certain segments of the business community. The city bosses, in other words, provided services to businessmen as well as to the urban masses. Particularly dependent on the machine were those business interests that profited by government decision making—transit operators, for example, who sought government franchises, or real estate interests that sold land to city governments, or construction companies that received contracts for buildings and other municipal projects.

Increasingly, new research suggests that most city machines promoted a wide range of urban development schemes. Such programs, of course, provided lucrative sources of graft, kickbacks, and payoffs. At the same time, however, urban development met many of the new demands of the growing industrial cities—demands for new streets, sewers, docks, bridges, parks, schools, transit and utility systems, and similar municipal facilities. Urban reformers, by contrast, often tended to be stingy with the public's money. Generally, they sought reduced municipal expenditures and lower taxes, as well as honesty in government. Thus, machine politicians and urban businessmen accommodated each other. The politicians made it possible for some businessmen to make big profits, while the businessmen kicked back money to the bosses. In the process, however, new streetcar lines, utility systems, and other municipal facilities were put into place. By some interpretations, the bosses were great city builders.

The functional view of the machine advocated by Merton and others addresses another important link between politics and business—in this case, illegal business. According to the reform interpretation, urban vice flourished during boss-dominated municipal administrations. The machine not only tolerated vice but profited enormously from gambling, prostitution, and liquor law violations. Middle-class reformers, of course, were morally outraged by such developments.

Functional analysis suggests a different way of looking at this situation. As Merton has written: "Just as the political machine performs services for 'legitimate' business, so it operates to perform not dissimilar services for 'illegitimate' business." Essentially, gamblers, prostitutes, saloon operators, and other purveyors of vice were urban entrepreneurs. They provided goods and services for which there was a demand. Morality aside, the machine simply organized and rationalized the delivery of these services in the same way that it organized and rationalized urban transit and utility systems. The bosses profited from urban vice much the way they profited from the granting of streetcar franchises and construction contracts. Payoffs and graft oiled the system, but the machine created some order amid the chaos of the industrial city.

Thus, an important thrust of recent scholarship has been to portray the city boss as a decisive, centralizing figure. At the beginning of the industrial era, municipal government was weak and fragmented. Only the political boss, several scholars have argued, could overcome urban disorder and the constitutional diffusion of municipal power. Controlling the diverse strands of power and lubricating the wheels of government with payoffs, the boss provided needed coordination and centralization.

Such a view was argued most energetically by historian Seymour J. Mandelbaum in his path-breaking study, *Boss Tweed's New York* (1965). By Mandelbaum's interpretation, the infamous Tweed was more than simply a colossal and audacious crook. He was that, to be sure, but he also centralized urban power and decision making, modernized city politics, promoted urban development, and provided a sort of positive government. Tweed achieved all this at a time when the fragmented structure of New York City's government impeded effective action through legitimate channels.

In the past few years, however, some historians have begun to challenge the functional view of the boss as a provider of positive government. It has never been proven, historian Terrence J. McDonald has argued, that the "latent functions" of the machine were sufficient to keep the bosses in office. Ethnocultural voting analysis explains little when abstracted from the political issues which angered, pleased, or motivated the voters. More research is needed, Jon C. Teaford has written, to discover "to what degree the boss actually bossed." Teaford's important book, *The Unheralded Triumph: City Government in America, 1870–1900* (1984), contended that in most cities the bosses had less impact than city engineers, landscape architects, public health officials, and other urban professionals and technicians. The historians' emphasis on the battle between bosses and reformers, Teaford argued, has obscured "the complexities of municipal rule and the diversity of elements actually vying for power and participating in city government."

THE TWEED RING

To a certain extent, the picture of the city boss as a powerful, decisive, and centralizing figure in urban politics has been overdrawn. With a few exceptions, most of the 19th-century machines were based on coalitions of ward organizations. In Tweed's New York, for instance, the citywide Democratic Party organization known as Tammany was loosely structured and decentralized. Political power was widely diffused and held by the Tammany ward leaders, who controlled local ward politics. Local primaries and caucuses in the wards produced delegates to party conventions and nominees for the city council and state legislature. Tammany itself was ruled by the Tammany General Committee, composed of three delegates from each ward. These ward bosses often fought among themselves over local political issues and the spoils of office. Boss of New York's seventh ward, Tweed also served as chairman of the Tammany General Committee by the mid-1860s. But despite his personal power and magnetism, Tweed never did create a fully centralized city-wide machine.

Tammany's structure remained weak and decentralized under Tweed and, indeed, throughout much of the remainder of the 19th century. As historian Kenneth Fox observed in his study of municipal reform, *Better City Government* (1977), Tammany's ward bosses were "bound together primarily by their common interest in winning elections and obtaining the spoils of electoral victory." Tweed never completely dominated his fellow Tammany ward leaders. Instead, Fox noted, "he managed the coalition of leaders through his control over City Hall patronage, through direct cash contributions to their ward organizations, and through an intricate hierarchy of status distinctions."

Despite the structural weakness of most citywide machines, bosses like Tweed had a shaping influence on 19th-century urban politics and city development. Tweed himself remains an endlessly fascinating figure in American urban history. A small businessman and an aspiring local politician, Tweed built a base of popular support as the brawny and brawling foreman of the Americus Fire Engine Company. In 1851 he was narrowly elected to the Common Council from the seventh ward. Tweed and his fellow aldermen were soon labeled the "Forty Thieves" by the reform press. The council raised taxes, increased municipal spending, and granted a number of lucrative omnibus, horsecar, ferry, and railroad franchises. Tweed and other aldermen became wealthy men virtually overnight. Not especially successful as a brush manufacturer and chairmaker, Tweed had developed an elegant lifestyle by the mid-1850s and was worth about $100,000. The excesses of Tweed and his fellow aldermen earned the opprobrium of the *New York Tribune,* which called them "the most debased, corrupt and disgraceful body of men ever invested with legislative power, at least in this country." In 1853, during a spasm of political reform, the voters chased all 40 of them out of office.

But Boss Tweed had barely begun. He was elected to Congress in 1853, but national politics held little excitement for him. In 1855 Tweed returned to the local political wars in New York City, getting himself elected to the board of education. Two years later, he was elected to the board of supervisors, a powerful body that served as the New York County legislature. At a time when the city's governmental structure and constitutional powers had been weakened by legislative meddling, the board of supervisors supplied an important base of political power for Tweed. During the late 1850s and early 1860s, Tweed assumed a number of additional offices which strengthened his power and patronage-dispensing abilities. As deputy street commissioner and commissioner of public works, Tweed had thousands of public jobs at his disposal. As a state senator, he was in a position to shape state legislation, tax policies, and other programs which affected the metropolis. As a member of the board of fire commissioners and as a commissioner of deeds, Tweed strengthened his links to business, insurance, and real estate interests. By 1867, one scholar has pointed out, Tweed held 17 different city offices simultaneously. This pattern of multiple office holding enabled Tweed to centralize power and decision making.

Tweed's political strength ultimately derived from his links to Tammany's district and ward leaders. Building on a base of patronage and payoffs, Tweed became chairman of the New York County Democratic Central Committee in 1861, chairman of the Central Committee of Tammany Hall in 1863, and "Grand Sachem" or nominal head of the Tammany Society shortly thereafter. By the election of 1868, the Tweed ring was firmly in control. Members of the ring included Mayor A. Oakey Hall—a respectable and well-educated, but exceedingly ambitious, politician. A dandy who loved being in the public spotlight, Hall served as Tweed's link to the city elite. Two other

Tweed lieutenants were Peter B. "Brains" Sweeney, an Irish politician, lobbyist, and saloon keeper who effectively manipulated Tammany power in backdoor deals, and Richard "Slippery Dick" Connolly, another Irish ward boss with important connections to Tammany district leaders. By 1868, with Hall in the mayor's office, Tweed was in control of the board of supervisors, the board of aldermen, and the board of public works. Completing the ring, Sweeney was appointed city treasurer and Connolly was installed as city comptroller.

The ring concentrated its power even further in 1870. State Senator Tweed spent upwards of $600,000 in bribes to fellow legislators in securing passage of a "reformed" city charter for New York. The new Tweed charter eliminated many independent commissions and agencies, strengthened the power of the mayor, and expanded the city's taxing, bonding, and spending authority. It also established a board of audit, whose function was to audit and approve all city expenditures. The members of the board of audit were none other than Tweed, Hall, Sweeney, and Connolly. By 1870, the ring not only pulled many of the political strings, but it had virtually unlimited access to the city treasury.

The reform opponents of Tweed and Tammany were certainly correct about one thing—the Tweed ring engaged in municipal corruption on a gigantic scale. Its period of control was relatively short, lasting from about 1868 to 1871. Nevertheless, Tweed, Sweeney, Connolly, and the others were ambitious grafters. Unlike later municipal bosses in New York and elsewhere, they sought political power not for its own sake but for the financial rewards it made possible. Estimates of the Tweed ring's graft range up to $200 million, much of it raked off by the bosses at the top of the machine's hierarchy. Typically, the city's new authority to issue bonds provided great opportunities for the grafters. Between 1867 and 1871, New York's bonded indebtedness increased from $30 to $90 million. Perhaps $10 to $15 million of the increase went into actual building projects, while $45 to $50 million was shiphoned off in kickbacks and payoffs.

Businessmen and builders with city contracts were instructed to pad their bills and kick back money to the ring. A new courthouse constructed during the Tweed years soaked up $13 million in city funds by 1871, and the building was still unfinished; it was supposed to cost $250,000. During one year, a plasterer received $500,000 for his work on the courthouse, along with an additional $1 million for "repairs." On a single day in 1870, four workmen were paid $164,000 for repairs at an armory. The ring profited from assessments to open or widen streets, phony bills charged against the city, fees extorted from storekeepers, small businessmen, tavern owners, and brothels, and a myriad of other sources of graft. As historian Alexander B. Callow noted in his careful study, *The Tweed Ring* (1966), the ring was distinguished by its "keen sense in exploiting every opportunity, high or low, big or little, that suggested a chance for plunder. What might have escaped the attention of less artistic thieves, was made into a bountiful harvest by the Ring."

Tweed and other Tammany leaders extracted additional graft by going into business for themselves and then contracting with the city. For instance, Tweed bought up a controlling interest in the New York Printing Company in 1864 and then directed all the city's printing business to the company, charging outrageous prices. The ring also controlled the Manufacturing Stationers' Company, which supplied paper and office supplies to the public schools and the city government. In 1870 the company was paid $3 million, including a $10,000 bill for a few ink bottles, six reams of paper, and several boxes of rubber bands. Tweed and his cohorts also speculated extensively in urban real estate and invested heavily in the stock market. Tweed was a director and active participant in several streetcar and transit companies that received city franchises. He was also on the payroll of the powerful Erie Railroad (which received special privileges in New York City) and served as president or director of several banks, insurance companies, and utilities. Thus, Tweed was something of a businessman as well as a politician. His career demonstrates the easy cooperation between business and politics during the machine era—a symbiotic relationship in which both the boss and the urban entrepreneur got rich while they shaped and controlled the growing industrial cities.

Boss Tweed's Tammany machine consolidated its political power through its appeal to the city's immigrant and working class voters. Indeed, the urban machine was made possible not only by the decentralization of municipal government in the mid-19th century but by the rise of ethnic political power during the years of heavy European immigration. By 1860, the foreign-born made up 47.6 percent of New York City's population, with the Irish and the Germans predominant among the immigrants. As late as 1920, the foreign-born and their children comprised 76 percent of the city's population. Most other big cities in the industrial era, and some smaller ones as well, had similarly large proportions of immigrants and immigrant children. Based in the wards and the precincts, the decentralized political machines cultivated the foreign-born and served their interests. At a time when middle-class and elite reformers denigrated the newcomers, the urban machines helped them through troubled times, speeded their naturalization, and earned their votes on election day.

Tweed's Tammany served as a sort of unofficial social welfare agency for the urban lower classes. A portion of the ring's graft trickled down to the poor. During the winter of 1870, for instance, Boss Tweed distributed $50,000 to the poor of his own seventh ward. Thousands of additional dollars were distributed by other ward leaders for winter fuel and Christmas turkeys. The philanthropy of the ward bosses became especially important after the early 1870s, when many cities abandoned official public relief altogether, despite a number of harsh depressions. Similarly, Tweed used his power in the state legislature to get appropriations for Catholic parochial schools and Catholic charities in New York City. These appropriations—about $1.4 million between 1869 and 1871—solidified working-class support for Tammany, particularly among the city's Irish and German Catholics.

In addition, the urban machines were strengthened by the extensive patronage at the disposal of the ward and district leaders. For several decades, aldermen in New York appointed police, teachers, and other municipal employees. In the days before civil service, Boss Tweed is reputed to have had about 12,000 patronage jobs at his disposal. The urban development schemes of the city machines created even more jobs for construction laborers and artisans. Moreover, by taking popular stands on the issues of importance to the urban masses—by encouraging unions, for example, or by supporting the Irish opposition to the British—Tweed added to his appeal in the immigrant wards. Recent historical research, particularly voting analysis by Allswang and others, clearly demonstrates that despite some vote fraud, Tammany could depend on immigrant and working class support during the Tweed years and long after. The machine, in short, supplied important social services to the urban masses, which in turn produced a persistent level of support for the machine's political candidates.

Some historians have also emphasized Boss Tweed's role as a city builder—as a promoter of urban development. The machines, of course, rose to power at a time when the industrial cities were expanding physically on a large scale. As the cities spread outward from the center, new pressures emerged for the construction of streets and bridges, transit and utility systems, parks and schools, and many other municipal facilities. Most bosses supported a variety of schemes for urban development. Tweed was no exception in that he used his position as a power broker and a central decision maker, particularly in the board of public works, to promote numerous building projects. These ranged from the building of Central Park and the Brooklyn Bridge—no mean achievements—to extensive new street and dock construction and new sewer and transit systems. These building programs provided jobs for the machine's loyal supporters and kickbacks for the bosses. They also began to put into place the infrastructure of public works and public utilities needed in the modernizing city. Historians such as Seymour Mandelbaum have argued that in the decentralized and fragmented city, only the political boss had sufficient power and decision-making authority to undertake urban development and public works projects successfully. By this interpretation, Boss Tweed was more than just a big crook; he was a great city builder as well.

The debate about Tweed continues to rage among the academic historians. One recent scholar, Leo Hershkowitz, has written an elaborate and unabashed defense of Tweed, claiming that the boss was not a crook at all but a victim of his political enemies. In his book, *Tweed's New York: Another Look* (1977), Hershkowitz contended that Tweed had been "a pioneer spokesman for an emerging New York" and "a progressive force in shaping the interests and destiny of a great city and its people." So far so good, and not so different from the central thrust of the Mandelbaum thesis. But Hershkowitz goes on to argue that the idea of a political ring pillaging the city treasury was a great myth and that there has never been any direct evidence proving Tweed's thievery.

Few urban historians would carry the revisionist argument that far. Indeed, it was the public revelation of Tammany corruption on a grand scale that led to the downfall of Tweed and his cronies in 1871. For some time Tweed had been pilloried on a regular basis in Thomas Nast's hard-hitting political cartoons in *Harper's Weekly*. Tweed's early response had been to throw down an insolent challenge to his reform critics: "What are you going to do about it?" By the early 1870s, however, some reformers had taken up the challenge. Although it had earlier praised Tweed, the *New York Times* joined the crusade against the ring in 1871, printing evidence of graft supplied by a disgruntled county auditor. As a result of these exposures, the Tweed ring collapsed. Tweed himself was arrested and died in prison in 1878.

TAMMANY AFTER TWEED

The rise and fall of the Tweed ring provides a fascinating case study of machine politics in the industrializing city. Taking advantage of the decentralization of government and the fragmentation of power, Tweed imposed a degree of order on urban political organization and on the city itself. Tweed would fall, but Tammany survived and grew more powerful as a citywide Democratic machine. Tweed's Tammany successors were both more modest and more successful as political leaders. "Honest John" Kelly, who followed Tweed as Tammany leader, and Richard Croker, who headed the organization in the 1880s and 1890s, both concentrated on winning elections and holding office, on patronage and power. They were pragmatic politicos. They often cooperated with the Democratic Party's reform wing, permitting "respectable" or reform candidates to head the Tammany ticket.

After Tweed, Tammany developed new techniques for getting and keeping political power. By the 1880s, the machine came to be organized around New York City's 24 assembly districts, which in turn were subdivided into more than 800 election districts. Croker delegated considerable appointive power to the assembly district leaders, extracting greater party discipline in return. The assembly district leaders comprised Tammany's inner circle of power brokers. Since state assemblymen were elected annually, the machine maintained a constant state of readiness, bringing cohesion and continuity to the organization. In addition, as political scientist Martin Shefter has pointed out in an important article on Tammany, the perfection of district political clubs in the 1880s and after strengthened Tammany's hold over Democratic voters. These clubs, with their meeting houses and yearround social and political programs, institutionalized the base of Tammany's support.

Interestingly, the Tammany machine also drew on widespread popular interest in sports, particularly baseball. Tammany sponsored numerous amateur and professional baseball teams, including the New York Giants. Machine politicians supported the building of large city parks, which were used for urban sports. In addition, they often abrogated laws restricting Sunday baseball. Many baseball magnates were both machine politicians and streetcar operators. They often used political influence to obtain transit franchises and then profited from streetcar routes to the ball parks. In New York and other cities, the close links between politics and sports such as baseball, boxing, and horse racing (as well as criminal activity such as gambling) revealed the new efforts of the machine to appeal to the urban electorate. Baseball, sports historian Stephen Hardy suggested in a recent study of Boston, "helped to cement the structures of urban political power."

One Tammany baseball player who rose up through the ranks of the machine was Charles Francis Murphy, Tammany boss from 1902 until his death in 1924. Under Murphy's leadership, the pattern of pragmatic politics was intensified. Murphy's Tammany began to support social reforms that had appeal in the immigrant wards. Thus, the machine gradually put its political weight behind such reform legislation as housing reform, factory safety legislation, workmen's compensation, women's suffrage, consumer protection, and closer regulation of the utility, banking, and insurance industries. Rising from the ward politics of Murphy's Tammany were such future reform leaders as Robert F. Wagner, who served in the U.S. Senate in the depression era, and Alfred E. Smith, who became governor of New York in the 1920s and ran a losing campaign for the presidency in 1928. By the early 20th century, as historian J. Joseph Huthmacher has suggested, Tammany had begun "to bank on its record of support for reform measures as its most effective appeal for votes at election time."

At the same time, the brazen corruption of the Tweed era was tempered. The ward bosses generally remained satisfied with "honest graft." As district leader George Washington Plunkitt confided to a journalist at the turn of the century, Tammany politicians "didn't steal a dollar from the city treasury. They just seen their opportunities and took them." With its ties to various ethnic and business groups, with its new interest in electioneering and sports, and with its new commitment to popular social reforms, Tammany's political formula usually succeeded. Indeed it succeeded so well that between 1854 and 1934 antimachine reformers managed to capture New York's municipal government for only 10 out of 80 years.

THE VARIETIES OF BOSSISM

While New York City's Tammany Hall may have been the most notorious of the political machines, in most other cities, the machine pattern generally conformed to the functional model offered by Merton and other revisionist scholars. That is, the bosses provided essential services to the voters, cooperated with business interests, and promoted wide-ranging schemes for urban development. Tweed, too, provided this sort of positive government, but his achievements were tempered by his weakness for graft.

One of Tweed's contemporaries was Alexander R. Shepherd, who emerged as a powerful boss in Washington, D.C., in the early 1870s. A former Washington alderman, Shepherd became president of the city's board of public works after a governmental reorganization in 1871. From this position of power, he distributed patronage jobs on a large scale. He also embarked on an ambitious campaign of urban physical development. Shepherd had grandiose plans for the civic beautification of the capital city. At the time, according to historian William M. Maury, Washington was little more than "a swampy mudhole" and "a physical mess of unpaved and ungraded streets, open sewers, and disorganized building." Several hastily arranged multimillion dollar bond issues financed an extensive program of laying sewers and water mains, grading and paving streets, planting trees, and building bridges.

As in New York, these building projects served important urban needs. They also provided marvelous opportunities for contract peddling, bill padding, kickbacks, and "honest graft," to use Plunkitt's terminology. Just as Tweed did, Shepherd moved easily between public and private roles, between politics and business. He headed a number of paving and stone companies that contracted with the city. He served as president or director of numerous banks, railroads, and streetcar companies. Like the honest grafters in most cities, Shepherd speculated heavily in Washington real estate. As Maury has suggested, "his ability to see the direction of growth the city was taking enabled him to buy sizable tracts of land at quite low prices for profitable later sale." Not unlike Tweed and other powerful bosses, Shepherd actually determined how and where the city would develop.

Boss Shepherd's board of public works spent $20 million in two years and brought some significant civic improvements to the capital city. Washington's bonded indebtedness sky-rocketed, but even Shepherd's critics begrudgingly praised his accomplishments. However, the depression of 1873 forced financial cutbacks, stimulating an investigation of fiscal irregularities in Shepherd's administration of public works. Shepherd was eventually ousted from his position of power. His power base, the board of public works, was abolished in 1874, ending an era of reckless urban development. Subsequently, Shepherd declared bankruptcy, moved to Mexico to head a mining company, and became a millionaire once again.

There are obvious differences between Tweed and Shepherd —Shepherd did not have a ward-based political organization geared toward winning local elections, for instance. Nevertheless, the parallels between the two bosses are too strong to ignore. Both men promoted urban development on a vast scale, both worked easily with business interests, and both became rich through contracting and graft. Interestingly, a statue of Alexander R. Shepherd now stands on Washington's Pennsylvania Avenue. Shepherd is remembered by most Washingtonians as a great city builder. There are no statues of William M. Tweed in New York City.

Boss politics took a different form in Cincinnati. In the Ohio River city, George B. Cox's Republican machine came into power in the early 1890s and dominated city politics for about 20 years. As historian Zane L. Miller has noted in his book, *Boss Cox's Cincinnati* (1968), Cox began much like other machine politicians of the time. The son of British immigrants, Cox worked at a succession of low-wage, unskilled jobs as a young man. Nursing political ambitions, he became a saloon keeper. Eventually, he rose to a position of political leadership in Cincinnati's inner-city 18th ward, serving several terms as a Republican alderman.

Unlike New York's Tammany bosses, who virtually owned the immigrant vote, Cox at first was unable to crack Democratic control of the central city immigrant slums. Rather, he fashioned a Republican coalition with reform-minded voters in the city's outer residential zones and suburbs. Cox's machine also depended on the votes of central city blacks, who generally voted Republican—the party of Abraham Lincoln. The Cox coalition relied, too, on the political clout of Cincinnati's utility and transit companies. Later, Cox forged an alliance with Democratic ward bosses, and the immigrant slums became a source of Republican political strength, as well.

Cox maintained his power by delicately balancing traditional machine activities with a variety of moderate urban reforms. He promoted such urban development schemes as street and sewer construction, park building, and the expansion of municipal services. As elsewhere, these programs provided patronage and graft, appealed to local business interests, such as construction and real estate, and served the needs of the rapidly expanding city. Cox also supported housing reforms, the expansion of educational facilities, civil service in some municipal departments, and such voting reforms as the secret ballot. To attract and keep the middle-class vote, he kept the tax rate low and even imposed some controls on gambling, liquor, and central city vice operations. As George Cox himself noted in 1893, the boss was "not necessarily a public enemy."

Not all of Cincinnati's reformers were persuaded on this point, however. Cox's political alliance between the center and the periphery was short-lived. Reform opponents consistently depicted the Cox machine as immoral and corrupt. They eventually won over the middle-class and suburban Republican voters. Cut off from the original sources of its political strength, the Cox machine ultimately collapsed amid charges of financial scandal. Nevertheless, over two decades George B. Cox had imposed some control and order on a fragmented government and a disorderly city. Boss Cox brought positive government to Cincinnati and even became something of a reformer.

A slightly different pattern of boss-dominated politics prevailed in late-19th century Baltimore. Isaac Freeman Rasin, Baltimore's boss, began as a salesman and shopkeeper, joined the Democratic political club in his ward as a young man, and in 1864 was selected to represent the ward in the party's citywide executive committee. By the early 1870s, Rasin had assumed leadership of the committee, which became the power base of his Baltimore machine. From this position, he distributed patronage, selected the party's ward bosses and city council nominees, and organized the dispensation of contracts and franchises. Using a combination of power, patronage, and persuasion, Rasin dominated the city council as well as Baltimore's mayor, who was usually drawn from the city's elite but friendly to the machine. Such was the case with Ferdinand C. Latrobe, a seven-term Baltimore mayor between 1875 and 1895 but essentially controlled by Rasin. As did Cincinnati's Cox and other bosses, Rasin promoted urban development and the construction of public facilities. According to historian James B. Crooks, author of a study of urban reform in the city: "For the Baltimoreans who repeatedly elected its candidates, the machine served the public interest." Rasin remained the Baltimore boss until ousted from party leadership by Democratic reformers in 1895.

Many urban bosses preferred to run their machines from behind the scenes rather than from city hall. Not so for Martin Behrman, who served five terms as mayor of New Orleans between 1904 and 1926. Behrman worked his way slowly up through the ward system, first holding a number of minor posts and then emerging as Democratic ward boss in the city's 15th ward. The city's 17 Democratic ward bosses made up the executive committee of the Choctaw Club, as the regular Democratic organization was known in New Orleans. Behrman soon came to rule the Choctaw Club, which gave him power to select party nominees for a whole range of city and state offices. This power base enabled Behrman to run successfully for the mayoralty.

Behrman's New Orleans machine was more centralized than most. The ward bosses had some freedom and patronage, but had to deliver the vote on election day or face retirement. Like other bosses, Behrman promoted the development of urban facilities and services, and he had close connections with local business, utility, and traction interests. He was critical of the elitist or "silk stocking" reformer "who knew all about municipal government because he read magazines and books." As Behrman noted in his memoirs: "The high class silk stocking always knew what led to the fall of the Roman empire, but he did not seem to know that the bulk of the voters were more interested in schools, police, firemen, the charity hospital, the parks and squares and labor troubles than the Roman empire." Because the Behrman machine paid attention to such things, it kept the support of the voters for over 20 years.

The political machine was not limited to the older cities of the East and Midwest. As Denver approached big-city status, with a population surpassing 100,000 by 1890, machine politics took hold. Denver's boss Robert W. Speer, writes Thomas Noel in *The City and the Saloon: Denver, 1858–1916* (1982), "established a large following among a wide variety of voters, ranging from the barroom, blue-collar crowd to the business elite of the Denver Club." Appointed in 1891 to the Denver Fire and Police Board, Speer quickly came to control the police department, the vice interests which depended on police nonenforcement, and the saloon keepers in the downtown wards who helped get out the vote. He also engaged in typical machine philanthropies. Although a Democrat, he developed a cozy relationship with Denver's mostly Republican business interests. After a decade and a half of pulling the political strings from behind the scenes, Speer exploited his power base in a successful campaign for the mayoralty in 1904. By 1920, when his third mayoral term expired, Speer had bossed Denver for 30 years.

The varieties of the machine tradition are numerous and fascinating. Some big cities of the industrial era never developed a powerful and centralized boss-dominated machine, such as New York's Tammany or Martin Behrman's New Orleans' machine. In Boston and Chicago, for instance, the proliferation of ethnic communities strengthened the hand of the ward bosses, who worked together in loose coalitions but carefully protected their local power bases. Thus, although popularly called the "czar" of Boston in the late 19th century, Martin Lomasney was in reality only the long-time boss of the city's eighth ward. According to Harold Zink, author of an early study of machine politics entitled *City Bosses in the United States* (1930), Boston politics was characterized by "a sizable band of powerful ward and local leaders who have warred so vigorously and yet survived so stubbornly as to render impossible the emergence of a single all-powerful boss." The Boston ward bosses carved out their own little empires and divided patronage and other spoils of office, never yielding power to a centralizing political leader.

The situation was more complex in Chicago, where tremendously rapid population growth (from 300,000 in 1870 to over 2 million in 1910) caused constant change and flux in residential patterns and political life. Most of Chicago's newcomers were European immigrants, and the city had become by the early 1900s a series of ethnic villages. Moreover, the Republican and Democratic parties remained evenly balanced throughout the industrial era. The ethnic residential pattern, as John Allswang has pointed out, created "the basis for an ethnically specific and decentralized political organization," while the strong two-party tradition prevented any single machine from dominating, at least until the 1930s.

In this heterogeneous and sprawling midwestern boomtown, then, machine politics remained decentralized, with ward bosses sometimes competing, sometimes cooperating. Graft was also decentralized, as Lincoln Steffens noted in 1904 in *The Shame of the Cities*. Chicago, Steffens wrote, "was a settlement of individuals and groups and interests with no common city sense and no political conscience. . . . The grafting was miscellaneous and very general. . . . It never was well organized and orderly. The aldermen had 'combines,' leaders, and prices, but, a lot of good-natured honest thieves, they were independent of party bosses and 'the organizations,' which were busy at their own graft."

Some charismatic political leaders did emerge in industrial

Chicago. These included Democrats Carter H. Harrison and his son, Carter H. Harrison, II, who each served in the mayoralty for five terms between 1879 and 1915; Republican William Lorimer, who rose from Cook County Republican committeeman from the sixth ward in 1885 to U.S. Senator in 1909; and William Hale "Big Bill" Thompson, a three-term Republican mayor between 1915 and 1931. But as Kenneth Fox has suggested in *Better City Government,* Chicago's "weak charismatic mayor" pattern reflected political realities. Power remained concentrated at the ward level. Ward bosses such as "Hinky Dink" Kenna and "Bathhouse John" Coughlin, who ruled Chicago's first ward from 1890 to 1940, jealously guarded their patronage and graft while looking out for the interests of their constituents. The division of power among the ethnic ward bosses kept Chicago politics fragmented and decentralized. This pattern prevented the creation of a citywide machine on the Tammany model, and it also made reform victories more frequent. Only in the 1930s, with the arrival of the New Deal, did Chicago Democrats put together a powerful citywide organization, led first by Anton Cermak, then Edward J. Kelly, and later inherited by Richard J. Daley.

The boss and the machine, then, became ubiquitous urban institutions during the industrial era. From Frank Hague in Jersey City to Ed Crump in Memphis, Ed Butler in St. Louis, Jim and Tom Pendergast in Kansas City, and Abe Ruef in San Francisco—the city boss confronted the disorderly city and often shaped the urban future. More often than not, rising from the immigrant slums, the bosses viewed politics as an avenue of upward mobility, a means of achieving status, power, and wealth. They usually worked their way up through the hierarchical ranks of the local political organization, mastering the mysteries of the machine at each level. Most came to have a remarkably tenacious grip on the levers of local power. They drew strength from the votes of the burgeoning immigrant and working-class wards. They provided jobs, social services, and special favors in return. They politicized the masses, helped integrate newcomers into the American mainstream, and offered central city residents a vehicle for political expression.

The most successful bosses never forgot their roots. However, they could expand their power on a citywide basis only by winning over elements of the local business community and segments of the urban middle class. Thus, the successful urban political machine, by necessity, became involved in urban development projects, tried to keep a lid on property taxes, and sought to improve the delivery of transit, utility, and other services. Practical and pragmatic, the bosses tolerated vice, graft, and corruption while also promoting a variety of social reforms. They had no fixed ideology, and they had few goals other than achieving and maintaining power. The bosses simply discovered what the cities and their citizens needed or wanted, and then set about satisfying those demands.

Almost two decades of historical scholarship on the boss and the machine has established the primacy of the functionalist interpretation. "The key structural function of the boss," as Robert Merton put it, was "to organize, centralize, and maintain in good working condition" the fragments of power dispersed throughout the city's political structure. The machine, in short, represented a positive response to the structural weakness of urban government and to the disordered conditions of the industrial city.

The remarkable similarity of the machine pattern in cities throughout the nation suggests that the functional interpretation is more than simply plausible. The system had its unsavory characteristics, to be sure, but the bosses did confront the problems of the growing big cities and they did get things done. As a result, they satisfied many divergent and often conflicting interests. Of course, there were many in every city who could never be satisfied, who could never accept the political machine. Many continued to believe, with reformer Clinton Rogers Woodruff, that "the real purpose of the machine is to plunder the public for the personal profit of the politicians." Although not always very successful, various groups of urban reformers posed alternatives to the boss and the machine.

SIX

The Varieties of Urban Reform

The ethnic-based machines often shaped political culture and municipal administration in the big-city era of the late 19th century. They were challenged almost everywhere by an incredible variety of reformers and reform organizations. The reform impulse culminated in the so-called progressive movement of the early decades of the 20th century. Historians have had a field day with the reformers, rarely agreeing on their motivations and purposes. The general thrust of recent research, however, suggests that urban reform was a complex, constantly shifting, multidimensional movement. Reformers, it seems, came from all social and economic classes, and they supported a diversity of often conflicting reform legislation, programs, and causes. The political arena, of course, provided the battleground for the shifting reform conflicts and coalitions of the industrial era.

MUGWUMPS AND GOO GOOS

The earliest reform challenge to the boss and the machine came from the civic reform clubs and the good government leagues of the late 19th century. These organizations, which sprouted between the 1870s and the 1890s, represented the so-called mugwump tradition in urban reform. Generally wealthy, well-educated, and upper-class business or professional types, men of the mugwump persuasion were galvanized by the independent Republican movement of the 1872 presidential election and the reform candidacy of Democrat Grover Cleveland in 1884. Concerned about immorality, corruption, and government fraud during the "Gilded Age," the urban mugwumps battled the political machine. These elite reformers had a clear vision of the imperatives of good government, but the machine politicians denigrated them as "goo goos."

Several unifying patterns marked the mugwump movement to clean up city government. Most of the men involved were elitist and patrician in social outlook, Protestant in religion, and old-stock Anglo-Saxon or Yankee in family background. They were politically and economically conservative. They looked back to an earlier era in which men of their class and standing possessed power, authority, and status. As a group, historian Richard Hofstadter wrote in *The Age of Reform* (1955), "they found themselves checked, hampered, and overridden by the agents of the new corporations, the corrupters of legislatures, the buyers of franchises, the allies of the political bosses." They were men such as E. L. Godkin, editor of *The Nation,* an influential and respected weekly magazine founded in New York City in 1865.

A personification of the mugwump personality, Godkin lamented the passing of traditional values and ideals in the industrial age. He believed that the great concentration of wealth made possible by corporate capitalism led to economic and political abuses, which in turn undermined the nation's moral fibre and democratic values. Municipal government, as Godkin saw it, was corrupted by businessmen and entrepreneurs seeking favoritism. Immigrants who sold their votes to the political machines shared the blame. Of the German immigrants, for instance, Godkin wrote: "In politics they are apt to go in the cities with the party which meddles least with their beer." The Irish were just as bad: "The way they take to low political intrigue and jobbery is something extraordinary and to me inexplicable."

This analysis of the urban problem led to the mugwump version of municipal reform and good government. They hoped to dilute lower-class political power by imposing literacy and property qualifications for voting. They sought to keep America ethnically pure by restricting immigration. To destroy the patronage system that kept the bosses in power, they promoted civil service for government employees. They wanted nonpartisan elections, the short ballot, the strong mayor system, and the separation of city from state and national elections. Finally, Godkin and other "genteel" mugwump reformers believed that only by electing the "best men" could the power of the machine be broken.

In New York City, urban reformers of the mugwump type first organized in response to revelations of the Tweed ring's corruption. A Committee of Seventy, appointed at a massive gathering of concerned citizens in September 1871, became the chief vehicle for the reform attack on the Tweed machine. Composed of a variety of Tweed enemies, anti-Tammany Democrats, and professional elites, the Committee of Seventy launched the successful reform candidacy of William F. Havemeyer for mayor in 1872. A wealthy banker and sugar refiner, as well as a New York mayor in the 1840s, Havemeyer moved quickly in reaction to the financial excesses of the Tweed years. His administration of urban government was dedicated to honesty, efficiency, economy, and low taxes. An adherent of free-market economics, Havemeyer drastically cut the urban development projects initiated by the Tammany machine under Tweed. In the midst of the depression of 1873, Havemeyer slashed virtually all public relief programs to the urban poor. As Seymour Mandelbaum noted in *Boss Tweed's New York* (1965), "in the wake of the Tweed Ring, New York was engaged in a headlong pursuit of economy."

Havemeyer and his fellow reformers also reversed the centralization of municipal administration begun by Tweed. For example, Havemeyer pushed a new city charter through the state legislature. The new charter severely limited the powers of the city council and concentrated policy-making authority in several interdepartmental boards, such as the board of estimate and apportionment. This new body, which represented a dispersal of municipal power, controlled all budgeting, spending, taxing, and bonding. The idea, of course, was to weaken the machine's aldermanic base in the wards and to strengthen the hand of the reformers appointed to the new interdepartmental boards. At the same time, however, Havemeyer's 1873 city charter diffused executive power, undercutting his own authority as a reform mayor.

By the end of Havemeyer's two-year term, the Committee of Seventy had disbanded, Tammany had reorganized, and the Democrats had swept the reformers out of office. Nevertheless, New York City's good government zealots continued their efforts, particularly after formation of the City Reform Club in 1882. Young Theodore Roosevelt, a reform Republican state legislator in the 1880s, provided much of the early energy for this new "goo goo" club. Typically, the City Reform Club challenged the Tammany machine and promoted nonpartisan elections, honesty and efficiency in government, and rigorous enforcement of purity legislation. Dozens of similar organizations sprouted elsewhere between 1870 and 1890: a Citizens' Reform Association in Philadelphia (1871), the Citizens' Association of Chicago (1874), the Baltimore Reform League (1885), the New Orleans Committee of One Hundred (1885), the Citizens' Association of Boston (1887), the Milwaukee Municipal League (1893), the Civic Federation of Detroit (1894), and many others. More than 80 such good government associations had been established by the mid-1890s.

Almost uniformly, these good government clubs addressed the problems of the city from an elitist, mugwumpish, business-oriented perspective. The bosses and the machines were the enemy; honesty, efficiency, and morality in urban administration the chief objectives. Occasionally, the good government groups ran their own reform candidates for municipal office, but usually they endorsed the best candidates of existing parties. Sometimes they were successful, as in the election of Grover Cleveland as mayor of Buffalo in 1881 and Seth Low as mayor of Brooklyn in 1882. More often, however, the good government types were defeated by the party machines, which had wider electoral appeal among the mass of urban voters.

The urban mugwumps generally sought to obtain a greater degree of home rule and to institute strong-mayor government. They hoped to counter the decentralized machine by beefing up mayoral powers and undercutting city council authority. Brooklyn's reform charter of 1882, for instance, concentrated appointment and removal powers in the mayor's office, along with veto power over city council actions. In Philadelphia, a new charter in 1877 invested the mayor with considerable authority as a chief administrator.

Toward the end of the 19th century, numerous other cities adopted strong mayor charters, hoping thereby to crush the machines and achieve good government. The strong mayor plan was not a perfect solution, however, since its success depended on the election of the "best men." As Kenneth Fox noted in *Better City Government* (1977): "Although the strong mayor system became quite popular as a reform model, it was far from an adequate solution to the municipal problem." After all, even Boss Tweed supported the strong mayor plan.

The late 19th-century urban reformers also emphasized civil service reform. For the mugwumps, the spoils system symbolized all that was wrong with American politics at every level. As one mugwump reformer put it, the patronage system "perverts public trusts into party spoils, . . . ruins the self-respect of the public employees, destroys the function of the party in a republic, prostitutes elections into a desperate strife for personal profit, and degrades the national character by lowering the moral tone and standard of the country." Obviously, the political power of the urban machines partially depended on extensive patronage. From the reform perspective, the merit principle in government employment would cut the power of the bosses, making urban administration more honest and efficient. Civil service legislation became the panacea of the mugwump reformers.

Civil service reform as an organized movement began in 1877 in New York City with the establishment of the New York City Civil Service Reform Association. After a few meetings, the association lagged until 1880, when a new infusion of reform energy began to produce results. Headed by George William Curtis, a mugwump leader and editor of *Harper's Weekly,* the New York group actively publicized the merit principle and encouraged the establishment of similar organizations in other cities. Within a year, civil service reform associations had been formed in at least 30 big cities. These organizational efforts culminated in 1881 with the creation of the National Civil Service Reform League, also headed by Curtis of *Harper's Weekly.*

The growth of the civil service reform movement coincided with the assassination of President James A. Garfield in 1881 by a disappointed office seeker. Garfield's assassination pushed the civil service issue into national prominence, assuring Congressional passage of the nation's first federal civil service law, the Pendleton Act, in 1883. The reform impulse also spilled over to the state level, resulting in state civil service legislation in New York (1883) and Massachusetts (1884) where the mugwump reformers had been most active. The New York law authorized, but did not require, the civil service principle for police, fire, health, and legal departments in all of the state's 25 cities. Civil service commissions were set up to administer the law in each city. A similar law in Massachusetts covered additional categories of workers and established a single statewide civil service commission rather than separate bodies in each city. Elsewhere limited civil service provisions were introduced in Philadelphia and Milwaukee in the 1880s and in Chicago, Toledo, New Orleans, and Seattle in the 1890s. Yet, the entire movement was sagging by the mid-1880s, when civil service reform measures failed in a dozen states. Not until the 20th century did municipal civil service become standard administrative practice.

The merit principle aroused the ire and contempt of the machine politicians—"snivel service," they called it. In the view of George Washington Plunkitt, the voluble Tammany chieftain, civil service was nothing less than "the greatest curse of the day," a false reform which would destroy democratic and responsive government. Nevertheless, the political machines were often able to turn this mugwump reform to their advantage. In New York City, for instance, the army of Tammany patronage appointees might now be protected from the "clean sweep" of the occasional Republican or reform administration. The story was the same elsewhere, as the city bosses realized they could not only live with civil service but use it effectively to entrench their supporters in the urban bureaucracy. Ultimately, therefore, the zealous and single-minded mugwump faith in a professionalized urban civil service was misplaced.

Lacking mass appeal, mugwump reform efforts remained fragmented and localistic. Their campaigns were usually specific to a single city or community, and they functioned outside of the regular party organizations. Their successes often resulted from short-lived bursts of reform zeal or depended on the energy of a few committed leaders. In the final analysis, the electoral popularity and functional success of the political machines dictated the ultimate failure of the civil service and good government reformers.

In 1890, after almost two decades of rather fruitless urban reform, President Andrew D. White of Cornell University provided an epitaph of sorts for the goo goos. Writing on "The Government of American Cities" in the *Forum* magazine, White sadly concluded: "Without the slightest exaggeration we may assert that, with very few exceptions, the city governments of the United States are the worst in Christendom—the most expensive, the most inefficient, and the most corrupt." Not all have agreed with White's judgment about American city government, but it seems clear that urban reform between 1860 and 1890 was rather ineffective.

THE STRUCTURAL REFORMERS

The mugwumps paved the way for the more successful urban reformers of the progressive era. In the 1890s, for the first time, municipal reformers overcame their localist orientation in the establishment of a new national organization dedicated to good government principles—the National Municipal League (NML). Supporters of this new national group were primarily structural reformers. By tinkering with the framework of city government, they sought to achieve their goals of honesty, efficiency, economy, and centralized decision making. The decade of the 1890s witnessed the early flowering of alternative reform traditions, as well. For instance, social reformers appeared on the urban scene, promoting not civil service or charter revision but improvements in housing, working conditions, and social welfare generally. Both groups of reformers generally distanced themselves from the moral or "purity" reformers who sought a legislated morality.

Thus, as the progressive era began, three distinct reform orientations emerged from late-19th century mugwumpery. Structural reformers, social reformers, and purity advocates competed with one another, as well as against the boss or businessmen. These three reform traditions occasionally overlapped with one another, as progressive coalitions formed, broke up, and reorganized with each new reform issue. Essentially, however, each set of reformers sought to impose a distinctive and particularistic brand of progressivism on the industrial city.

Structural progressives advocating a variety of political and administrative solutions quickly moved into the reform mainstream during the 1890s. The establishment of the NML in 1894 reflected the nationalization of the municipal reform impulse. Goo goos in New York and Philadelphia jointly sponsored the first national Conference for Good City Government in January 1894. Some 150 delegates commiserated with one another over the sad state of urban government, then agreed to establish a national organization, hold annual meetings, and promote municipal reform. Within two years, 260 local civic and reform organizations had affiliated with the NML. The new outfit provided a central focus for the municipal reformers, but it also bureaucratized the entire movement. In this sense, the NML typified the emerging administrative society—a society dominated by big bureaucracy, administrative control, and the impersonality of corporate capitalism and the industrial city.

The NML represented administrative and structural reform, pure and simple. NML reformers believed that the chief problems of the city could be rectified through changes in the structural framework of municipal government. The bureaucratic mentality was firmly in control of the organization by 1899, when the NML issued its first model city charter. The model charter built on the existing faith in the strong mayor plan and civil service reform, but added a few new wrinkles as well. The NML called for extensive home rule from state legislative interference, a unicameral city council, secret ballot elections, and separation of municipal from state and national elections. Urban fiscal control, the source of corruption under the political machine, should be entrusted to an elected and administratively independent city controller, the NML contended. Another source of corruption, utility and transit franchises, would be more strictly regulated and granted only for short periods of time. Finally, the NML model charter called for at-large elections for aldermen—this a direct attack on the power base of the machine in the districts and wards.

This sort of administrative tinkering with city charters often reflected an elitist, antidemocratic spirit. The at-large constituency, for instance, generally undermined the localistic, ethnic-bloc politics of the ward system and delivered the city council into the hands of the business and professional elites. Clearly, the structural reformers of the NML sought not only to destroy the bosses, but to rob the urban masses of their electoral power. The NML's model city charter, in short, provides a classic example of the administrative mentality of the structural reformers.

In addition to the NML, several other agencies promoted the administrative and structural reform of city government. For example, in 1902 the U.S. Census Bureau began collecting urban fiscal statistics. This information, reported annually in a comparative format, soon established standards for municipal taxation, budgeting, and administrative practice. As Fox put it in *Better City Government:* "The bureau mounted a major program of comparative statistical reporting and research designed to advance the new approach to municipal administration, and to make structural and administative innovations accessible to city governments."

The Census Bureau's model for good city government called for a centralized administrative structure headed by a strong mayor committed to professionalized delivery of municipal services. Along with the NML, the bureau promoted a uniform accounting system for cities. Budget controls would make machine corruption more difficult and bring a new degree of fiscal accountability and efficiency. Like the NML, the Census Bureau hoped to standardize, rationalize, and professionalize city government.

Similar goals were promoted by the bureaus of municipal research established in many cities during the progressive era. The first such agency, the New York Bureau of Municipal Research, was founded in 1907 by a group of administrative reformers interested in greater municipal efficiency. Typically progressive in their faith in research, experts, and statistical methods, the organizers of the New York bureau viewed the corporation as a model for reorganizing municipal administration. They believed, historian Martin J. Schiesl wrote in *The Politics of Efficiency* (1977), "that the technical side of running a government could be analyzed and developed on a factual basis in the same way as a business." They advocated centralized decision making along the lines of the corporate pattern and hoped to apply Frederick W. Taylor's idea of scientific management to city government. Thus, the New York agency made numerous studies of governmental and administrative problems in New York and other cities.

The idea caught on. Similar municipal research bureaus were set up in Philadelphia, Cincinnati, Dayton, Akron, Denver, Rochester, San Francisco, and other cities. Chicago reformers established a Bureau of Public Efficiency in 1910; Milwaukee's city administration set up a Bureau of Economy and Efficiency in 1910; Detroit's municipal leaders created a Bureau of Governmental Research in 1916. These municipal research agencies generally reflected the view of the wealthy elites and business classes that good city government was a matter of efficiency, technical expertise, and businesslike administration.

Early in the 20th century, political reformers fastened on two additional methods of restructuring municipal administration—the city commission form of government and the city manager plan. The city commission plan began in Galveston, Texas, in 1901, after a severe hurricane and tidal wave devastated the city, destroying 4,000 homes and killing 6,000 residents. At the request of the city's business elite, the state legislature quickly established a five-man commission to substitute for the mayor-council government, which had collapsed during the disaster. Each commissioner headed one of the municipal departments, thus defining clear lines of responsibility for municipal affairs. Because the commission had both policy-making and administrative powers, urban decision making was streamlined.

Within a few years, Galveston had been rebuilt and business leaders in other Texas cities (including Houston, Dallas, Fort Worth, El Paso, and San Antonio) had secured similar commission charters. Labeled at first the Texas idea, the city commission plan fit perfectly the political reformers' goals of nonpartisanship, centralization, and businesslike efficiency. "Developed and led by business groups," Schiesl has suggested, "the commission movement was integrating the methods and values of the corporation into urban government."

The commission plan spread rapidly throughout the nation. Its appeal increased substantially after a modified commission charter was implemented in Des Moines, Iowa, in 1907. The Des Moines plan tempered the antidemocratic and centralizing features of the Texas idea by incorporating such techniques of direct democracy as the initiative, referendum, and recall. This modified commission idea (also known as the Galveston-Des Moines plan) seemed the answer to the structural and administrative reformers' prayers.

By 1917, according to Bradley R. Rice's book, *Progressive Cities* (1977), nearly 500 cities had adopted the commission form of government. Most of these places, however, were smaller and newer cities with relatively small immigrant and working-class populations. Machine government had always been weaker in such towns. At the same time, local business elites had greater power than in big cities where ethnic voting blocs were strong, political parties well established, and the business community often divided. Only a few large cities outside of Texas adopted the commission plan, including Kansas City (1910), Oakland (1911), Omaha (1912), Denver (1913), St. Paul (1914), Jersey City (1913), Newark (1914), and Buffalo (1916). In any event, the commission movement was a "reform contagion" that swept the nation's small and medium-size cities in the decade or so after 1907. The new plan promised to deliver municipal government into the hands of technicians, bureaucrats, and businessmen, placing it permanently above politics.

By the second decade of the 20th century, another type of administrative reform was becoming popular, too. The city manager plan centralized administrative decision making in the hands of an appointive manager, presumably an expert technician, engineer, or public administrator. When linked with a nonpartisan council or commission elected at-large, the city manager plan provided a model of corporate decision making. In its ideal form, the plan separated policy making from administration and insulated both from partisan politics—long a goal of the structural reformers. First adopted in Dayton in 1913 after a successful charter reform campaign, the city manager plan attracted national attention and soon supplanted commission government as an administrative panacea.

Generally, local business and professional elites became the biggest boosters of the city manager plan. Indeed, as historian Ernest S. Griffith noted in his detailed study, *A History of American City Government, 1900-1920* (1974), "the backing of the business community was usually the decisive factor in its adoption." In Dayton, for example, chief support for the city manager plan came from the local chamber of commerce and executives of the National Cash Register Company, which had its headquarters in Dayton. While the business community liked the city manager plan, established political party leaders became its main opponents. Typically, representatives from Dayton's Democratic and Socialist parties criticized the city manager plan as a "scheme of the business interests to gain perpetual control of the government." They were right, of course, which explains the widespread popularity of the city manager plan among the structural and administrative progressives.

Lukewarm to commission government, the National Municipal League endorsed the city manager plan and in 1919 officially incorporated it into a revised model city charter. By 1920 some 158 cities had adopted the new plan; three years later, the total had increased to 270. Most manager cities were small or medium size (only four cities over 100,000 population had the plan in 1920), relatively new, and predominantly native-born American in population. With the exception of Cleveland, Cincinnati, and Kansas City, which adopted the city manager plan in the 1920s, most big cities resisted both the commission and manager plans and retained a ward-based and partisan mayor-council system of municipal government.

Even in the big cities, structural reformers tinkered around with the mayor-council charters and sought to improve administrative efficiency. Most of the anti-Tammany reformers in New York City, for instance, were administrative types interested in honesty, efficiency, and economy. Typical of the genre was Seth Low, a wealthy businesman, a former mayor of Brooklyn (1882–1885), and mayor of a consolidated New York in 1902 and 1903. An advocate of businesslike municipal government, Low pushed civil service reform and home rule, promoted charter reform to streamline administration, cut city taxes and spending, and, in characteristic fashion, zealously attacked gambling, vice, and Sunday drinking.

A decade later, Mayor John Purroy Mitchel (1914–1917) brought a similar passion for business efficiency and scientific management to New York's municipal government. Mitchel clamped strict controls on city spending, centralized fiscal procedures, and introduced dramatic administrative reforms in most city departments. He sought, unsuccessfully, to implement the controversial Gary school plan in New York, primarily because of its money-saving features. In a classic structural reform maneuver, he secured a reduction in the size of the school board from 46 to 9. Neither Low nor Mitchel paid much attention to the kinds of economic and social issues that stirred interest among immigrant and working-class New Yorkers— cheap transit fares, municipal ownership of utilities, or housing, labor, and social justice reforms. Not surprisingly, each man served only one term, each succeeded by a regular Tammany Democrat.

In both small and large cities alike, then, the structural reformers sought a businesslike government geared toward efficiency, economy, and scientific management. To achieve centralization and coordination on the corporate model, they tinkered with city charters or boosted new forms of municipal government like the commission and city manager plans. Not coincidentally, these new techniques of city government were designed to destroy the influence of the political machines and consolidate power in the hands of the urban elites. The move-ment for structural reform, technical expertise, and profes-sionally administered city government was part of a growing standardization and bureaucratization of American society. These objectives appealed to urban business and professional people—to those who had money, power, and influence. As a result, structural and administrative goals came to dominate the thinking and the practice of political reformers during the progressive era.

THE SOCIAL REFORMERS

Structural reform promoted by the urban business community staked out the mainstream of the movement for municipal betterment. In some cities, however, social reformers rose to political prominence and power. The introduction of strong-mayor government often facilitated the emergence of reform bosses—social reformers who built ethnic-based political organizations and defended the interests of the urban masses.

The urban masses had a serious interest in social reforms that would improve living and working conditions, and in economic reforms that would bring greater state regulation or intervention in the economy. In his book, *Urban Liberalism and Progressive Reform* (1973), historian John D. Buenker made a convincing case for "new-stock" or immigrant support for such reforms as workmen's compensation, child labor laws, old age pensions, unemployment insurance, factory safety legislation, tax reform, protection of labor unions, and state regulation of such businesses as utilities, banking, and insurance. By contrast, the elite and business groups usually associated with progressive reform generally opposed this sort of social reform and economic intervention.

One of the first successful social reformers was Hazen S. Pingree, a four-term mayor of Detroit (1889–1897) and later a two-term governor of Michigan (1897–1900). A wealthy boot and shoe manufacturer, Pingree ran for mayor as a Republican good government candidate with the backing of the Michigan Club, an organization of Detroit's downtown businessmen. He came into office dedicated to honesty and efficiency, and to applying business principles to municipal administration. According to urban historian Melvin G. Holli, author of *Reform in Detroit* (1969), the new mayor made substantial progress during his first term: "Pingree rooted out dishonesty and inefficiency in a fashion that excited civic uplifters. . . . He brought the power of his administration to bear on crooked contractors, bad workmanship, and the lax policies of municipal departments." His efforts to keep utility rates and streetcar fares down brought him into conflict with local gas, electric, and transit companies, eventually converting him into an advocate of municipal ownership.

Pingree began as a typical businessman in politics, but the devastating 1893 depression turned him into a social reformer. Confronting massive unemployment and severe human problems, Pingree expanded public welfare programs, initiated public works projects for the unemployed, and built new schools, parks, and public baths. He earned nationwide recognition for his "potato patch plan"—a depression program that turned empty city lots over to the poor for gardening. He achieved municipal ownership of an electric lighting plant, fought for low streetcar and utility rates and better services, and urged higher taxes for railroads and corporations and state regulation of all utilities. In addition, he downplayed the purity issues which outraged old-stock, middle-class reformers. Thus, as in machine days, Pingree's police paid little attention to Sunday saloon-closing laws and generally ignored gambling and prostitution. As Pingree noted in an 1894 speech: "The most dangerous enemies to good government are not the saloons, the dives, the dens of iniquity and the criminals." Rather, in a passage that presaged Lincoln Steffens, Pingree contended that most of Detroit's problems could be "traced to the temptations which are offered to city officials when franchises are sought by wealthy corporations, or contracts are to be let for public works."

In short, Hazen Pingree became a defender of Detroit's working class and poor citizens. As his stock in the business community declined, his popular support rose, enabling him to build a powerful political organization based on ethnic and working-class voting power. Pingree was a reformer with a difference—one who emphasized social reform rather than the sort of structural reform advocated by the business reformers of the good government clubs and civic reform leagues. Pingree began with all of the attributes of a structural reformer, but the realities of urban life in the 1890s depression quickly turned him into a social reformer or reform boss.

Urban social reformers of the Pingree variety also emerged in Cleveland and Toledo. Samuel "Golden Rule" Jones, a wealthy manufacturer of oil-drilling equipment, became mayor of Toledo in 1897 and was reelected three times until he died in office in 1904. Like Pingree, he had originally been supported by Republican politicians and business groups. However, Jones refused to go along with the party organization in providing special favors to the streetcar and utility companies. Abandoned by the Republican machine, Jones gradually built a base of working-class support and ran successfully for reelection as an independent. His mass voter appeal was based on his social reform program. He pushed for municipal ownership of utilities, built new parks and schools, and instituted an eight-hour day and a generous minimum wage for city workers. Moreover, Jones did not believe in legislated morality and cut back enforcement of liquor, gambling, and vice laws. Jones's successor, Brand Whitlock, pursued a similar reform program, drew electoral strength from Toledo's working-class wards, and served five terms as mayor.

In Cleveland, Mayor Thomas L. Johnson carried out an equally reformist urban social program. Another wealthy businessman in politics, Johnson served in the mayoralty from 1901 and 1909, when he was narrowly defeated for reelection. Like the structural reformers, Johnson believed in government efficiency, but thought it might best be achieved when municipal government was decentralized, democratic, and close to the people. His reform program included lower streetcar fares, public baths, an extensive park and playground system, milk and meat inspection, and other kinds of government intervention for social welfare. Like Pingree and Jones, Cleveland's Tom Johnson criticized the corrupting role of business in city government, strongly advocated municipal ownership of utilities, and generally ignored rigorous enforcement of purity legislation. According to Lincoln Steffens, who investigated most of the nation's big cities, Johnson was "the best mayor of the best-governed city in America."

These social reform mayors in Detroit, Toledo, and Cleveland focused on the human problems of the industrial city. They resisted the movement to impose middle-class morality on the mass of immigrant and urban workers. They blamed business interests for corrupting urban government while seeking franchises, contracts, low taxes, and other special favors. They did not perceive the chief problems of the city in structural terms. Instead, they had considerable faith in popular democracy and popular control of government. The business and moral reforms emphasized presumed inadequacies of governmental structure and evils of the saloon and urban vice. By contrast, reformers such as Pingree and Johnson were successful precisely because, like the political machines, they engaged the social and economic problems of the urban masses.

A distinct variety of urban social reform emerged in Milwaukee, one of the few big cities ever to elect Socialist mayors. By the 20th century, Milwaukee's heavily German immigrant population had developed a strong working-class consciousness which, according to historian Sally M. Miller, led them to perceive "the unions to be their economic arm and the Socialists their political arm." Thus, in 1910 Milwaukee voters sent Victor Berger, reputed by some to be the city's "Socialist boss," to the House of Representatives for the first of six terms. In the same year, they elected a second-generation German socialist, Emil Seidel, to the mayoralty, along with a socialist city attorney, city treasurer, comptroller, and 21 of 35 aldermen. Seidel was ousted in a close vote after one term, but in 1916 another socialist, Daniel W. Hoan, was elected mayor. He remained in office until 1940.

Milwaukee's Socialist mayors shared with the structural

reformers an interest in honest government, administrative efficiency, and the use of experts. Seidel, for instance, created a Bureau of Economy and Efficiency to help streamline municipal government. The similarities ended there. Both Seidel and Hoan opposed structural reforms like the commission and city manager plans, at-large elections, the short ballot, the strong mayor system, and nonpartisan elections. Such political reforms, they argued, undermined democracy and limited the power of the people.

The lack of effective home rule hampered both Seidel and Hoan, frustrating their efforts to achieve municipal ownership of utility and streetcar companies. As Hazen Pingree had discovered earlier in Detroit, the power of the urban business interests often thwarted popular democracy in Milwaukee. Daniel Hoan dramatized the chief problem in a speech during the 1916 election: "The main issue of this campaign is whether the flag of the street car company will float over the City Hall instead of the Stars and Stripes."

Despite heavy opposition from local business interests, Milwaukee's two socialist mayors embarked on wide-ranging programs of social reform. These included establishment of a housing commission, factory safety and housing inspections, extensive public health measures, new park development and recreational facilities, a city-run employment office, union wages and an eight-hour day for city employees, city-sponsored strike arbitration, rate reductions for some utilities, even free public musical concerts. Left-wing socialists attacked Hoan as a "sewer socialist"—a contemptuous dismissal of the long-term mayor's emphasis on achieving municipal ownership and providing better services instead of frontally assaulting the capitalist system. Municipal socialism as implemented in Milwaukee represented a version of progressive social reform.

The longevity of municipal socialism made Milwaukee unique, but numerous other cities experienced socialist administration for shorter periods. In 1911, for instance, a Protestant minister and long-time social crusader, George R. Lunn, was swept into a two-year term as mayor of Schenectady, New York.

A Christian socialist rather than a Marxian ideologue, Lunn attacked the local grafters, campaigned for lower trolley fares and gas rates, promoted municipal ownership, and, once in office, implemented a variety of social reforms.

In Minneapolis, voters in 1916 elected socialist labor leader Thomas Van Lear to the mayoralty, but controversy over American participation in World War I undermined his program for municipal socialism. During the high tide of socialism in America, from about 1910 to 1920, socialists won 174 mayoral elections. Most of these socialist political victories occurred in smaller cities and towns, but municipal socialists also won in such industrial cities as Haverhill, Massachusetts; Lackawanna, New York; Flint, Michigan; Granite City, Illinois; and Butte, Montana.

Even in big cities such as New York, socialist candidates for municipal office gained extensive electoral support. In 1917, for example, socialist Morris Hillquit finished a close third in a four-way race for the mayoralty, achieving the highest vote ever for a citywide socialist candidate in the metropolis. During the campaign, Hillquit conducted a relentless attack on incumbent John Purroy Mitchel, for whom, Hillquit said, "the administration of a great community like New York is nothing but dry and cold-blooded business, the business of the business interests." Hillquit and other urban socialists often differed in the extent of their commitment to Marxism, but virtually all advocated extensive programs of social rather than structural reform. Sewer socialism it may have been, but it was clearly focused on improving the lives of urban people rather than reorganizing or restructuring urban government.

Social reform, then, represented an important and dynamic political thrust from the 1890s to about 1920. The social reformers sought to use the political system to make American life safer, more democratic, and more socially just for the urban masses. They emphasized issues such as municipal ownership of utilities. They displayed little interest in the administrative and structural reforms promoted by the business and professional elites. They derived their political strength from immigrants and workers, often creating reform machines to organize the urban neighborhoods and get out the vote. Moreover, they had important nonpolitical allies among settlement house workers, housing and health reformers, educators, playground advocates, and city planners. These reform constituencies also focused on the urban environment and its perfectibility. Taken together, the social reformers and their supporters posed an alternative both to the political machine and to elitist administrative reform.

THE MORAL REFORMERS

The industrial era also engendered a third reform tradition—the effort to bring moral reform to the big city. Motivated by Protestant pietism, the purity reformers sought to impose a legislated morality on the American people. With its corrupt political machines and hordes of new immigrants, the industrial city became the chief target of the moral reformers. They launched attacks on the saloon, the brothel, and the gambling den—three urban institutions which violated traditional Protestant, middle-class values. These moral reformers often became overtly political, and they found allies among other types of municipal reformers. The battle against the saloon, for instance, was also an assault on the machine and the rising political power of the immigrant masses.

Historians have debated the degree to which prohibition and the coercive purity movement were really reformist in character and objectives. In *The Age of Reform,* Richard Hofstadter contended that prohibition was a "pseudo-reform," "a ludicrous caricature of the reforming impulse," and "a symbol of the moral overstrain" of the progressive era. Others have disagreed. In his study, *Prohibition and the Progressive Movement, 1900–1920* (1963), James H. Timberlake described prohibition and other moral crusades as "an integral part of the progressive movement." Similarly, historian Paul Boyer, in his important *Urban Masses and Moral Order in America, 1820–1920* (1978), concluded that the antisaloon and antiliquor impulse drew on the same crusading idealism, the same sort of moral indignation, aroused by corrupt bosses and machines. These moral purity efforts overlapped with other municipal reform movements and attracted the same nativist, Protestant, middle-class support. As Boyer put it: "In the 1890s, moral reform and political reform converged, and they would remain interwoven for years."

However, not all urban reformers were converted to the tenets of moral coercion. Issues such as prohibition often split reformers into two camps. Historians have defined cultural-religious divisions that dictated one's stand on purity matters. A distinction has been made, for instance, between "pietists" and "ritualists." Pietists held to a rigorous and crusading Calvinist position—one which viewed the world from a position of moral absolutism. Ritualists generally accepted the world as it was and believed that moral conduct should be determined by individual conscience. The old-stock, Anglo-Saxon, Protestant groups and some Protestant immigrant denominations fell into the pietist tradition. The new-stock Catholic, Christian Orthodox, and Jewish immigrants, along with some Protestants (German Lutherans, for example), comprised the ritualist orientation. Moral purity legislation generally divided native, old-stock, middle-class pietists from the ethnic, new-stock, working-class ritualists. Thus, one's religious and cultural orientation usually dictated one's stand on purity issues.

Moral reforms of various kinds were perfectly acceptable to most middle-class and elitist advocates of municipal reform. The goo goos and later administrative reform types found it difficult to see much contradiction between these two reform impulses. The machine and the saloon, bosses and booze, represented the twin evils of the industrial city. Municipal reform and moral repression represented the twin solutions. By contrast, social reformers with strong political support among the urban masses remained distinctly hostile to moral crusading, cultural conformity, and a coercive, legislated morality.

Throughout the industrial era, the liquor evil dominated the thinking of the purity reformers. The disparate temperance movement of the early 19th century was supplanted in the post–Civil War era by a national crusade against alcohol, led largely by native-born, Protestant, middle-class women—the female counterparts of the mugwumps and goo goos. A short-lived Prohibition party entered the political lists in the 1870s and 1880s, but without much result. Organizations such as the Women's Christian Temperance Union (1874) and the Anti-Saloon League (1895), however, successfully institutionalized the coercive drive to outlaw alcohol.

Protestant, rural America almost uniformly lined up with the prohibitionists, but as Boyer observes, a surprising degree of antisaloon support could be found in the cities, as well. Between 1895 and 1913, some 31 states, ten of them predominantly urban, enacted local option laws. By 1917, alcohol had been prohibited entirely in 26 states, five of them more than half urban in population. Rural dominance in the state legislatures often led to these prohibition victories, but this does not explain why many cities went dry on their own. In 1911, the Anti-Saloon League identified 52 American cities which had abolished the saloon. By 1918, local referenda had made dry cities of Worcester, Haverhill, Lynn, Richmond, Birmingham, Duluth, Denver, Albuquerque, Portland, Seattle, Tacoma, Spokane, and Long Beach, among others. In Chicago, where a no-license option applied down to the precinct level, half the city was dry by 1908. In 1916, prohibitionists were nearly successful in drying up Boston. The wealthiest and poorest wards voted heavily against Boston's prohibition measure, while the primarily native, middle-class wards gave it majority support. Good government reformers everywhere pushed prohibition as a means of purifying municipal politics and cleansing the American city. Of course, the larger cities of the Northeast and Midwest, with their heavy concentrations of ritualistic immigrant groups, held out against the antiliquor crusade.

The moral reformers emphasized the link between the saloon and such other urban problems as prostitution, gambling, police corruption, and machine politics. In New York City, for instance, the Reverend Charles H. Parkhurst initiated a passionate campaign against the saloon and the brothel in the 1890s. Parkhurst's sermonizing on liquor, prostitution, and the "slimy, oozy soil of Tammany Hall" stirred up a hornet's nest. As a result, the city's newspapers went on a reform binge. Parkhurst himself formed a City Vigilance League in 1892 to purify government and society. Pursuing Parkhurst's charges, a state legislative commission investigated police corruption in the metropolis in 1894.

The wave of moral fervor also swept Tammany out of power in the municipal elections of that year, bringing into the mayoralty William L. Strong, an old-stock, Yankee Protestant representative of the city's business and professional elite. In retrospect, one of Strong's notable actions was the appointment of Theodore Roosevelt as police commissioner. The young and aggressively moralistic Roosevelt tramped the streets at night with his friend, journalist Jacob Riis, searching out saloon violations, streetcorner prostitutes, and delinquent patrolmen. But the moralistic crusade of Parkhurst and Roosevelt did not survive the torrents of ethnic pluralism and machine politics. Two years later, Tammany was back in power while the purity forces regrouped for another assault on the saloon and the machine.

A similar moral crusade swept Chicago at about the same time. The catalyst for the purity crusade in the Midwest metropolis was the 1893 visit of William T. Stead, an English reformer and journalist noted for his sensational exposés of prostitution in London. Stead spent six months investigating Chicago's low life in saloons, brothels, and gambling dens, publishing his findings in 1894 in a sweeping moralist tract, *If Christ Came to Chicago*. Stead's call for moral regeneration stimulated the organization of the Chicago Civic Federation, a typically pietist, middle-class effort to clamp down on liquor and vice as well as rescue municipal government from machine domination. This new agency also provided the early momentum for the National Civic Federation, founded in 1900 to promote a businesslike approach to social, economic, and political problems. As these organizational efforts suggest, the link between moral reform and political reform remained close throughout the progressive era.

The purity crusades touched off by Parkhurst in New York and Stead in Chicago had their counterparts in dozens of cities. Local vigilance leagues, law-and-order societies, and social-purity alliances sprang up all across the urban landscape, each focusing on prostitution, gambling, and other forms of urban vice. In the 1890s, purity reform had all the attributes of a mass movement. In 1895 vice reformers institutionalized this brand of urban reform by establishing a new national organization, the American Purity Alliance. The same pietist impulse sparked the founding of the National Vigilance Society in 1911, headed by Clifford G. Roe, a young Chicago attorney and antivice crusader. Thus, purity advocates breathed a new urgency into the reforming spirit of American voluntarism.

They also sought to enlist government in the crusade to impose a coercive, pietist morality on the urban masses. Typical was the work of the Chicago Vice Commission of 1910–1911, which investigated prostitution in the city and produced a massive report on *The Social Evil in Chicago* (1911). The Chicago study provided impetus for congressional passage of the Mann Act prohibiting interstate traffic in "white slavery" (an early 20th-century euphemism for prostitution). During the progressive era, over 100 cities established vice commissions following Chicago's model. The purpose, of course, was to destroy the purported links between organized prostitution, the political machine, and police on the take.

In its various guises, moral reform represented a powerful thrust of the progressive era. The saloon and the whorehouse were not the only urban evils. Purity reformers found a menace to morality in lotteries, gambling, pornography, birth control, boxing, horse racing, college football, Sunday baseball, cigarette smoking, card games, dance halls, amusement parks, vaudeville shows—virtually every aspect of modern urban life posed dangers to pietist morality and values. Not unrelated was the surge of hostility toward immigrants in the 1890s and the growth of new nativist organizations such as the American Protective Association. The drive to close America's gates to the newcomers drew on the prevailing pietist ideology, the same sense that the immigrant masses of the big cities threatened social order and traditional American values. Indeed, as historian John M. Allswang observed in *A House for All Peoples* (1971), a study of ethnic politics in progressive-era Chicago, purity issues and prohibition became an important part of the nativist assault on ethnic pluralism. "Prohibition was the greatest ethnic issue," according to Allswang.

The passage of the Eighteenth Amendment in 1918, outlawing the manufacture, sale, and use of alcoholic beverages, represented the high point of reform moralism. It was also a great defeat for Americans of the ritualistic persuasion and for social reformers interested in cultural tolerance and civil liberties. Perhaps more than any other issue, prohibition revealed the divergent and contradictory nature of progressive urban reform.

BEYOND REFORM

The political history of the industrial city illustrates the growing complexity of urban government and urban society generally. Mid-19th century egalitarianism created a power vacuum in city government, making the rise of the political machine possible. The urban bosses of the post–Civil War era were often corrupt, but modern historians now recognize that they provided centralized decision making and positive government of sorts. As population and problems mounted rapidly in the big cities of the late 19th century, even the antimachine reformers saw the need for decisive executive authority as well as honest urban government. Thus, civil service reform and the strong mayor system emerged as the chief proposals of the mugwump and good government reformers.

The urban reform movement splintered as the progressive era heated up in the 1890s. Political reformers emphasized administrative and structural changes to streamline municipal government, to make it more honest, efficient, and scientific. Social reformers promoted legislation at various levels to improve housing, social welfare, working conditions, and urban life generally; they also sought a greater degree of economic regulation and a more egalitarian politics. Finally, drawing on the principles of pietist Protestantism, the purity reformers hoped to impose a legislated morality on the American city.

Urban reform clearly built on a complex, often contradictory, and even ideologically incompatible set of impulses. As urban historian Blaine Brownell has suggested, "progressivism and reform meant different things to different people, and it produced, not surprisingly, a variety of different coalitions on an array of issues in scores of communities across the country." Similarly, John Buenker found a bewildering diversity among progressives: "Like all else in this volatile and complex period, political reform was characterized by a myriad of groups pressing for a plethora of reforms for even more variegated motives." The three main strands of reform thought and action often overlapped. Many individual reformers fought one another, but others shifted easily from one type of reform activity to another.

Several decades of historical research, then, have illuminated the diversity and even conflict among those generally considered reformers. As a result, the traditional practice of portraying urban politics as a sharply defined struggle between bosses and reformers seems less useful now than it did a decade or so ago. If reformers with different goals fought each other vigorously, if many reformers supported antidemocratic programs, and if many bosses were really social reformers in disguise—where does this leave the historian seeking to understand and explain the urban political history of the industrial era? Clearly, the boss-reformer model does not correspond perfectly with the political realities of the age. The now perceived weaknesses of this interpretive framework have forced historians to pose new questions and view the evidence in alternative ways.

Some recent scholars, for instance, have begun addressing the issue of political power, particularly its distribution and its uses. Although historians are relatively new to the study of power, political scientists have long been interested in this question. Generally, the views of political scientists about power fall into one of two interpretive frameworks. One position holds to the dominance of local elites—society has been stratified by economic class, and power tends to follow wealth. Other political scientists believe that power has been more or less widely dispersed among competing social groups. This pluralist interpretation contends that a multiplicity of interest groups exert their power in the political arena, battling and compromising with one another for a share of the benefits, services, and other amenities provided by urban government.

Historians are just beginning to investigate the distribution of political power in the cities of the industrial era. The results are meager so far, but promising. One important study of power, Carl V. Harris's *Political Power in Birmingham, 1871–1921* (1977), typifies this new approach to the history of urban politics. Harris focused on two interrelated aspects of political power: which groups obtained power through office holding, and which groups profited by government decision making. He concluded that in Birmingham electoral success generally was proportional to economic wealth, and that office-holding was concentrated among the richest 20 percent of the city's population.

Yet, office-holding patterns did not always dictate public policy outcomes. Harris demonstrated that decision-making power was distributed in rather complex ways. Depending on the particular policy issue (taxation, services, public improvements, economic regulation, social regulation, utility regulation, and the like), Birmingham's politics were complicated by shifting alliances among and within economic groups, and by religious, ethnic, and racial influences. Thus, neither the power-elite thesis nor the pluralist interpretation matched perfectly the political reality in this growing industrial city of the New South. Nevertheless, by avoiding the boss-reformer framework and by posing new questions, Harris was able to bring a fresh perspective to urban political history.

Similar conclusions were reached by David C. Hammack in a second important study of political power in the industrial city, *Power and Society: Greater New York at the Turn of the Century* (1982). Hammack examined both the pattern of mayoral politics and the conflicts surrounding three big public policy issues: the consolidation of greater New York City in 1898, the building of the city's first subway, and the centralization of the public school system. The city's increasing ethnic and economic heterogeneity, Hammack argued, "hastened a shift from a politics based on the direct participation of particular economic and social elites, to a politics of competing elite and nonelite economic, social, and cultural interest groups mediated and managed by specialized professional politicians."

Several forces coalesced to undermine the earlier dominance of power elites. First, the elites were divided among themselves, as was also the case in Harris's Birmingham. They often had different economic interests and competing political ambitions. Second, as the city's population grew through immigration and economic diversification, varied nonelite groups (ethnic communities, small businesses, labor unions, and so on) developed into active pressure groups. The community-based political parties which represented these interest groups siphoned off political power from the elites. Finally, as the political arena became a place where different interests were compromised and mediated, technical experts, professionals, and bureaucrats came to exercise a great degree of governmental authority.

The powerful and decisive role of urban professionals and experts is also emphasized in Jon C. Teaford's *The Unheralded Triumph: City Government in America, 1870-1900* (1984). More important than bosses or reformers, Teaford contended, the growing army of city bureaucrats and technicians may have been the real shapers of the new city. Public policy making depended on what was technically or financially feasible. The politicians came to rely on the experts, who by the 20th century staffed the administrative departments in city government. Neither the bosses nor the reformers, perhaps, had as much power or influence as historians once believed.

By focusing on power and professionalism, recent scholars have forced urban historians to consider alternatives to the boss-reformer interpretive framework, Urban historians will continue to think of the industrial city as a political battleground between bosses and reformers. But they can no longer ignore the new questions about power and professionalism. The chief interpretive thrust of these new studies is that political decision making reflected the economic, ethnic, and cultural complexity of the cities. Depending on the political or policy issues involved, coalitions formed, broke up, and reformed as the changing perceptions of the major political actors and interest groups dictated policy shifts and compromises. At the same time, the range of political authority was being narrowed considerably, as technical expertise and professionalism came to determine administrative decision making. The new city of the industrial era, in short, was shaped by the continual political interaction of competing elites, pluralistic interest groups, and technical experts.

This sort of dynamic interpretive framework is one which can accommodate disparate reform movements as well as machine politicans with distinctively different approaches. It is a framework which has room for antidemocratic reformers, moral reformers, even reform bosses. The new American city of the industrial era became a stage on which contending ideological and political forces exerted their power and asserted their fears, their hopes, and their urban dreams. It was, predictably, an exciting and eventful drama.

III.

City and
Society

SEVEN

The Problem of Social Order

The rapid pace of growth and change in the late 19th century reshaped the urban social order. Even before the great surge of immigration and industrialization in the 1870s, the American city had experienced substantial social change. The colonial town had been orderly, deferential, and relatively homogeneous in population. A powerful sense of localism prevailed. Change and innovation came slowly. Above all, society was characterized by widely shared values and a strong sense of community.

By the mid-19th century, however, these social patterns

began to erode before the twin forces of urbanization and industrialization. The centralization of government authority by the early 20th century, for instance, began to rob local communities of autonomy and power. The rise of the corporate-industrial system destroyed the local and regional economic pattern of earlier years. The new capitalist order enhanced the role of the national marketplace and promoted the bureaucratization of American society. Technology and the factory system altered the social organization of work, depriving the new industrial artisans of skills and weakening their control over the workplace. The impact of change intensified with the surge of rural American and European newcomers to the city—heterogeneous groups of migrants unaccustomed to urban ways of life and work. As the industrial era progressed, urban society became increasingly segmented, divided, and disorderly. In these and other ways, the big city of 1900 bore little resemblance to the small town and seaport center of the preindustrial era.

MODERNIZATION THEORY

Borrowing from the social sciences, American historians in the 1960s began to use modernization theory in interpreting U.S. social history and social change. Modernization theory posits a linear progression over time from a traditional, agrarian, and preindustrial society to a more modern, urbanized, and industrial society. According to this analysis, traditional societies were highly localized and autonomous, characterized by a strong sense of social unity and community. Kinship and communal networks regulated the social experience of the people. Primary or face-to-face relationships prevailed. The pace of life was dictated by sun and season, and social patterns were determined by communal folkways of long standing.

Modernization theory goes on to suggest that traditional patterns of society erode, break down, and are transformed by the forces of change unleashed by urbanization and industrialization—by the city and the factory, and by migration and mobility. As Cyril E. Black put it in his innovative study, *The Dynamics of Modernization* (1966): "The construction of a new way of life inevitably involves the destruction of the old." In the modernizing society, power and authority become centralized, communal patterns give way to competition and conflict, primary relationships are replaced by indirect and impersonal contacts. Social order and stability are undermined as new urban and industrial ways dictate how people live and work. According to the theory, the modernizing society is characterized by human dislocation, social disorganization, instability, disorder, and alienation. The city, by this analysis, becomes an artificial, impersonal, even evil place—one which destroys the organic social unity, the group solidarity, and the communal folk and family pattern of the traditional community.

Some American historians have applied these ideas about modernization in order to understand the social history of the industrial era. One of the most influential of these efforts, Robert H. Wiebe's *The Search for Order, 1877–1920* (1967), reinterpreted post–Civil War American history according to the tenets of modernization theory. Essentially, this study postulated the erosion of the cohesive community and the growth of loose, disorderly, and impersonal human relationships in the urban, industrialized society of the late 19th century. The new society was national rather than local, centralized rather than autonomous. It was formal, specialized, and bureaucratic rather than informal and premodern. The new social and economic conditions, according to Wiebe, fostered a quest for order and direction. Some individuals sought to restore familiar patterns and defend the old order; others tried to build new institutions, to develop more cosmopolitan relationships to replace the communal network patterns prevalent in the old localized island community.

In a later book, *The Segmented Society* (1975), Wiebe refined these ideas, portraying a shift in 19th-century America from a cohesive and communal society to one composed of disparate social and economic units, each divided from one another. The segmented society, Wiebe wrote, was "a configuration of small social units"—networks or groupings organizing around family, occupation, ethnicity, and locality. Further modernizing change occurred in the 20th century, as the segmented society became centralized, hierarchical, and bureaucratic.

Another historian, Samuel P. Hays, also used modernization theory in a number of influential writings on the industrial era. In his book, *The Response to Industrialism, 1885-1914* (1957), and in several important articles, Hays described an urban America in which "everything was in flux, nothing seemed permanent, and traditions became lost in the midst of rapid change." Society in industrial America, Hays wrote, had become impersonal, bureaucratic, and specialized. An "organizational revolution" emerged in response to the new forces of the industrial age, reshaping American life in the process. Many aspects of human behavior came to be regulated by large-scale administrative systems and by a variety of functional organizations. As Hays put it in *The Response to Industrialism:* "For the millions of people torn from accustomed rural patterns of culture and thrust into a strange, urban environment, the meaning of industrialism lay in a feeling of uprootedness, in the disintegration of old ways of life and the loss of familiar surroundings."

In other writings, Hays conceptualized even further about the impact of modernizing change. Drawing on the earlier work of sociologist Robert K. Merton, author of the influential *Social Theory and Social Structure* (1957), Hays suggested that the local-based society with its communal patterns was being supplanted in the industrial era by a less traditional and more cosmopolitan society. Transcending the local community, the cosmopolitan orientation was attuned to the larger structural changes in American political, economic, and social life. For Hays, the transition from a traditional to a modern society was accompanied by shifts from local to wider and more cosmopolitan patterns of social relations. As a rather unified body of writings on American social history, his work has been much influenced by modernization theory.

Similarly, in an important essay on "The Social System" (*Daedalus,* 1961), historian Oscar Handlin used modernization theory to explain the urbanization pattern of the industrial era. "The stupendous growth of the modern city in the nineteenth century," Handlin wrote, "destroyed the old hierarchical order based on the defined relationships of corporately organized households. The social system that then emerged was loosely structured through a large number of autonomous and scarcely articulated associations." Thus, the social system of the new city became fragmented and disorderly. Much of the new urban population remained "a drifting, isolated mass, the elements of which belonged to no larger group." Handlin's article offered a classic statement of modernization theory applied to the 19th-century city.

Modernization theory had a powerful impact on the writing of American social history in the 1960s and 1970s. More recently, however, Thomas Bender suggested the dangers of an undiscriminating application of sociological theory. In his book, *Community and Social Change in America* (1978), Bender criticized historians who "mechanically inserted historical data into the framework supplied by the essentially ahistorical logic of change offered by modernization theory." Bender concluded that the transition from traditional to modern society was never as neat and precise as the theory would suggest. Rather, social change was occurring at different levels of human experience simultaneously, often at varied speeds and with varied degrees of intensity. As a result, traditional folkways and modern urban patterns coexisted in the same society. Some aspects of society and social interaction had been modernized, specialized, and centralized; others remained localized, communal, and traditional. As Bender put it, "the mass of Americans became involved in two distinct but intertwined patterns of social relations, one communal, the other not." In other words, the sense of community and elements of a traditional lifestyle still existed for most Americans in some aspects of life, but in others the forces of modernization had permanently altered old social patterns.

Bender's argument is supported by a considerable body of recent research. We now know, for instance, that most immigrant groups retained old world culture and premigration folkways long after arrival in industrial America. Blacks who migrated to the cities of the industrial North maintained the traditional folk patterns of the rural South, even as the urban ghettoes grew and spread. Industrial laborers adhered to preindustrial work routines even in the new factory system. Kinship and family networks were often strengthened during the industrial period; the family may have provided an emotional shelter from the fearful realities of the industrial city.

Thus, modernization theory may disguise as much as it explains about the growth of modern industrial America. Nevertheless, it remains a useful conceptual framework for analyzing the processes of change. Bender's reformulation, in particular, provides great insight, a way of understanding the social history of the city in the industrial era.

Clearly, urban society in the industrial period was multifaceted and pluralistic rather than one dimensional, homogeneous, and uniform in character. While some segments of urban life remained localized and communal, others had been transformed and modernized. As a result, people and groups responded in different ways to the city, the factory, and the other dynamic forces of modern life.

These responses to urbanism and industrialism took at least three forms. First, as Wiebe has suggested, some sought to control the emerging society, particularly its most threatening and disorderly elements. This sort of thinking explains the attack of reformers on the political machine and the saloon, the hostility of native-born Americans toward the immigrants, and the concern of industrialists over labor radicalism. Second, while some advocated new forms of social control, others hoped to alter or reform the environment of the industrial city. Shaping the environment through housing reform or city planning, for instance, represented an alternative means of controlling and directing the disorderly forces of urban-industrial life.

The persistence of communalism represented a third important response to the change and disorder of the modernizing society. Here, the response to the disorderly and threatening industrial world was to cling to the old traditions and familiar folkways. Thus, social control, environmentalism, and communalism represented three distinctly different responses to urban change and to the disorder of the modernizing city.

DEPRESSION AND DISORDER

The modernization of American society in the late 19th century was accompanied by unprecedented levels of economic and social disorder. The rapid population growth of the cities created tremendous human and social problems—jobs and housing, schooling and social welfare, public health and public order. A large proportion of the new urbanites of the era had rural and even peasant origins, which made adjustment to the modern industrial city even more difficult. Industrial growth was uneven as the American economy became increasingly dependent on the ebb and flow of international trade. During the industrial era, the great corporations carried the capitalist system to new heights of organization and profit, but the period also witnessed high levels of business failure.

A repetitive cycle of boom and bust buffeted the American economy. Economic depressions hit with regularity, bringing severe problems of unemployment, poverty, labor violence, and social dislocation to the cities. As historian John A. Garraty has observed in *Unemployment in History* (1978): "In the late nineteenth century, cyclical depressions associated with industrialization were making unemployment more severe. At the same time, slum conditions, the lack of steady work, the regimentation incidental to machine methods of production, and other social pressures were dashing the hopes and undermining the sense of loyalty to the community of many people, making them poor workers and worse citizens." Clearly, much of the social disorder of the industrial city was intimately linked to economic conditions—to the instability of the free market and the uneven pace of industrial development.

In the 30 years between 1870 and 1900, the United States

experienced three periods of prolonged economic depression. The depression of 1873–1878 brought the most serious economic downturn in American history to that time. The impact was most apparent in the industrial cities of the Northeast and Midwest. During the winter of 1873–1874, for example, about 40,000 laborers in Philadelphia were thrown out of work, while in New York City almost 100,000 workers—one fourth of the labor force—went jobless. In November 1874, according to the American Iron and Steel Institute, unemployment reached at least 1 million. By the winter of 1877–1878, unemployment nationwide peaked at 3 million. Labor reformer William G. Moody estimated that one-half of the nation's working population was either wholly or partially unemployed in 1878.

These economic conditions brought serious social unrest, labor discontent, and political agitation. In many cities, jobless workers established unemployed councils and breadwinners leagues. They organized mass marches and demonstrations and demanded work, relief, and economic reform. Occasionally, these mass meetings and demonstrations resulted in violence, such as the Tompkins Square Riot in New York in January 1874, in which ten to fifteen thousand labor demonstrators were attacked and dispersed by police. The depression also stimulated radical politics and radical labor unionism. The mid-1870s witnessed the emergence of the national Greenback–Labor party, the Socialist Labor party, the Knights of Labor, and other political and labor groups. Layoffs and wage reductions brought a rash of work stoppages and labor violence, culminating in the great railroad strikes of 1877. State militias and even federal troops were called out to put down the striking railroad workers, but at great cost in lives—55 workers and soldiers were killed in Pittsburgh alone. Thus, the combination of depression, massive unemployment, labor discontent, and radical agitation produced unprecedented social turmoil and urban disorder during the 1870s.

A similar social and economic pattern prevailed during the depression of 1882–1886. Although less severe than that of the previous decade, this downturn in the business cycle was clearly an industrial depression rather than a business or financial panic. Its chief characteristics were wage cuts, layoffs, and unemployment among urban and industrial workers. By October 1884, according to one survey, unemployment reached 350,000 in 22 northern states, or about 13 percent of the work force. Wage cuts averaging 20 to 30 percent affected those still working. By 1885, the newly created U.S. Bureau of Labor reported 1 million workers unemployed, while Terence Powderly of the Knights of Labor insisted that the depression had idled at least 2 million. Unemployment and wage cuts intensified discontent and unrest among the working classes and stimulated new strike activity. Some 8,584 recorded strikes and labor actions took place during the 1880s. Symbolic of the social disorder of the decade, Chicago's notorious Haymarket Riot in 1886 touched off fears of radicalism and violence from below.

The 19th century ended with yet another period of depression and disorder. Like its predecesors, the depression of 1893–1897 brought bank and business failures, along with wage cuts and unemployment for workers. The depression of the 1890s also stimulated mass demonstrations, social and political radicalism, strikes, and violence. An economist at the University of Chicago surveyed unemployment in 60 cities in November 1893 and reported 100,000 people out of work in Chicago; 85,000 in New York City; 50,000 in Philadelphia; 38,000 in Boston; 35,000 in Brooklyn; 25,000 in Detroit; 20,000 in St. Louis; 18,000 in Milwaukee; 15,000 in Cleveland, Buffalo, and Newark; and 10,000 in Baltimore, Providence, Paterson, and Rochester. Estimates of aggregate unemployment during the devastating winter of 1893–1894 ranged from 1 to 4.5 million. While these statistics remain unproved, especially the larger figures offered by labor, they suggest the relative magnitude of the depression of the 1890s.

The economic disaster of the decade created extensive social disorder. Unemployed workers tramped the country in search of work. They demanded public jobs, food, and relief; they organized mass meetings and demonstrations; they went on strike to oppose wage cuts and layoffs. According to the U.S.

Bureau of Labor Statistics, more than 14,000 strikes involving about 3.7 million workers occurred during the 1890s. Many unemployed and discontented men supported political change through populism, socialism, and other radical or utopian schemes. Led by Jacob Coxey and others, thousands of men demanding work and relief formed industrial armies and marched on Washington. As historian Jerry M. Cooper noted in his study, *The Army and Civil Disorder* (1980), "a massive breakdown of local, state, and federal law enforcement took place" in 1893 and 1894. The depression of 1893 was marked by the most serious industrial conflict of the late 19th century—the Pullman strike—which pitted federal troops against striking railroad workers, left dozens dead and wounded, and generated widespread fears of class conflict and revolution.

Rising economic prosperity generally marked the first two decades of the 20th century. However, labor strife, urban disorder, and violence continued, peaking in 1919, when according to recent estimates, over 4 million workers went out on strike. This was the year of the Seattle general strike and the Boston police strike. Some 250,000 striking steel workers shut down blast furnaces and rolling mills in Pittsburgh, Cleveland, Chicago, Gary, and other steel centers. Thousands of textile workers, led by the radical International Workers of the World, struck in Lawrence, Massachusetts, and other mill towns in the Northeast. John L. Lewis led 300,000 miners in a strike of the bituminous coal industry, and only the threat of a federal injunction prevented a nationwide railroad strike.

In addition to labor strife, severe race rioting broke out in Chicago and Omaha in 1919. Whites began responding with violence to the surge of black population out of the rural South. Immigrants and political radicals became targets of a new nativist hostility at the height of the great "red scare," a period of political reaction emerging in the backwash of World War I. The Ku Klux Klan—an urban Klan now—was on the rise again, and a vast Americanization movement spread across the land, hoping to assimilate immigrants quickly and dissolve their ethnic ghettoes in the cities. The fear of social upheaval which prevailed throughout the late 19th century subsided during the progressive era, but the events of 1919—with the Russian Revolution as a backdrop—renewed the old anxieties about social turmoil, disorder, and violence.

CATACLYSMIC THOUGHT

The social disorder of the industrial era generated widespread fears of approaching apocalypse and doom. In his study, *Doubters and Dissenters: Cataclysmic Thought in America, 1885–1918* (1964), historian Frederic Cople Jaher identified the problem: "Although cities were growing, immigrants arriving, corporations forming, unions agitating, and artisans already giving way to factories before the Civil War, not until the 1880s did these forces come to dominate American life. To many who thrived on memories of a rural, agricultural, native-born, and small-propertied community, these elements embodied the threat of modern times—they were the manifestations of the cataclysmic trend of industrial capitalism."

Many Americans shared these perceptions. The powerful social forces of the industrial era—the city, the factory, unchecked immigration, corporate capitalism, labor radicalism, and community breakdown—threatened to plunge American society into a new dark age. Many social critics of the time believed that the inequalities of wealth and power would ultimately result in disorder, catastrophe, even class war. The apparent loss of the old values nourished by Protestantism and republicanism had ominous implications. Greed, materialism, moral decay, and political corruption dredged up constant reminders of the decline and fall of the once powerful Roman Empire. Amid the social disorder of the industrial era, as John L. Thomas put it in *Alternative America* (1983), "the ghost of Rome returned to haunt the American people."

The fear of urban crime, violence, and rioting pervaded the late 19th century. This fear of social upheaval was reflected in the 1870s, for instance, in Charles Loring Brace's book, *The*

Dangerous Classes of New York (1872). Brace, a social reformer, was particularly concerned about "outcast street-children" who grew into adult criminals preying on the city's respectable citizens and their property. By the 1880s, the surge of immigration and the emergence of working-class activism caused additional apprehension.

A pamphlet published in 1886, *Riots in Cities and Their Suppression,* written by a retired general, typified this new urban paranoia. In this manual for the suppression of riots, published soon after the shocking Haymarket Riot, General E. L. Molineux predicted inevitable social revolution in the cities. According to Molineux, "the restless and implacable association of Socialists, Communists, and Nihilists that have taken root in our midst . . . sooner or later, must inevitably precipitate a conflict upon us." Only ruthless and effective police and military action could preserve order in the cities. "The strong arm of moral and physical suppression" was society's only protection. The mob and the riot, it was generally believed, posed mortal dangers to urban life. The city itself, one writer asserted in the *Atlantic* magazine in 1895, was the nation's "deadliest menace."

Perhaps the industrial era's most alarming document of doom was Ignatius Donnelly's nightmarish antiutopian novel, *Caesar's Column: A Story of the Twentieth Century* (1890). A farmer, eccentric writer, and Populist politician in Minnesota, Donnelly had a passionate sense of social justice. *Caesar's Column* envisioned a futuristic urban and industrial civilization, complete with air ships, air conditioning, television, electric transit, and other technological wonders of the year 1988.

But Donnelly also portrayed a social system brutalized and dehumanized by capitalism and modernizing change:

Life is a dark and wretched failure for the great mass of mankind. The many are plundered to enrich the few. Vast combinations depress the price of labor and increase the cost of the necessaries of existence. The rich, as a rule, despise the poor; and the poor are coming to hate the rich. The face of labor grows sullen; the old tender Christian love is gone; standing armies are formed on one side, and great communistic organizations on the other; society divides itself into two hostile camps; no white flags pass from one to the other. They wait only for the drum-beat and the trumpet to summon them to armed conflict.

As Martin Ridge observed in his biography of Donnelly, *Caesar's Column* "depicted in a biting pyrographic style a degraded society devoid of reform's influence, with the rich in complete control, the laboring classes reduced to a horrible quasi-barbaric poverty, ending in a revolution more bloody and violent than any that had preceded it."

Donnelly's fiction represented one man's vision of what was wrong with modern industrial society. However, the popularity of *Caesar's Column*—it sold almost 700,000 copies within a decade—suggests that Donnelly's message found a wide and perhaps fearful audience. *Caesar's Column* was a book which raised powerful apprehensions about the decline of social order in modernizing America.

In some ways, Ignatius Donnelly was right. Great disparities of wealth and poverty marked the industrial era. Recurring cycles of boom and depression created an unstable economy and uneven employment for millions of workers. Riots, strikes, and labor conflicts reflected a growing militancy among the urban masses. The incessant flow of immigrants from the European peasant village and migrants from the American farm, and the mingling of all these groups in the great American city, made social cohesion difficult. With its new skyscrapers and streetcars, the city was changing physically. With its new population pattern, and with people living in dismal slums and working in brutal factories, mills, and sweatshops, the city was changing socially, as well. Maintaining social order in the new city emerged as a dominant issue of the late 19th century. In responding to the problem of social order, urban Americans variously pursued new methods of social control and new ways of reforming the environment, as well as older and more traditional patterns of communalism.

EIGHT

Social Control

In the depression-filled decades of the late 19th century, urban America experienced unprecedented levels of labor violence and social disorder. Writers, social critics, and prophets of disaster predicted worse to come. It was inevitable, they argued, given the clash of cultures and values between rural and urban, rich and poor, native-born and immigrant, communal and capitalist, traditional and modern. With society in flux and older values eroding, governments and established institutions tried to maintain order and control. Mass demonstrations, strikes, and violence were dealt with through such traditional social controls as law, penal institutions, police, state militias, even federal troops.

154

At the same time, new mechanisms emerged for social regulation and control. In the preindustrial past, institutions such as family and church had effectively maintained social order and cultural conformity. In the new city, wealthy and powerful elites found alternative ways of extending cultural domination over potentially threatening subordinate groups. Those who did not share traditional nativist, Protestant, and pietist visions of social order, for instance, were subjected to vigorous efforts to shape values and behavior. Public schooling offered one new method of imposing social and moral conformity on the rising generation, especially immigrant and working-class children. Newer forms of charity and social welfare similarly emerged as powerful instruments of urban order and social regulation.

SOCIAL WELFARE
AND SOCIAL ORDER

The late 19th century was a crucial period in the history of American social welfare. During the industrial era, social welfare and philanthropy became specialized and scientific. State boards of charities emerged in most states to supervise administration of poorhouses and more specialized state welfare institutions. The charity organization movement—an effort to systematize and coordinate private relief-giving at the local level—also sprouted. Toward the end of the period, social workers began establishing urban settlement houses to serve the immigrant and urban masses.

Simultaneously, a great debate raged about the merits of "outdoor relief," or welfare assistance to the noninstitutionalized poor. Public attitudes toward the poor were often uncharitable, to say the least. Most 19th-century Americans accepted the distinctions generally drawn between the so-called worthy or deserving poor and those considered unworthy and thus undeserving. The American gospel of individualism fostered the belief that any hard-working, virtuous man could support his family in independence and dignity. Those in need, it was generally believed, had come to their dependent state through such personal failings as immorality, ignorance, idleness, and alcoholism.

Many agreed with industrialist Andrew Carnegie that poverty was a positive, character-building virtue. Those with initiative and foresight would overcome their humble beginnings— this was the rags-to-riches theme of the popular Horatio Alger novels. The Social Darwinism of the time promoted acceptance of poverty and economic inequality as part of the natural order of things and cast doubt on the usefulness of public relief and private charity. Adherents of this "survival of the fittest" theory of social relations believed, as one writer in *The Nation* put it in 1894, that the solution to poverty could be found in "nature's remedy"—"work or starve."

If anything, public attitudes toward the poor hardened between 1870 and 1900. Ironically, as unemployment and poverty intensified during the industrial depressions, hostility to public assistance of any kind became stronger. Indeed, a number of major cities abandoned public assistance completely; for example New York City suspended public outdoor relief in 1874. Except for small appropriations for the indigent blind, the practice was not resumed for the remainder of the 19th century. The 1898 charter of the newly consolidated Greater New York actually prohibited the distribution of outdoor relief. Brooklyn, the nation's third largest city, abolished outdoor assistance in 1878, followed by Philadelphia in 1879. Seth Low, Brooklyn's tight-fisted reform mayor, opposed welfare assistance as "a vast political corruption fraud." Private charity, Low suggested, was "equal to the burden of such outdoor relief as may be actually needed."

Political leaders in other cities apparently agreed. By 1900 outdoor relief had been abandoned in Baltimore, St. Louis, Washington, San Francisco, Kansas City, New Orleans, Louisville, Denver, Atlanta, Memphis, and Charleston. Several other big cities—Cincinnati, Jersey City, Indianapolis, Pittsburgh, Providence, and St. Paul—budgeted only miniscule amounts for this kind of public assistance. The depressions of the late 19th century, rather than loosening public purse strings for the unemployed and the poor, actually hardened antipauperism attitudes and imposed new demands on private charity.

The economic and social changes of the period also brought new patterns to private philanthropy. The charity organization movement supplies a key to understanding how social welfare was used to regulate the urban masses and shape their behavior. The movement officially began in 1877, when Samuel Humphreys Gurteen, a transplanted English clergyman, founded the Buffalo Charity Organization Society (COS). The new scientific philanthropy spread rapidly throughout urban America. At least 25 cities had established charity organization societies by 1883. This number grew to 100 by 1895. According to social welfare historian Roy Lubove, author of *The Professional Altruist: The Emergence of Social Work as a Career, 1880-1930* (1965): "The swift expansion of the charity organization movement represented one response of a troubled middle class to the social dislocations of the post–Civil War industrial city."

Underpinning the entire COS movement were two fundamental beliefs. COS leaders contended that poverty and dependency resulted from individual moral and character defects. They also believed that indiscriminate charity merely strengthened pauperism by discouraging the poor from making any efforts in their own behalf.

This analysis of the problem dictated COS solutions. First, the COS urged the coordination of urban charity to eliminate duplication of effort. Second, relief applicants had to be investigated carefully before being assisted. Third, relief should be minimal, temporary, and tied to work. Finally, the COS sought to regulate and reform the morals and the behavior of the poor. In the words of social welfare historian Blanche Coll, the COS "emphasized personal failure as the major cause of dependency, believed that no one would work unless goaded by fear of starvation, investigated every aspect of an applicant's life, reduced relief to the lowest possible level, and provided close supervision of any family on its rolls."

Most recent historians of the COS movement have agreed on the social control purposes of the new charity. COS philanthropy was built on the work of "friendly visitors"—middle-class female volunteers who went into the slums to counsel the poor and guide them onto the paths of work and virtue. These COS workers hoped to end pauperism and associated evils by cultivating such values as thrift, honesty, work, self-reliance, sobriety, piety, and respect for authority. Moral uplift and character building through friendly visiting represented nothing less than the shaping and regulating of behavior. COS advocates optimistically contended that this sort of moralistic paternalism —or maternalism—would improve the lot of the poor. They also believed that it would restore social unity, strengthen family ties, protect wealth and property, counter socialist and radical schemes, and safeguard against revolution from below. As Lubove put it in *The Professional Altruist:* "Charity organization represented, in large measure, an instrument of urban social control for the conservative middle class."

While demanding virtue from the poor, COS leaders castigated public assistance and in many cities led the successful drive against public outdoor relief. Josephine Shaw Lowell, a founder of the New York COS and a vigorous propagandist for the entire movement, argued that any sort of relief "should be surrounded by circumstances that shall . . . repel everyone, not in extremity, from accepting it." Relief was a last resort for the helpless poor, she believed and even then the COS should "refuse to support any except those whom it can control." Even work relief, Lowell contended, was "dangerous"; to effectively counter pauperism and dependency, work relief had to be "continuous, hard, and underpaid." The relief system, in other words, should serve as a deterrent, one which would force the poor to work and support themselves. "The great lesson we want to teach people," Josephine Shaw Lowell wrote, "is to depend on themselves." Moralism, work, and self-reliance— with these weapons the COS movement sought to control the urban masses.

The new state charity boards also worked to regulate the

behavior of the poor. Charity officials in virtually every state attacked the outdoor relief system, seeking instead to build character, morality, and self-reliance among the poor. Most dependency stemmed from intemperance, the Pennsylvania state charity commissioners typically asserted in 1871. Thus, "the victims of appetite, and lust, and idleness" had to be trained "to know and revere the precepts of the Bible, and to form habits of industry, frugality, and self-restraint." Hoping to make the lower classes pious, temperate, thrifty, and industrious, the state charity boards emerged alongside the COS as an important force for regulating the urban poor.

In some ways, the settlement houses also approached the urban masses from a manipulative and moralistic perspective. In the late 1880s, these social service and reform institutions began popping up in the immigrant slums of most industrial cities. By 1900 more than 100 such settlements had been founded. Generally, they were staffed by middle-class, college-educated women who resided at the settlements, permitting them to take a more active role in the neighborhood life of the city. Living in the slums often engendered a more sympathetic and practical understanding of the problems of the urban masses. For most social workers in the nonsectarian settlements, environmentalism gradually replaced morality as an analytical explanation for poverty and social disorder. Thus, Jane Addams of Chicago's Hull-House, perhaps the most famous of the settlements, spent much of her time promoting various social and political reforms. The settlements, historian Allen F. Davis suggested, became "spearheads of reform in the progressive era."

But there was another side to the settlement house movement. Settlement house workers generally perceived slum residents through a lens of middle-class, Protestant morality. They were outraged as much by the saloon as by the run-down and overcrowded tenement house. Opposition to drinking, gambling, and urban vice brought most settlement residents into the mainstream of the moral purity crusade. In addition, settlements, such as Hull-House, aimed for social "conciliation" and the prevention of class conflict. Closely linked to these goals, the settlements sought to Americanize, and sometimes to Protestantize, the immigrants and their children.

Typically, in the new and rapidly growing steel city of Gary, four settlement houses were established between 1909 and 1917. Each had religious affiliations and viewed the immigrant community as a missionary field ripe for proselytization. All four settlements developed wide-ranging Americanization and moral-uplift programs. The Gary Neighborhood House, for instance, a Presbyterian settlement headed by a Presbyterian minister, conducted Bible study classes and Protestant Sunday schools in several languages for immigrant children. Settlement residents distributed Bibles in the immigrant communities, propagandized for temperance and prohibition, and promoted Americanization through recreational and educational programs. The Gary-Alerding Settlement House, a Catholic agency founded in 1917, expended considerable effort in "counteracting the socialistic and bolshevistic tendencies of certain elements among the foreigners." These settlements, to be sure, performed important social services for the urban immigrants, but they approached their tasks from a paternalistic perspective. They wanted to help the newcomers, but they also wanted them to become patriotic Americans who worked hard, stayed sober, went to church, and sent their children to Sunday school.

These sectarian settlements were excluded from membership in the National Federation of Settlements because of their religious affiliations. As a result, they were isolated from professional and progressive influences in the settlement movement. It seems quite likely that Jane Addams's Hull-House was not a typical settlement. More representative, perhaps, were the 2,500 settlements and urban missions established by the Catholic Church by 1915. These agencies, along with parallel institutions created by evangelical Protestant denominations, sought to Americanize the immigrants, proselytize among newcomers to the city, and bring moral purity to the urban slums. Most such institutions provided social services, but ethnic assimilation and moral uplift remained at the heart of this sort of religious benevolence. In various ways, then, agencies of charity, benevolence, and social welfare served the purpose of social order.

PUBLIC SCHOOLS
AND SOCIAL ORDER

From the beginning of the common school movement in the early 19th century, public schools served as instruments of socialization and social order. Amid the social and economic changes of the industrial era, public schools came to be viewed as increasingly important agencies for inculcating behavioral conformity. They promoted patriotism and Protestant piety, assimilated immigrants, and, above all, helped to maintain social stability. Public schools, of course, have always had cognitive functions—the teaching of basic skills, such as reading, writing, and mathematics, which are necessary for social and occupational living. But they have also served to transmit mainstream American culture and values across the generations. In this sense, the schools generally reflected the interests and values of those who possessed economic and political power.

By the late 19th century, urban school systems began to undergo a process of centralization and bureaucratization paralleling the reorganization of the corporate economic structure. Indeed, some big city school administrators conceived of the schools as educational factories, in which the principles of scientific management could be applied to the training of children. The purpose was to extend the influence of the school as widely as possible.

By the 20th century, kindergarten programs had been established in many large cities as a means of expanding the socialization function of the schools, especially in the immigrant slums. The kindergarten, one writer asserted in 1903, presented the "earliest opportunity to catch the little Russian, the little Italian, the little German, Pole, Syrian, and the rest and begin to make good American citizens of them." Similarly, high school programs became widespread, extending the schools' influence beyond the traditional grammar school curriculum. City schools initiated night school programs for adults, who were offered citizenship and English-language instruction, along with vocational training. The urban population explosion of the industrial era was accompanied by a substantial expansion of school programs.

The new urban school systems sought to impose an institutional order and discipline on the growing mass of urban children, particularly immigrant children. Fearful of the social consequences of mass immigration, most native-born Americans viewed the public school as a homogenizing agent, one which would break down immigrant cultures and traditions and secure adherence to more acceptable American habits, dispositions and beliefs.

Elwood P. Cubberley, one of the nation's leading educators, articulated the goals of the public-school Americanizers in a 1909 book, *Changing Conceptions of Education:* "Our task," Cubberley wrote, "is to break up these groups or settlements, to assimilate and amalgamate these people as a part of our American race, and to implant in their children, so far as can be done, the Anglo-Saxon conception of righteousness, law and order, and popular government, and to awaken in them a reverence for our democratic institutions and for those things in our national life which we as a people hold to be of abiding worth." For Cubberley and most other urban school officials, the schools were primarily responsible for attainment of these objectives. The public schools became, as Boston school superintendent Frank V. Thompson wrote in *The Schooling of the Immigrant* (1920), "the chief instrument of Americanization."

Along with Americanizing the immigrants, the urban schools took on the larger task of establishing and maintaining social order. As historian Selwyn K. Troen has noted, "builders of public school systems had an overriding fear of chaos and disorder." These concerns led the public schools to establish numerous programs to shape values and behavior. In particular, work was promoted as a satisfying and ennobling virtue. Vocational courses and shopwork trained boys for industrial and factory work. Classes in typing, bookkeeping, sewing, cooking, and home economics prepared girls for their special niche in the new industrial order. Student government instructed children in the mechanics of democracy, but denied them any real power. School savings banks promoted thrift as a capitalist virtue. Most schools encouraged patriotism and piety through musical, dramatic, and auditorium programs. Through intelligence testing and curriculum tracking, the schools sorted children for appropriate slots in the social and economic structure. Segregated schools and second-rate facilities taught blacks where they stood in white American society.

As socializing agents seeking to produce loyal citizens and willing workers, the schools manipulated behavior and values. This sort of socialization, or adaptation to the prevailing economic and social system, educational historian Joel Spring wrote, usually entailed "shaping a social character that would submit to the authority and order of a role within the bureaucratic enterprise." For immigrant and native-born children alike, then, the public schools developed programs promoting conformity, cooperation, industriousness, thrift, temperance, cleanliness, patriotism, punctuality, self-discipline, respect for authority, and other values considered important in an orderly, industrial society. Most educational reformers agreed, historian David Nasaw noted in *Schooled to Order* (1979), that "the route to social amelioration lay in adjusting the people to fit the new productive order, not the reverse." Thus, the role of the school became one of preparing workers and citizens for a life of cooperation and conformity in the new urban and industrial age.

If educators promoted work as a means of achieving social stability and industrial order, they also conceived of play in similar terms. Physical education in the schools and supervised municipal playgrounds for children became part of a larger nationwide movement for child training and child saving. Contemporary theories of childhood psychology emphasized that children could be trained effectively for social roles through rigorous physical drills and through organized team sports. As

Dominick Cavallo suggested in *Muscles and Morals: Organized Playgrounds and Urban Reform, 1880–1920* (1981), "children's play was too important to be left to children." Thus, team games such as baseball, with clearly defined rules and roles, were envisioned by play organizers as a means of socialization and social control. As Cavallo put it, playground reformers promoted baseball as a perfect way of teaching "respect for law, order, and justice" and restoring "the social cohesion damaged by urban mobility and anonymity."

It seems hardly likely that city kids thought of baseball in exactly these terms. Nevertheless, the logic seemed persuasive and compelling to educators, social workers, and others alarmed about urban disorder. By the progressive era, the movement to organize children's play had been institutionalized in the Playground Association of America, founded in 1906. Urban officialdom bought the playground idea as well. Between 1880 and 1920 municipal governments throughout the United States spent over $100 million on city playgrounds. The movement was particularly strong in Boston, New York, and Chicago. The activities of the playground reformers suggested that play as well as work might be turned to the task of rebuilding social stability and urban order.

One final child-saving technique—the juvenile court program—illustrates the widespread effort to control children and turn them into productive, orderly citizens. As the old social order trembled under the impact of industrial and urban change, reformers confronted the reality of juvenile delinquency in the cities. The growth of a deviant and criminal class among city children and teenagers seemed clear evidence of the breakdown of morality and self-discipline. Schools and playgrounds had already failed for such delinquents; other alternatives became necessary. Some programs, such as those promoted by reformer Charles Loring Brace, took delinquents from city streets and sent them to rural homes in the West. Founded in New York City in 1853, Brace's Children's Aid Society placed about 90,000 homeless and delinquent city kids in country homes by 1890.

The juvenile court, first established in Chicago in 1899, presented another alternative. Progressive social reformers emphasized that rehabilitation was possible for delinquents. This ideal of rehabilitation and reform spurred the creation of juvenile courts, as well as the use of probation and counseling in the family setting for adolescent offenders. The goal, of course, was to rescue children from evil city influences by restoring traditional morality and behavioral patterns. As sociologist Anthony M. Platt contended in *The Child Savers* (1969), the juvenile reformers succeeded "in extending governmental control over a whole range of youthful activities that had previously been ignored or dealt with informally."

Thus, public schools and related child-saving agencies served the purpose of social order during the turmoil of the industrial age. To be sure, schools also provided avenues of upward mobility for the talented and ambitious, keeping alive the ideal of a fluid and democratic society. At the same time, however, few American institutions (except perhaps the family) exercised such a powerful socializing influence over so many during their formative years.

The new city of the industrial era, then, was characterized by rapid change and disorder. Various middle-class and elite groups responded to the problem of order by building a new set of social welfare institutions, typified by the charity organization societies. Sprouting rapidly throughout the nation by the 1880s, these agencies sought to shape and regulate the attitudes and the character of the urban poor. Urban settlement houses often brought a similar paternalistic purpose to welfare work in the city slums. New urban school systems took on the task of character building. In addition to Americanizing immigrant children, public schools regulated behavior and promoted such desirable virtues as work, morality, and patriotism. Related child-saving agencies, such as the juvenile court, extended society's molding influence into the neighborhood and the family. For the dominant economic and cultural groups of the new city, the emerging institutional apparatus in charity and schooling represented an important means of order and control.

NINE

Environmentalism

Social welfare programs, public schools, and other child-saving agencies represented a coercive, or at least manipulative, response to the social turmoil of the industrial city. A different response to social disorder—one seeking change and reform in the urban environment—emerged by the end of the 19th century. But because it challenged deeply held theories of science, economics, and society, environmentalism took root only gradually.

THE CHALLENGE TO
SOCIAL DARWINISM

The application of Charles Darwin's theory of evolution to contemporary society and social relationships strengthened the conservative, laissez-faire outlook of the industrial age. The English sociologist Herbert Spencer and his American follower, William Graham Sumner, popularized Social Darwinism. These views fostered the fatalistic belief that human progress was a matter of gradual evolutionary change—a process that took generations, even centuries.

By this theory, existing patterns in the distribution of wealth and power stemmed from natural evolutionary laws, such as the "struggle for existence" and the "survival of the fittest." Thus, oil magnate John D. Rockefeller could write: "The growth of a large business is merely a survival of the fittest. . . . It is merely the working-out of a law of nature and a law of God." Social Darwinism was buttressed by widespread belief that there were natural economic laws, as well—David Ricardo's "iron law of wages," for instance, which justified subsistence incomes for industrial workers. Taken together, these natural economic and social laws represented a powerful set of ideas—a "steel chain of ideas," one historian has suggested—legitimizing ruthless economic competition and blocking governmental intervention and reform.

But Social Darwinism did not go unchallenged. By the end of the 1870s, socialists, liberal clergy, labor leaders, and varied social critics had begun to mount an attack on the prevailing orthodoxy of social determinism. Increasingly, they attributed the poverty, crime, and disorder of the industrial city to the environment in which people lived and worked. Unwilling to wait decades or centuries for evolutionary progress, they wanted environmental reform—and they wanted it now. They advocated a reform Darwinism which would improve the individual, eliminate poverty and misery, and ensure social order. As Eric F. Goldman put it in his classic study of modern American reform, *Rendezvous with Destiny* (1956), "legislating a better environment, particularly a better economic environment, could bring about a better world, and bring it about before unconscionable centuries.''

In 1879, a journalist turned reformer named Henry George jolted the conservative defenders of the status quo with his immensely popular book, *Progress and Poverty*. Posing one of the earliest challenges to Spencer's Social Darwinism, George directed a withering assault on social injustice, the free market, and inequities in the distribution of wealth. "Social maladjustments," not natural law, had created poverty and injustice, George wrote, and "in removing their cause we shall be giving an enormous impetus to progress." In particular, George sought to curb monopoly power and abolish private property in land. He also anticipated later environmentalists by linking social progress to governmental reforms in education, labor, housing, and public health. From Henry George's perspective, the urban social order could be rebuilt through economic and environmental reform.

Edward Bellamy, a journalist and utopian novelist, posed a second significant challenge to the established economic and social system. In 1888, Bellamy published *Looking Backward, 2000–1887,* a novel with a romantic and anticapitalist vision of the future—a future based on economic equality, social harmony, and communal democracy. *Looking Backward* took the nation by storm, ultimately becoming one of the most popular books in the 19th century. The story of Julian West, a genteel Bostonian who wakes from a hypnotic trance in the year 2000, the novel presented a relentless indictment of capitalism and the free market economy. It was a system, Bellamy wrote, which encouraged social injustice and human exploitation, which pandered to man's worst instincts.

By contrast, Bellamy's futuristic society had abolished private profit and wasteful economic competition in favor of a system based on economic cooperation. In Bellamy's utopia, each individual contributed equally and was rewarded equally. Although idealistic and impractical, Bellamy's anticapitalistic vision nevertheless inspired a wave of sentiment for change and reform. Above all, Bellamy's challenge to economic orthodoxy strengthened the idea that human life was not determined by immutable economic forces.

Over the course of the late 19th century, the writings of Henry George and the utopian vision of Edward Bellamy exerted a powerful influence on American thought. By the turn of the century, writers and reformers alike had expanded the environmentalist attack on Social Darwinism. Jane Addams and other settlement house workers who lived in city slums soon came to recognize that the urban poor were victims of the economic system. In their social work and their writings, they publicized the need for social and economic reform. Liberal religious leaders became vocal critics of an economic and social system that condemned the urban masses to a life of poverty and deprivation.

The 1893 depression, with its devastating and long-term impact on the urban working class, moved many clergy to begin preaching the social gospel—a form of applied Christianity. Typically, Protestant social gospelers such as Washington Gladden and Walter Rauschenbusch urged social activism as a Christian duty. They promoted such reforms as minimum wage laws, old age pensions, income and inheritance taxes, housing reform, and government ownership of railroads, mining, and other important industries. The movement for social Christianity affected the Catholic church, as well. Catholic activist Father John A. Ryan, for instance, emerged as a powerful advocate of labor reforms and social justice legislation. Addams, Rauschenbusch, Ryan, and the others all rejected Darwinian social determinism in favor of an environmentalist approach to the problems of the industrial city.

The crusading journalists of the period buttressed the environmentalist argument for social and economic reform. In this vein, New York newsman and photographer Jacob Riis exposed the horrible living conditions of the city's tenement slums in an arresting book, *How the Other Half Lives* (1890). With its dramatic style and poignant photographs, especially of poverty-stricken children living in cellars and alleys, Riis's book shocked comfortable middle-class readers. Three years later, another journalist; Benjamin O. Flower, described the wretched and degraded conditions in Boston's slums in *Civilization's Inferno, or Studies in the Social Cellar* (1893).

Both men attributed much of the poverty, crime, and disorder of the modern American city to filthy and inhumane living conditions. Riis, in particular, continued the attack on the slums in books, articles, and speeches until his death in 1914. Both Riis and Flower, however, shared the widespread moralism of the time and never became complete converts to the environmentalist position. Their chief contribution was to dramatize the shocking conditions of slum life, to establish for millions of Americans the reality of poverty and despair among big city tenement dwellers.

THE PROGRESSIVE ASSAULT

The environmentalist position advanced considerably during the early years of the 20th century. The investigative journalists of the mass periodical press—the muckrakers, as President Theodore Roosevelt called them—exposed both political corruption and economic exploitation. In a flood of articles after 1900, they focused on such issues as child labor, overworked women, low wages, industrial accidents, ruthless employers, poor housing, and consumer fraud. From 1900 to about 1912, mass circulation magazines such as *Collier's Weekly, Cosmopolitan, Munsey's, McClures,* and *Everybody's* carried the muckraking crusade to every corner of the nation. This early literature of exposure gave a powerful impetus to social and economic reform.

The excesses of industrialism also stimulated an important shift toward realism in the writing of American fiction. For example, Upton Sinclair's powerful novel of working-class realism, *The Jungle* (1906), depicted with relentless and devastating detail the brutalizing working conditions in the Chicago meat-packing industry. A fictional counterpart to muckraking journalism, *The Jungle* also described the insanitary methods used in the meat-packing business. The ensuing public outcry eventually led to a government investigation and passage of federal pure food legislation. In *The Jungle* and in later novels, such as *The Metropolis* (1908) and *The Money Changers* (1908), Sinclair emphasized the link between industrial capitalism and the filth, disease, poverty, and degradation of the urban environment.

Similarly, novelists Stephen Crane, Theodore Dreiser, Frank Norris, and Ernest Poole wrote about the underside of city life in industrial America. About his novel, *Maggie: A Girl of the Streets* (1896), Stephen Crane wrote: "It tries to show that environment is a tremendous thing in this world, and often shapes lives regardlessly." In *Sister Carrie* (1906), Theodore Dreiser's protagonists are constantly battered and ultimately overpowered by the sordid reality of the urban environment.

These writers as a group, Robert Bremner noted in *From the Depths: The Discovery of Poverty in the United States* (1956), portrayed "the whole people squeezed and twisted out of shape by monstrous economic forces and suffering from a fearful insecurity." They addressed a number of significant themes illustrating the jarring impact of city life on European newcomers and American migrants. They portrayed the industrial city as wracked by social disorder and the breakdown of community; they focused critically on the materialism of modern city life; and they described the devastating impact of industrialization and mechanization on the individual. Along with muckraking journalism, the realistic fiction of the progressive era strengthened the movement for environmental reform.

Realism in American literature was paralleled by a similar movement in art. Throughout the late 19th century, graphic illustrations of the seamy side of city life filled the pages of the widely circulated *Harper's Weekly* and the *New York Daily Graphic*, the nation's first fully illustrated daily newspaper. By the 1890s, newspaper and periodical graphic arts had come to center in Philadelphia, where a group of newspaper illustrators provided instant sketches of urban scenes and events to accompany newspaper stories. Displaced by photography after 1900, several of these graphic artists shifted to painting and moved to New York City. The most influential, Robert Henri and John Sloan, became the primary figures of a new genre of realistic painting, sometimes known as the ash can school.

Rebelling against New York's genteel art establishment, the ash can artists painted slum streets and tenement alleys, street urchins and street walkers, and other realistic slices of city life. Most of them had a genuine social consciousness. Their paintings reflected the progressives' concern for the urban environment. In similar fashion, Jacob Riis and Lewis Hine pursued a form of documentary photography, dramatically portraying slum children, tenement life, and industrial workers on the job in factories, mills, and mines. Art Young, a popular cartoonist for the radical journal, *The Masses,* offered an even more biting indictment of urban and industrial reality. As Henry Bamford Parkes suggested in his classic study of American culture, *The American Experience* (1955), realism in the arts "meant a concentration on social conditions as they actually were, emphasizing their more sordid and gloomy aspects and demonstrating, at least by implication, the inapplicability of the accepted economic, political, and moral dogmas." For many Americans, realism in literature, art, and illustration provided a special kind of insight about urban life and social problems.

The progressive era demand for facts and information also stimulated the social survey movement. Typical was the exacting Pittsburgh survey of 1907–1909—an unprecedented effort by a team of social welfare experts to study microscopically the industrial life of a single city. The Pittsburgh survey resulted in six published volumes and, according to historian Walter I. Trattner in *From Poor Law to Welfare State* (1974), "revealed the cost and consequences of low wages, preventable diseases, industrial accidents, ramshackle housing, and lack of urban planning." As one of the survey experts put it, working-class life in industrial Pittsburgh was "very unfavorable, very disastrous." The Pittsburgh survey, and subsequent investigations in dozens of other cities during the progressive era, provided raw evidence for reformers who hoped to reshape the environment.

The search for facts pervaded the reform literature of the progressive period, strengthening the advocacy position of the environmentalists. For example, in a pioneering piece of social investigation titled simply *Poverty* (1904), social worker Robert

Hunter provided a dispassionate account of economic dependency and life at the edge of subsistence and despair. One of every eight Americans lived in poverty, Hunter asserted, but in New York and other large industrial cities the proportion rarely fell below one in four. To solve the problem, Hunter recommended a long list of reforms to improve the living and working environments of city people.

In his book, *Misery and Its Causes* (1909), the influential social work professor Edward T. Devine offered a similar analysis. Poverty and misery, Devine wrote, stemmed not from personal moral failings but from economic and social maladjustment. The problem lay "not in the unalterable nature of things, but in our particular human institutions, or social arrangements, our tenements, . . . our politics, our industry and our business." The message delivered by Hunter, Devine, and others was clear —a decent and orderly society required governmental intervention for social and economic reform.

Progressives established dozens of reform agencies pursuing the same environmentalist goals. These included the National Consumers' League (1899) and the National Women's Trade Union League (1903), both of which advocated improved wages and working conditions for women, and the National Child Labor Committee (1904), which lobbied to get working children out of the factories, mills, and mines. Reform journals and magazines such as *The Survey,* an important medium for social welfare and settlement workers established in 1909, promoted the whole spectrum of social reform and social action. As the progressive era deepened, intellectuals, journalists, and social workers increasingly established the link between the evils of the urban and industrial environment and the necessity for reform programs.

HEALTH, HOUSING, AND PLANNING

Three separate but interrelated reform efforts—for public health and sanitation, housing reform, and city planning—best illustrate the movement for environmental change. The rise of the industrial city, for instance, created serious and life-threatening public health problems. As the industrial machine geared up and as city populations increased rapidly, American urban dwellers began to suffer the consequences of unfettered urban and economic growth. These public health problems included useless sewage disposal methods, undrinkable water, smoky air, ear-shattering noise, heaps of smelly garbage and solid wastes, and unconscionably high mortality rates from epidemic disease. As Martin V. Melosi suggested in *Pollution and Reform in American Cities, 1870–1930* (1980), "industrial cities were experiencing an environmental crisis on a scale not encountered before in America." Since both rich and poor were endangered by filth and disease, public health reforms enjoyed a large and supportive constituency.

Remarkably, given the political battles of the industrial era, municipal governments made substantial progress in sanitary reform. Advances in science and medicine, particularly the discovery of the germ theory in the 1880s, authoritatively linked contagious disease to environmental conditions. At the same time, new technology provided the mechanism for reform. Thus, late 19th-century cities replaced cesspools and backyard privies with newly built sewer systems. By 1907 virtually every American city had installed sewers. By the progressive era, most big cities were using filtration and chlorination to assure pure water supplies. New methods were applied to street cleaning, garbage disposal, and smoke pollution.

New transportation technology had a positive impact on city sanitation. As historian Joel Tarr noted, "the predecessor of the auto was also a major polluter." The horse—the chief beast of burden in the 19th-century city—contributed heavily to urban filth. Every city was home to thousands of horses, each leaving an estimated 20 to 30 pounds of manure on city streets every day. New city residents were not unknown to remark that the city often smelled like a barnyard. The shift to electric transit in the 1890s eliminated one of the worst sources of urban filth.

A new kind of expert, the municipal engineer, played a

particularly vital role in achieving technological advances in sanitary reform. Some of these municipal and sanitary engineers —Ellis S. Chesbrough in Chicago, George E. Waring in New York, Charles V. Chapin in Providence, and George H. Benzenberg in Milwaukee, to name only a few—shaped the urban environment as much as any politician or planner.

In Chicago, for instance, Chesbrough played a decisive role in sanitary engineering during the city's years of most rapid growth. Chicago's chief sanitation problem early in the industrial era stemmed from the use of Lake Michigan for both water supply and sewage disposal. These intertwined problems were solved through a series of sequential engineering decisions. The first significant decision came in 1855, when the city council adopted a sewerage plan recommended by Chesbrough. Before this time, Chicago had no sewers; garbage and waste was simply dumped into roadside ditches.

Chesbrough's plan required the building of graded, underground sewers that emptied into the Chicago River, which in turn flowed into Lake Michigan. The plan was unique in that it necessitated the raising of street grades substantially. Since the city had been built originally on very low land, sewers were laid at street level and the streets then raised 10 feet through an extensive filling operation—a plan that also required raising most of the city's buildings by means of an elaborate screw-operated lifting system. The main problem with Chesbrough's sewer plan was that the sewage entered Lake Michigan quite close to the city's water supply intake.

After the sewer system became operable, Chicago's water supply worsened and waterborne diseases increased. These problems brought a recognition of the interdependence of water supply and sewage disposal, dictating new engineering decisions in 1863. Chesbrough, now chief engineer of the city's Board of Public Works, supervised construction of a tunnel under Lake Michigan to a water-intake point in deep water two miles from shore. As the city's water supply needs increased, additional tunnels were constructed, as well as a pumping station and an underground system of mains and pipes for distribution.

Preservation of a pure water supply from Lake Michigan became an absolute requirement. Future sanitation decisions focused on improving methods of sewage disposal. In the 1880s, engineers reversed the flow of the Chicago River and connected it with the Illinois-Michigan Canal and a newly built sanitary canal. Both flowed southward into the Illinois River and then the Mississippi. By this means, Chicago preserved the Lake Michigan water supply while dumping its sewage through the Mississippi River drainage area. Further advances in sanitation were made early in the 20th century, especially the construction of sewage and water treatment facilities. Every big city, faced with massive sanitation problems, ultimately applied engineering know-how to assure pure water supplies and to dispose of sewage, garbage, and other waste products.

Urban sanitation problems were closely linked to the slum housing conditions that prevailed throughout industrial America. Jacob Riis's 1890 exposé of tenement house life in New York City stimulated the movement for housing reform. Some earlier reformers advocated the construction of model tenements by philanthropic builders willing to accept marginal profits. A few projects of this sort were carried out, but the model tenement idea had little impact on building patterns during the industrial era.

Reformers next turned to restrictive housing legislation. As Gwendolyn Wright noted in *Building the Dream: A Social History of Housing in America* (1981), "those who wanted to uplift the victims of poverty now viewed tenement-house reform as a key to changing the residents' lives." New York tenement house investigations in 1894 and 1900 provided the factual evidence housing reformers needed. Lawrence Veiller, an aggressive New York reformer, subsequently pushed a tenement reform law through the New York state legislature in 1901. This landmark legislation outlawed the notorious dumbbell tenement, with its narrow airshaft and inadequate access to light and air. Instead, the law stipulated a new type of tenement architecture incorporating an open courtyard, the size of which depended on building heights. It also required sanitary facilities in each apartment and fire escapes and other fire-protection measures for every tenement building. Finally, the law included tough new provisions for inspection and enforcement.

Housing reform of the Veiller variety quickly spread to other cities. In Chicago, an investigation in 1901 by the City Homes Association, a housing reform group, revealed serious congestion and sanitary problems in the city's slums. The report focused public attention on housing conditions and led to passage in 1902 of a restrictive tenement law similar to New York's. But, the ordinance lacked effective enforcement provisions. Chicago's housing reformers continued to push for tougher controls on construction and building maintenance, with moderate success over the progressive years. Regulatory housing codes soon became law in Boston, Philadelphia, Washington, Baltimore, St. Louis, San Francisco, and other big cities.

Lawrence Veiller's success in implementing the New York tenement law of 1901 propelled him to the forefront of the housing reform movement in the United States. Over the next two decades, Veiller traversed the country advising municipal governments and local reformers on restrictive housing codes. Aided by the Russell Sage Foundation, he founded the National Housing Association in 1910—an organization Veiller turned into a powerful advocate of environmental reform. By 1912, housing reform associations had been established in 38 cities, and by 1920, some 40 cities had enacted housing legislation. As Roy Lubove suggested in *The Progressives and the Slums* (1962), "Veiller left as a permanent legacy to the nation the principle of a community's right to high minimum standards of restrictive housing legislation." It should be emphasized, however, that the main thrust of progressive housing reform was restrictive and regulatory only. Even the most ardent housing reformers—such as Lawrence Veiller himself—were willing to leave the provision of decent housing to the private building market.

The rise of the comprehensive city planning movement in the early 20th century represented a third important reform dimension. Early planners such as Frederick Law Olmsted and Daniel H. Burnham had emphasized urban park systems, civic center development, and neoclassical municipal architecture. Twentieth-century planners demonstrated greater interest in planning the total urban environment.

The city beautiful ideas inspired by the 1893 Chicago World's Fair gradually gave way to the city efficient and city useful concepts of progressive era planners. New urban planners such as John Nolen and Benjamin C. Marsh emphasized the practical and utilitarian. They addressed problems of street arrangement and traffic control, the tangle of overhead wires and underground utility systems, population congestion, building development, and orderly urban growth. They especially argued for rational and efficient systems of urban transportation, thinking that cheap mass transit would permit the urban masses to move from crowded city slums to less congested suburbs. Indeed, as planning historian Joseph L. Arnold has written, "of all the schemes for banishing the slum, decentralization appeared at the time to offer the best hope."

In their efforts to control the city, planners of the progressive era focused especially on the garden city idea and zoning legislation. Based on the work of British town planner, Ebenezer Howard, the garden city concept called for economically self-sufficient population clusters of about 32,000 surrounded by permanent agricultural greenbelts. Laid out with parks, boulevards, and civic spaces, and with land owned cooperatively, the garden city was to abolish the slum and bring urban life into balance with nature. Planners also discussed an alternative called the garden suburb—a planned residential suburb on the unbuilt fringes of the metropolitan area. These ideas were captivating, of course, but highly utopian and impractical in the United States. In city and suburban development, private real estate interests still reigned supreme.

More influential was zoning—the idea of designating segments of urban space for specific residential, commercial, or industrial uses. First used widely in Germany after 1900, zoning appealed to landowners and real estate developers as a way of achieving order and stability in the urban land market. But reform-minded planners envisioned zoning (mistakenly, as it turned out) as a tool for improving urban housing and eliminating congested living conditions. New York City implemented the nation's first zoning ordinance in 1916, establishing specific land use areas, building height limits, and lot usage restrictions. Zoning caught on quickly, and within a decade, some 591 cities had adopted zoning ordinances.

Thus, the city planning movement offered an alternative to disorderly and haphazard urban development. Planners believed that the environment could be shaped and controlled. By 1920, some 300 cities had established city planning commissions. Ultimately, however, planning did not eliminate the slums or grapple effectively with the urban housing problem. Only a few neglected voices called for constructive housing legislation—that is, for government built or subsidized public housing. "Restrictive housing legislation prevents superlatively bad conditions," but "it cannot produce good ones," housing investigator Edith Elmer Wood wrote in *The Housing of the Unskilled Wage Earner* (1919). Since the private building market failed to provide good housing for the urban masses at affordable rents, Wood contended, a government housing program remained the only alternative to industrial slums. Few reformers carried the environmentalist position that far. Social Darwinism had lost its legitimacy by 1920, but free market capitalism remained a powerful force in the industrial city.

By 1900, close observers of the American city recognized that urban-industrial growth was accompanied by adverse environmental consequences. Thus, liberal reformers increasingly argued the case for altering and improving the environment— for better health, housing, and planning measures. As Scott Nearing, a professor at the University of Pennsylvania, put it in a study entitled *Social Sanity* (1916), "believers in progress are insisting upon a complete adjustment of the environment to the needs of man." The reformers who took this position sought not so much to manipulate the urban immigrants and workers as to shape and control the environment of the city.

TEN

Communalism

While some Americans sought to impose new forms of social control or to reshape the urban environment, others stood opposed to the modernizing trend of the industrial city. Americans were not uniformly wedded to technology, industrialization, and the idea of progress. Preindustrial and premodern lifestyles, folkways, kinship patterns, and work disciplines remained strong in many places and among some subcultures. The industrial revolution did not wipe out the traditional patterns of culture and community entirely. Manifested in a multitude of ways, this communal spirit represented a third important response to the change and social disorder of the modernizing city.

Essentially, communalism reflected the persistence of the values and social behaviors of the smaller, simpler, localized communities of the premodern era. In the preindustrial years, social order and cohesion was based on family and kinship networks, on neighborhood or ethnic or religious solidarity, and on a strong identification with community. Political power was decentralized, and social interaction occurred through primary, face-to-face relationships. The artisanal work pattern enhanced the importance of skills, ensuring the economic security of the preindustrial worker. The dictatorship and discipline of the factory bell and the time clock had not yet supplanted the seasonal labor routines and relaxed work customs of the premodern era. The general thrust of recent historical research suggests the surprising strength and persistence of the communal, preindustrial, premodern pattern, even in the midst of the drive toward industrialization.

ANTIMODERNISM

The communal pattern was manifested in numerous ways during the industrial era. The maintenance of premodern values, for example, encouraged a widespread rejection of technology, the machine, and the factory—indeed, of industrialism, capitalism, and consumerism. This antimodernism was at work on several different levels simultaneously. First, on a rather elevated intel lectual plane, the industrial revolution stimulated a preservationist arts and crafts movement, an antimachinery crusade which originated in mid-19th century England. Influential British writers and social critics such as John Ruskin and William Morris rejected industrialization and its consequences. They hoped to preserve handicraft skills and the decorative arts. Not exactly Luddites, the handicraft preservationists promoted the simple life of the premodern, preindustrial agrarian community.

The antiindustrial handicraft movement arrived in the United States in the 1890s. Beginning in Boston and Chicago in

1897, arts and crafts societies and even some rural handicraft settlements sprouted around the country—some three dozen by 1904. These groups romanticized the premodern artisan. They lamented the decline of handicraft skills and the degredation of work. The arts and crafts critique of the machine culture reflected a growing sense of industrial alienation—the idea that factory work was unsatisfying, dehumanizing, and morally empty. Yet, the handicraft ideology never caught on. It appealed mainly to an educated elite appalled by the crassness and materialism of modern life, but it never acquired a following among the urban working class. Nevertheless, in idealizing the values and lifestyles of the premodern past, the handicraft movement asserted and upheld the communal spirit in a society increasingly dominated by industrial capitalism.

More widespread and more popular was the reformist critique of industrial society espoused by organized labor in the post–Civil War decades. The onset of industrialization coincided with the emergence of two nationwide unions—the National Labor Union, founded in Baltimore in 1866, and the Knights of Labor, originated by garment cutters in Philadelphia in 1869. Both built on the reformist ideals of the earlier Jacksonian era labor movement. Both rejected the demeaning wage-labor system of industrial capitalism. Looking to the past, both unions promoted the ideal of a cooperative society in which capitalism and monopoly power had no place. In its push to abolish the wage system, for instance, the Knights of Labor established more than 100 cooperative enterprises by 1886, including groceries, newspapers, banks, and factories. As social historian Gerald Grob has noted, the Knights hoped to restore "the simple master-workman relationship of an earlier era where employer and employee performed similar functions."

The preindustrial orientation and reformist goals of the two unions had a widespread appeal. The membership of the National Labor Union reached 400,000 by the early 1870s. The Knights of Labor at the peak of its influence in 1886 had over 700,000 members. However, the utopian and reformist approach to labor problems ultimately failed, giving way to the more practical and perhaps more realistic trade union approach of the American Federation of Labor. The AF of L accepted the new industrial order and sought job-related gains in wages and hours. But the reformist unions with their preindustrial goals reflected the yearnings of new factory and mill workers for the premodern past, for a simpler time before the factory, the machine, and the time clock came to control the worker's life. The large membership of the two reformist unions suggested that workers did not passively accept the new factory system.

WORKING-CLASS CULTURE

New studies of working-class history have demonstrated that laborers resisted the new work disciplines of the industrial period. With its emphasis on efficiency and production, the new factory system imposed rigorous demands on the industrial work force. As the industrial era wore on, factory managers viewed time in monetary terms and sought to discipline workers to the time clock and the stop watch. But as Daniel T. Rodgers noted in *The Work Ethic in Industrial America, 1850–1920,* "there is ample evidence that large numbers of industrial workers failed to internalize the faith of the factory masters." The irregular work rhythms of preindustrial craftsmen persisted in the new factories and mills, even as the American economy was industrializing.

Workers demonstrated adherence to the values and traditions of the preindustrial artisanal past in a number of ways. They demanded shorter hours, joining popular crusades for the eight-hour day in the late 1860s and the mid 1880s. In 1886, some 480,000 workers went on strike or cut back their work day in a nationwide demonstration for the eight-hour day. Factory laborers resisted the imposition of new work rules designed to speed up the work pace and achieve greater productivity. As Herbert Gutman and other specialists in working-class history have argued, the first generation of industrial workers often drank and loafed on the job, wandered in and out of the factory at will, and sought to control the speed and pace of work. They had high absenteeism rates, especially on Mondays after a weekend of drinking—thus the holiday known as "blue Monday." Periodically, industrial laborers took off from work to celebrate religious holidays and ethnic festivals. Recent research suggests the surprising strength and persistence of the communal, preindustrial work pattern.

Industrial workers resisted the new factory discipline in another way, as well—by quitting their jobs in astonishing numbers. Many industries suffered tremendously high rates of labor turnover, commonly surpassing 100 percent a year. In steel, meat packing, automobiles, textiles, machine tools, clothing manufacture, and other industries, factory workers abandoned their machines easily and often. "Unbroken to industrial discipline," Rodgers suggested, workers walked off the job in an ultimate act of resistance to the demands of the new factory system.

Rodgers' point is supported by a substantial body of research on immigrant workers in industrial America. This new work has depicted the immigrants of the period as virtual trans-Atlantic migrant workers—"sojourner" immigrants who came to America to work for a time and then return to the old country. These sojourner immigrants were highly mobile within the United States, as well, forming what the U.S. Immigration Commission described in 1911 as a floating immigrant labor supply. Fresh off the farm or the immigrant ships, the new industrial workers were quick to move on in the search for better opportunities.

The new working-class history, then, has revealed that modernization was not an all-powerful juggernaut, sweeping away the remnants of the past. On the contrary, recent research has shown that industrial workers adhered to the artisanal values of the past. By various means, they resisted the discipline and work rules of the new factory system. Trade unions often served to protect their traditional craft autonomy and work rules in the new factory setting. And they were quick to quit, moving on to another job in another place or, in the case of European immigrants, often returning to the old country. It seems clear, as

Thomas Bender noted, that "traditional values and patterns of behavior do not passively collapse before larger processes of social change."

ETHNIC SUBCULTURES

Communal traditions and values also persisted among the numerous ethnic subcultures in industrial America. Recent historians of ethnicity in the United States have been revising earlier interpretations of the immigration, adjustment, and assimilation process. Traditional views portrayed the immigrants as peasants displaced from the agricultural village with its communal patterns of life and work. Confronted by the unfamiliar and harsh demands of a foreign land and the new industrial workplace, the newcomers suffered social disorganization and the destruction of traditional culture. In the urban ghettos of industrial America, the new immigrants endured the shock of alienation. Over time they also became assimilated, as schools, politics, the mass media, and other American institutions silently Americanized the newcomers and their children. Historians of immigration and ethnicity have seriously challenged this social breakdown and assimilationist interpretation in recent years.

The historical scholarship of the past decade or so has provided new perspectives on the migration process, the creation of the ethnic village in the American city, and the development of immigrant institutional life. We now know, for example, that immigrants came to the United States not as a large indistinguishable mass, but as individuals in a chain migration process—that is, they joined relatives or villagers already in America, perhaps coming on a prepaid steamship ticket to a factory job already lined up in advance by a brother, cousin, uncle, or friend.

Typically, about half of the Italian immigrants to Cleveland in the 25 years prior to World War I came from only 10 villages in southern Italy. About 45 percent of the Italians who migrated to San Francisco between 1850 and 1930, according to a study by

Dino Cinel, came from 4 provinces in Italy; substantial numbers came from only 9 separate Italian communities. Similar chain migration patterns have been demonstrated for southern and eastern European immigrants throughout industrial America. Rather than weakening under the strains of migration and modernization, the ties of family, kinship, and community among immigrants remained strong in the industrial city.

Once in urban America, as immigration historian Rudolph Vecoli has argued, the immigrants revealed a "powerful tendency to reconstitute community in accordance with Old World origins." Thus, Chicago's "Little Italies" were in reality dozens of old country village groups reorganized and reconstituted in the new land. The *contadini,* the southern Italian peasant immigrants, transplanted their mutual benefit societies to the new land, as well as their commitment to traditional peasant religion with its devotion to symbol and ritual, magic and miracles. Italian peasant traits and customs "proved very resistant to change even under the stress of emigration," Vecoli noted. This same cultural heritage determined the nature of their adjustment to American industrial society.

Immigration historians have sketched a comparable picture of vibrant peasant cultures in other cities. By the early 20th century, for instance, Boston's Italian North End had become a collection of old country "enclaves" based on village and regional origins. Even marrige patterns reflected the powerful hold of the old culture in the American industrial city. Church records in Boston's North End Italian parishes showed that between 1890 and 1930, almost 90 percent of all marriages were between individuals from the same Italian region, and an astounding 50 percent from the same village. As historian William M. DeMarco put it in *Ethnics and Enclaves: Boston's Italian North End* (1981), "in terms of subcultural neighborhoods, the North End resembled the Italian countryside by 1920."

Similar patterns of neighborhood settlement prevailed among other European immigrant groups. For example, Caroline Golab's study of Poles in Philadelphia, *Immigrant Destina-*

tions (1977), noted that "the Poles' settlement and work patterns wherever they went strongly reflected their feudal past and peasant culture." Golab asserted that the Poles, like other southern and eastern European immigrants, were network people:

Their identity, security, self-control, and stimulation derived not just from their membership in a group but in a group that they could see, hear, touch, and smell at all times. They could not function without the constant presence of the group because a person became an individual only by belonging to and interacting within a group. The group provided mechanisms for social control and determined codes of personal behavior. For the Poles, who placed great importance on personal status within the group, status could be defined only by interacting with other Poles. . . . The world of network people, whether in the village of the Old Country or in the neighborhood of the New, was a walking world, highly dependent on oral, visual and personal interaction.

For most of industrial America's new immigrant groups, this sort of communal group behavior prevailed long after arrival.

While immigrants were rebuilding community in the American city, they often resisted Americanizing influences. It is now clear, for example, that public schooling was not as powerful an assimilating agent as historians once thought. While some immigrant groups accepted public education as a means of upward mobility in the new land, others just as clearly rejected public schooling. On the Minnesota iron range, for instance, Finnish and Slovenian newcomers opposed public schools because they propagated capitalistic values and undermined ethnic culture. Similarly, Slavic immigrants resisted public education because of their adherence to traditional ethnic culture and values. Italian immigrants often rejected public schooling in America because it indoctrinated their children with "ideas antagonistic to the traditional codes of family life." For these immigrants, historian John Bodnar suggested, "education for immigrant children was for the purpose of retaining the cultural, linguistic, and religious values of the ethnic group," not for becoming Americanized.

For such Catholic immigrants, many of whom remained

committed to the communal values of the premodern village past, the parochial school served as an alternative to public education. By 1920, between 20 and 40 percent of all school children in such immigrant cities as Boston, New York, Philadelphia, Chicago, and St. Louis attended Catholic parochial schools. Usually controlled on the local level by the ethnic groups themselves, the parochial schools taught the immigrant languages and culture and strengthened ethnic identity and the communal values of the old country. Among Jewish, Chinese, and Eastern Orthodox immigrant groups, a similar function was served by the ethnic folk schools which children attended after public school classes ended.

Ethnic groups in industrial America developed alternative educational institutions to preserve language, culture, and values. The immigrant church served similar communal purposes. In urban America, the ethnic or national parish became a crucial link to the old country and its preindustrial folkways. Among 19th-century German immigrants, for instance, the ethnic parish not only satisfied religious needs but reinforced group consciousness and helped preserve German culture and traditions. In a study of Italians in New York City, *Piety and Power* (1975), Silvano Tomasi contended that the ethnic parish provided continuity with the communal ways of the old country. As Tomasi put it, "the old dialects and language, religion, traditions and customs were preserved to protect the immigrant group from social disorganization and the shock of adjustment to the new culture." French-Canadians, Poles, Greeks, Serbs, Slovaks, Swedes, and others all found the ethnic parish or congregation an indispensable means of maintaining culture, community, and continuity with the past—a link with the communal village world of the old country.

Parochial schools and ethnic churches comprised an important part of a larger network of immigrant institutions in the industrial city. These included fraternal and benevolent societies, musical and dramatic associations, cultural and political groups, and foreign-language newspapers. These ethnic institutions muted the impact of industrialization and Americanization. Perhaps more important, they facilitated the maintenance of old country traditions, customs, and values. As Herbert Gutman put it in *Work, Culture, and Society in Industrializing America* (1976), "when so much else changed in the industrializing decades, tenacious traditions flourished among immigrants in ethnic subcultures."

It seems clear, however, that the maintenance of ethnic group solidarity had at least two other and perhaps unanticipated consequences. First, the persistence of ethnic subcultures tended to heighten conflict with other groups, particularly among those competing for jobs in the same industry and for housing in the same neighborhood. Second, the creation of new ethnic defense institutions (parochial schools, ethnic parishes, foreign-language newspapers, fraternal and other organizations), inevitably contributed to immigrant adjustment to modern industrial society. As John Bodnar suggested, "modernization may have involved a process of synthesis where traditional ways were integrated with working class pragmatism to produce distinctive behavioral patterns."

In other words, ethnic groups in industrial America fought to preserve their old cultures and traditions, but the struggle itself forced them to accommodate to new ways of thinking and behaving. The immigrant experience was one of both continuity and change. Communal traditions and beliefs persisted, but they also evolved in the new land. Some aspects of the old communal culture modernized more slowly than others, of course. The immigrant family remained especially impervious to the pressures of change.

THE FAMILY AS CUSTODIAN OF TRADITION

The persistence of communal values and traditions has been demonstrated in a number of recent studies in family history. The immigrant family pattern generally reflected the village folkways of the preindustrial culture. In a study of Italians in

Buffalo, Virginia Yans-McLaughlin noted that "even as different members entered industrial America's work world, the immigrant family remained remarkably untouched." In America, the Italians chose work "that put minimal strain on their accustomed family arrangements."

Among French-Canadian textile workers in Manchester, New Hampshire, family culture remained a powerful determinant of life and work. As family historian Tamara K. Hareven demonstrated in *Family Time and Industrial Time* (1982), French-Canadian working-class families at Manchester's huge Amoskeag mills not only maintained traditional kinship networks, but guided the recruitment, training, and adaptation of family members to industrial labor. The French-Canadians even "introduced some of their own traditions and work habits into the modern factory system." Hareven's massively detailed work effectively demolished the traditional view that migration and modernization caused social breakdown and the deterioration of traditional family patterns.

Other recent studies offered similar conclusions. Among immigrant groups in industrial Detroit, high rates of endogamous marriage and marital fertility tended to strengthen the ethnic family. A study of families with boarders and lodgers by historians John Modell and Tamara Hareven concluded that industrialization did not lead to the deterioration of urban family life. By contrast, the widespread practice of taking in boarders—common among both native American and foreign-born families—"not only was a sensible response to industrialization," but cushioned the "shock of urban life for newcomers." A parallel conclusion was offered by sociologist Richard Sennett, whose book *Families Against the City* (1970) examined the impact of industrialization on middle-class family life in the Union Park section of Chicago. Sennett's research in manuscript census material revealed that most Union Park residents lived in nuclear family units, that most families had few children, that children left home at a relatively advanced age, that they married late, and that occupational and social mobility across generations was limited. This evidence led Sennett to speculate that the nuclear family provided a haven from the fearful realities of the industrial city. The family, as Hareven put it, became a "custodian of tradition" during the process of modernization.

Immigrants were not the only newcomers to the industrial city who sought to keep alive the communal traditions of the premodern past. Among black migrants from the rural South to the industrial North, the old folkways and family patterns persisted into the 20th century. Buffeted first by slavery and then by modernization, the black family remained a strong and vital institution. Several historical studies have demonstrated that southern black migrants maintained stable, two-parent families, supported by extended-kin networks. In a study of blacks in Cleveland, historian Kenneth L. Kusmer discovered that the process of migration to the urban North actually strengthened the black family. In Cleveland, the two-parent nuclear family was more common than in the rural or urban South.

Urban ghettoes grew in Philadelphia, New York, Chicago, and elsewhere, but the rural southern blacks did not forget their roots. Storefront churches kept alive the religious spirit of the black southern churches, with their special brand of preaching and singing. The food, music, entertainment, and culture of the newly urbanized blacks reflected their rural southern origins. Like the European immigrants, the blacks established networks of benevolent, fraternal, and cultural societies. In Harlem, as historian Gilbert Osofsky noted, the rural black migrants "banded together to try to retain as much contact with the pattern of their former lives as possible."

The pattern was much the same in other northern cities on the receiving end of the black migration from the South. In an innovative study of blacks in Washington, historian James Borchert found a remarkable persistence of black folklife in the city. In the nation's capital, Borchert noted, "church services, communal singing, and communal recreation of songs enabled people to remember and pass on their heritage, as well as providing for adjustment to a harsh and difficult urban experience." If

Washington was at all typical, blacks in the urban North "were able to maintain their old cultural patterns in the new environment." Modernization, Borchert contended, did not destroy traditional black life. Rather, blacks in Washington "were able to maintain stability through their primary groups of family, kinship, neighborhood, community, and religion." Despite the economic and social dislocations of the industrial city, old traditions, customs, and ideologies died hard—both for the immigrants and for the black migrants from the South.

The communal spirit prevailed among many other groups, as well. For socialists and utopians of the late 19th century, the ideal of community—of a "cooperative commonwealth," as early socialist Lawrence Gronlund put it—remained a primary goal. The mass agrarian uprising, known as the Populist movement, according to recent interpretations, similarly advocated a democratic and cooperative society based on the shared communal values of the past. Social workers such as Jane Addams and environmental reformers such as Jacob Riis also upheld, even romanticized, the ideal of community. The settlement house leaders hoped through their work and example to rebuild neighborhood ties seemingly severed by the modernizing tendencies of the factory and the city. The reformers and utopians alike assumed that communalism was gone, a victim of time and progress. The historical research of the past decade or so provides substantial evidence to the contrary.

Indeed, the new research on families, immigrants, blacks, and working-class groups has altered significantly our understanding of urban life in the industrial era. Dramatic shifts in the structure of the economy did not erase all vestiges of the preindustrial world. The communal values of the artisan's workshop, of the rural village in Europe or the American South, and of the traditional family persisted. Modernization theory holds that the industrial revolution brought social disorganization and alienation—that it initiated a rapid shift away from traditional social patterns toward more modern ways of working and living. The thrust of recent historical scholarship, however, suggests that the theory must be modified by the reality of communalism in the industrializing world. While some aspects of urban life had been unalterably transformed, others remained imbued with the values and customs of the preindustrial past. Despite the onslaught of social and economic change, the old values of the small community lived on. For many urban Americans, the patterns of the past persisted; they remained the only reliable response to the bewildering changes of the industrial era.

The Twentieth-Century City

During the industrial era, the United States became an urban nation. The new city that emerged between 1860 and 1920 reflected the dynamic forces of the age. By the end of the industrial period, more than half of the American people lived in urban places. The city had become a powerful reality often shaping American economic, political, and social life. Whether this was a change for the good remained a question for many Americans. "The problem of the 20th century will be the city," social gospeler Josiah Strong predicted in 1898. Others had a more positive new. "The city is not only the problem of our civilization, it is also the hope of the future," reformer Frederic C. Howe wrote in 1905. Despite these divergent viewpoints, most observers agreed that the city would remain at the center of 20th-century change.

URBAN DEMOGRAPHIC SHIFTS

Urban growth continued at a rapid pace after 1920. Populations spread far beyond city boundaries, creating huge and sprawling metropolitan areas. By 1980, for example, more than 16 million people lived in the New York urbanized area; almost 12 million resided in the enormous urbanized region centered on Los Angeles. But this is not a story of growth pure and simple—rather the urbanization process in recent America reflects some incredibly volatile patterns of demographic change.

The metropolitan demographic pattern has been marked by substantial population shifts within urban areas, as well as among regions of the United States. At least since 1940, for instance, most of the older cities of the industrial heartland have not only stopped growing, but they have been losing population to their suburbs. Detroit had a population of 1.8 million in 1950, but lost 600,000 people over the next 30 years. Cleveland's 1950 population of 915,000 had withered to 574,000 by 1980. St. Louis lost almost half of its central city population over the same time span, dropping from 857,000 to 453,000. Incredibly, St. Louis's population in 1980 was about the same as it had been in 1890.

A similar pattern of population deconcentration could be demonstrated for virtually every major city in the northeastern-midwestern industrial belt. The rate of population loss varied, to be sure, but the trend has been evident throughout the snowbelt region. Among larger cities, Pittsburgh lost 37 percent of its population between 1950 and 1980; over the same time span, Boston lost about 30 percent and Baltimore 20 percent of 1950 population. Smaller cities, too, followed the same pattern of population decline over 30 years—Buffalo, 38 percent; Providence, 37 percent; Youngstown, 31 percent; Minneapolis, 29 percent; Rochester, 27 percent; Newark, 25 percent; and Jersey City, 25 percent. Although substantial numbers of blacks have moved to the inner suburbs of some cities, most of those fleeing the central cities for the new suburban frontier have been middle-class and working-class whites.

As a result of the enormous deconcentration of white population, the shrinking central cities are populated increasingly by poorer, black, Hispanic, and new immigrant groups. Since World War II, for instance, almost 2 million middle-income residents have left New York City, while at least that many lower income people have moved in. New York and other cities, some now suggest, have developed a large and permanent underclass.

Similarly, blacks and Hispanics have become highly concentrated in the central cities. In most of the big snowbelt cities, the black population has at least doubled between 1950 and 1980. In Boston and Detroit, the black population quadrupled during the same years. The Hispanic population, too, has soared in cities such as New York and Chicago.

The economic and social consequences of this dramatic population turnover are predictable enough. The aging central cities have experienced heavy unemployment, racial conflicts, high crime rates, burdensome welfare costs, inadequate schooling and health care, deteriorating services of all kinds, and abandonment by business and industry. A declining tax base and higher costs for servicing low-income populations have brought many older cities to the edge of bankruptcy. New York City escaped default and bankruptcy in 1975 only when state and federal officials stepped in, borrowed from municipal employee pension funds, and created the Municipal Assistance Corporation to manage the city's debt crisis.

A few years later, Cleveland faced a similar fiscal crisis, barely avoiding bankruptcy. One recent study suggests that Detroit, St. Louis, Boston, Philadelphia, and Buffalo can also anticipate a troubled financial future. Along with New York and

Cleveland, these cities faced "net out-migration of population, loss of private jobs, high local tax burdens, a rising proportion of low-income households, and very small increases in per capita income." According to economist Ira S. Lowry, the future of the declining snowbelt cities appears dismal. The changes since 1970, Lowry wrote, suggest "that deterioration is spreading to more cities and accelerating in those where it has long been evident."

THE URBAN NEWCOMERS

These contemporary patterns of urban change have rather deep historical roots. The older central cities of the industrial belt have been experiencing substantial population turnover since the 1920s. Blacks began a great exodus from the South during and after World War I. The black migration slowed during the depression of the 1930s, but surged once again after 1940. Between 1940 and 1970, almost 5 million blacks migrated out of the South to the urban North and West. Aided by rising prosperity and favorable government housing and highway programs, and often pushed by the presence of expanding black neighborhoods in the urban core, whites moved to new suburban housing on the outer fringes of the metropolitan areas. As the whites moved out, the blacks moved in, taking over the aging and deteriorating inner-city neighborhoods.

For over more than half a century, the inexorable process of population succession has substantially altered the American city. By the 1980s, blacks had become a majority in such cities as Detroit, Baltimore, Newark, Gary, Atlanta, Birmingham, Richmond, New Orleans, and Washington, D.C. In a few other big cities—Cleveland, St. Louis, Chicago, and Philadelphia—black majorities are not far off. In 1900 blacks were the least highly urbanized of all racial and ethnic groups in America, but by 1980 they had become the most highly urbanized group.

Blacks are not the only newcomers to the 20th-century city.

In recent years, southern and western cities along with such northern cities as New York and Chicago have been on the receiving end of an enormous Hispanic migration. In Miami, where Cuban refugees have settled in large numbers since the Cuban Revolution in 1959, Hispanics made up about 56 percent of the population in 1980. In the Southwest, Mexicans and Mexican-Americans have settled heavily in such cities as San Antonio, El Paso, Corpus Christi, Houston, Albuquerque, Tucson, San Bernardino, San Jose, and Los Angeles. Almost 1.5 million Spanish-speaking people—mostly Puerto Ricans, but also hundreds of thousands of Dominicans and Columbians—have migrated to New York City. Hispanics in New York total about 20 percent of the city's population. Substantial numbers of Mexicans, Cubans, and Puerto Ricans have settled in Chicago, where Hispanics numbered about 423,000— some 14 percent of total population. Before the end of this century, it is likely that Hispanics will have surpassed blacks as the nation's largest minority group.

But the urban newcomers are not just Hispanics. Cities such as New York and Los Angeles have become magnets for hundreds of thousands of new immigrants. In 1983, for instance, the Los Angeles metropolitan area was home not only for over 2 million Mexicans and Mexican-Americans, but also for 200,000 Iranians, 200,000 Salvadorans, 175,000 Japanese, 150,000 Chinese, 150,000 Koreans, 150,000 Filipinos, 130,000 Arabs, and smaller but still sizeable concentrations of Israelis, Colombians, Hondurans, Guatamalans, Cubans, Vietnamese, East Indians, Pakistanis, and Samoans and other Pacific Islanders. With over 27 percent of its 1980 population foreign-born, Los Angeles has become a new immigrant city of incredible diversity.

Similarly, New York City has attracted astounding numbers of Asian, Caribbean, Hispanic, and other new immigrants and refugees. As the *New York Times* observed in 1981, "immigrants are coming to New York City from virtually every country, island, and territory on the globe, creating a city more diverse in race, language and ethnicity than it was at the turn of the century when immigrants from Europe poured through Ellis Island." Reflecting this new surge of immigration, the foreign-born made up almost 24 percent of New York City's population in 1980.

SUBURBIA AND EXURBIA

By contrast, the growing suburbs continue to be mostly white and mostly middle class. In the post–World War II era, the sub-urban migration was hastened by the vast increase in tract-house development on the urban periphery. An affluent economy through the early 1960s put suburban homeownership within reach of even the urban working class (which by then had middle-class incomes). Widespread automobile ownership enabled the new suburbanites to commute to jobs in the city. A multibillion dollar federal investment in interstate highway construction encouraged this suburban process, as did government mortgage programs and tax policies. By 1970, more Americans lived in the suburban rings than in central cities or in nonmetropolitan areas.

In the 1970s, moreover, population began pushing out beyond the fringes of suburbia. This is exurbia, or "ruburbia," as one writer suggested—small country towns barely within commuting distance of the central cities, often with brand new office buildings and factories of their own. Since 1970 these nonmetropolitan areas have been growing rapidly. Indeed, during the 1970s the growth rate of rural regions and small towns outstripped that of urbanized areas. As a recent demographic analysis put it, "the level of urbanization stopped increasing for the first time in the 1970s."

During the past decade and a half, rural areas have had a magnetic attraction for industry and other business activities formerly concentrated in the cities. Between 1947 and 1977, New York City lost more than 500,000 jobs, while Chicago lost about 400,000. Most of these job losses were in manufacturing and other blue-collar employment. But as metropolitan areas lost employment, new manufacturing jobs were created in nonmetropolitan areas—some 700,000 alone between 1970 and 1978. This shift in economic location has speeded the population growth of nonmetropolitan America—a pattern which is likely to continue until rising population fills in empty spaces and these distant areas, too, are pulled into the metropolitan orbit.

THE SHIFTING URBAN ECONOMY

The economies of the declining cities of the old industrial belt have suffered tremendously in recent decades. A great deal of manufacturing and employment either has been suburbanized or shifted out of the industrial heartland entirely. Multinational corporations have transferred production to less-developed nations such as Mexico, Taiwan, Singapore, and South Korea, where labor costs are much lower. Consequently, these corporations have been closing factories and mills in the urban Northeast and Midwest. Federal tax policies and a wave of corporate mergers have encouraged industrial shutdowns to improve company profits and reduce taxes. Foreign competition, rising oil prices, and economic recession in the 1970s helped to destroy industrial prosperity. Heavy unemployment has hit such basic industries as steel and automobiles. As the 20th century draws to a close, the aging cities of the industrial heartland have become increasingly obsolete.

Indeed, by the middle of the 20th century, the United States had begun to move toward a postindustrial society. The rapid growth of a service and information-processing economy has accompanied the decline of manufacturing. White-collar, professional, and service workers outnumbered blue-collar production workers in the United States as early as 1956. By the 1980s, the service economy employed twice as many workers as the manufacturing and production sector. The American postindustrial economy now revolves around governmental, financial, educational, informational, medical, recreational, and other services. Such staple activities of the contemporary

consumer society as retailing, merchandizing, travel and transportation, business services, and fast-food outlets have become
integral parts of the new service economy. Governmental
services, in particular, are an important ingredient in the new
American economy. By 1978, government at all levels employed
more than 15 million civilian workers.

The rapid and dramatic shift to a service and informational
economy has hastened a process now labeled deindustrialization
—plant closings, community abandonment, and the dismantling
of basic industry. Typically, Akron, Ohio—formerly the
rubber capital of the world—no longer produces automobile
tires. Although the major rubber companies retain their corporate offices in Akron, tire manufacturing has been decentralized
and moved primarily to southern states where labor costs are
lower. Meanwhile, some 40,000 rubber workers have lost their
jobs in Akron. In nearby Youngstown, Ohio—a steel town—
three steel companies shut down their blast furnaces and rolling
mills in the past few years—not because they were unprofitable,
but because they did not produce enough profit. Tens of thousands of steel workers organized to buy up these plants, hoping
to run them as workers' cooperatives. But the scheme smacked
of socialism and the corporations refused to sell. Ultimately, the
companies dynamited these steel mills to the ground and sold off
the remains for scrap. This pattern has been replicated in dozens
of old industrial cities in the Northeast and Midwest.

The links between population decline and the shifting urban
economy in the old industrial belt are well established. The cities
with large population losses have been caught in the transformation to a service and information economy. The newcomers to the old central cities—the blacks, Hispanics, and new
immigrants—suffer chronic high unemployment because they
are untrained for the new employment pattern. A mismatch
between high-skill jobs and low-skill workers has come to
characterize central city employment.

Nor will this problem go away in the future. According to
the report of the President's Commission for a National Agenda
for the Eighties: "The massive losses of industrial employment

probably will not be recouped, even during cyclical upswings in the nation's economy, and the middle class probably will not return to the central city in large numbers.'' The postwar shift in the economy, in short, has had an important and perhaps irreversible impact on the nation's aging industrial cities.

SUNBELT CITY GROWTH

Another important shift in the contemporary urban pattern has been the remarkable growth of the sunbelt cities of the Southeast and Southwest. By the early 1980s, 5 of the nation's 10 largest cities—Houston, Dallas, Phoenix, San Diego, and Los Angeles—were located in the Southwest. In 1890 the largest of these 5 cities was Los Angeles with a population of 50,000. By contrast, in 1980 the city of Los Angeles had a population of almost 3 million, while its entire metropolitan area totaled about 11.5 million. Between 1940 and 1980, the sunbelt states grew in population at almost triple the pace of the old industrial belt states. Cities such as Miami, Tampa, Atlanta, Houston, Dallas, Phoenix, and San Diego all at least quadrupled in size during the same 40 years.

At the same time, most sunbelt cities expanded in physical size through annexation of peripheral territory, some in spectacular fashion. San Antonio, for instance, covered 36 square miles in 1940, but annexations increased the city's size to 263 square miles by 1980. Between 1950 and 1980, Houston grew from 160 to 556 square miles; Oklahoma City from 51 to 603 square miles, and Phoenix from 17 to 324 square miles. In the automobile era, speedy population dispersal from the central city was commonplace throughout the sunbelt. Metropolitan growth often followed new highway construction and the decentralization of economic activities. As in the industrial heartland in the late 19th century, settlement and physical expansion of the urban periphery has been followed quickly by annexation.

Yet, annexation in the urban sunbelt, dramatic though it

has been, has not kept pace with metropolitan population growth. Virtually all of the major sunbelt cities have grown steadily and sometimes spectacularly throughout the postwar years. But despite the inexorable process of annexation, the outlying regions of most of the sunbelt cities have grown in population even faster than the central cities.

THE SUNBELT ECONOMY

Vast structural changes in the American economy have encouraged the explosive urban development in the sunbelt. The surging population growth of these cities has been based on the characteristic activities of the postindustrial service and informational economy. These are supplemented by such high-tech industries as electronics and computers, aircraft and aerospace production, and energy development (particularly oil), along with recreation, tourism, and retirement activities. The role of the federal government, especially the military establishment, has also been exceedingly important. During World War II, the federal government located a large number of air and naval bases in the sunbelt states. The continued military presence in the region, along with heavy defense spending throughout the cold war era, has helped to sustain economic prosperity and economic growth in the sunbelt region.

Most likely, the shifting American urban pattern will continue and intensify. The regional migration trends which in the 1970s saw 5.5 million people move out of the so-called snowbelt areas for the South and West will certainly intensify. According to most economic and demographic projections, urban areas in Florida, Texas, and California will grow most rapidly over the rest of the 20th century, and probably beyond. The older smokestack industries will decline further, and many more factories and mills will close down. Newer and cleaner industries and services will continue to concentrate in the sunshine states, which generally have low taxes, cheap labor, more amenities, and political climates favorable to corporate activity. Sunbelt city growth, it seems clear, is not a temporary phenomenon but a long-term reality.

THE FEDERAL-CITY RELATIONSHIP

While the demography and economy of the modern American city have been changing, important transformations have been altering the nature of urban political life, as well. One of the big changes in 20th-century America has been the tremendous expansion of federal government power and influence. Responding to the economic dislocations of the Great Depression, the federal government under President Franklin D. Roosevelt embarked on an unprecedented policy of federal intervention and activism. New welfare and public works programs, along with a river of social legislation, poured out of Washington during the New Deal years.

A new federal-city political partnership emerged during the 1930s, one which has persisted until the 1980s. Bypassing the state legislatures, cities increasingly looked to Washington for assistance in confronting urban problems and helping urban people. The fruits of this new federal-city relationship can be found in the various public housing programs begun in the 1930s, the urban renewal and expressway building efforts of the 1950s and 1960s, and the antipoverty, community development, employment opportunity, and model cities programs of Lyndon Johnson's Great Society years in the 1960s.

These federal programs have had a decisive impact in shaping metropolitan growth and change. But the effect has not always been positive. As historian James F. Richardson has noted, "many federal programs have detracted from rather than contributed to the health of core cities." Federal mortgage programs, for instance, encouraged middle-class and working-class whites to flee to lily white suburbs, leaving urban blacks and the poor behind. Some federal housing programs (the Home Owners Loan Corporation and the Federal Housing Administration, for example) adopted an appraisal system which led to redlining—the practice by banks and other lending institutions of refusing to grant mortages or other loans in older, poorer, and black neighborhoods. The Federal Housing Administration, according to housing scholar Charles Abrams in his classic *Forbidden Neighbors* (1955), "set itself up as the protector of the all-white neighborhood" and "became the vanguard of white supremacy and racial purity—in the North as well as the South."

Other federal programs have had a similarly devastating impact on the city. Extensive urban renewal programs since the 1950s have destroyed inner-city housing, but did not always deliver on promised new low-rent units for displaced families. In some quarters, urban renewal became nothing more than black removal. Huge public housing projects such as Pruitt-Igoe in St. Louis turned into large-scale disasters; ultimately, this enormous public housing project was dynamited to the ground. Federal expressway building has had comparable results. The interstate highways have driven straight to the urban cores, tearing the cities apart physically, destroying neighborhoods, and leaving large chunks of city space virtually unusable. Thus, the New Deal initiated a new era of federal-city cooperation. The city has been reshaped in the process, but not always for the better.

In recent years, the federal-city relationship has begun to experience substantial change. The decay of the older central cities and the changing distribution of economic activity led to an unfinished and essentially futile effort by the Carter administration to establish a coherent national policy. Some critics, however, saw in this policy-making process an attempt to write off the frostbelt cities, with their financially draining social problems and low-income, minority populations. In the 1980s, large-scale federal aid to the cities has been labeled a failure and is being cut back drastically. President Ronald Reagan has been reversing 50 years of federal activism in urban affairs. Reagan's goal is to return the city, and indeed the nation at large, to the vagaries of the free market.

THE NEW URBAN POLITICS

Other political changes have been taking place within the cities themselves. In some of the older industrial cities, the dominance of machine politics began to give way before the growing power of the black vote. In 1967, black mayors were elected in Cleveland and Gary—the first black mayors ever in large American cities. Since 1967, as the proportion of central-city whites declined, black mayors have been elected in Newark, Detroit, Los Angeles, New Orleans, Atlanta, Richmond, Birmingham, Washington, D.C., and most recently Chicago and Philadelphia. Chicago presents a classic case of this shifting pattern of race and urban politics. Virtually ruled since the 1930s by the Democratic machine of mayors Edward J. Kelly and Richard J. Daley, Chicago elected a black mayor in 1983. Congressman Harold Washington defeated the machine candidate in the Democratic primary and then rode into office on a wave of black and Hispanic votes. The campaign, however, was marked by bitter racial conflict and tension—a pattern which may intensify as the older industrial cities become less white and more black in the future.

The newer sunbelt cities have experienced dramatic political transformations, as well. Most of these newer cities had little in the way of a machine tradition based on ethnic voting power. Generally, their political structures had been dominated by local business and professional elites at least since the 1920s. Until the 1950s, these urban elites and chamber-of-commerce reformers pursued the booster tradition. They sought to control government and manage physical and economic growth so as to benefit central city business interests. By the 1950s, as suburban rings sprouted beyond central city boundaries, significant political strife emerged in the metropolitan sunbelt. These struggles were characterized by conflict between central city and suburban interests over such issues as annexation, consolidation, taxes, services, school integration, and highway and public housing location.

By the 1960s, however, the pattern of sunbelt city politics was changing once again. Ethnic, racial, and neighborhood conflict began to replace earlier city-suburban hostilities. Urban politics—North, South, East, and West—now seems to revolve around issues with heavy ethnic or racial overtones. In Miami, for instance, the most divisive political issues in recent years have included battles over bilingualism, Haitian and Cuban refugee resettlement, public housing location, and redevelopment of Miami's black ghettos—Liberty City and Overtown. Local communities within the urban region have become focal points for political discontent and activism. In cities as diverse as Chicago and Miami, ethnic and racial emotions have boiled over into the political arena, where they are likely to remain for some time to come.

In sum, then, the American city has experienced enormous change in the years since 1920. In every region of the nation, the cities have been reshaped by demographic shifts, vast structural changes in the economy, and the powerful role of the federal government. Whatever the future brings, it seems certain that, as in the industrial era, the American city will continue to be located at the cutting edge of political, economic, and social change.

Bibliographical Essay

This bibliography is designed to identify the chief sources on which this book is based and to suggest additional reading for interested students. For general overviews of American urban history, see especially David R. Goldfield and Blaine A. Brownell, *Urban America: From Downtown to No Town* (Boston, 1979); Howard P. Chudacoff, *The Evolution of American Urban Society*, 2d. ed. (Englewood Cliffs, 1981); Charles N. Glaab and A. Theodore Brown, *A History of Urban America*, 3d. ed. (New York, 1983); Bayrd Still, *Urban America: A History with Documents* (Boston, 1974); Sam Bass Warner, Jr., *The Urban Wilderness: A History of the American City* (New

York, 1972); Blake McKelvey, *American Urbanization: A Comparative History* (Glenview, Ill., 1973); Raymond A. Mohl and James F. Richardson, eds., *The Urban Experience: Themes in American History* (Belmont, Calif., 1973).

For theoretical and interpretive insight on the preindustrial city and the transition to a modern and industrialized society, read Gideon Sjoberg, *The Preindustrial City: Past and Present* (New York, 1960); Lewis Mumford, *The City in History: Its Origins, Its Transformations, and Its Prospects* (New York, 1961); Oscar Handlin, "The Modern City as a Field of Historical Study," in Oscar Handlin and John Burchard, eds., *The Historian and the City* (Cambridge, Mass., 1963), pp. 1–26; and Eric E. Lampard, "The Urbanizing World," in H. J. Dyos and Michael Wolff, eds., *The Victorian City*, 2 vols. (London, 1973), pp. 3–57.

Important period studies of the industrial era are Robert H. Wiebe, *The Search for Order, 1877–1920* (New York, 1967); Samuel P. Hays, *The Response to Industrialism, 1885–1914* (Chicago, 1957); and Ray Ginger, *Age of Excess: The United States from 1877 to 1914,* 2d. ed. (New York, 1975). A specific focus on the city during the industrial era is provided in Arthur M. Schlesinger, *The Rise of the City, 1878–1898* (New York, 1933); Blake McKelvey, *The Urbanization of America, 1860–1915* (New Brunswick, N.J., 1963); and Maury Klein and Harvey A. Kantor, *Prisoners of Progress: American Industrial Cities, 1850–1920* (New York, 1976).

THE DYNAMICS OF URBAN GROWTH

The population volumes of the U.S. Census for each decennial year between 1860 and 1920 are indispensable for reconstructing the demographic characteristics of the American industrial city. The Census Bureau has also published an extremely useful compendium, *Historical Statistics of the United States: Colonial Times to 1970,* 2 vols. (Washington, D.C., 1975).

Two classic studies of population growth and demographic

change are Adna F. Weber, *The Growth of Cities in the Nineteenth Century: A Study in Statistics* (New York, 1899), and Conrad Taeuber and Irene B. Taeuber, *The Changing Population of the United States* (New York, 1958).

On metropolitan growth, examine R. D. McKenzie, *The Metropolitan Community* (New York, 1933), and Amos H. Hawley, *The Changing Shape of Metropolitan America* (Glencoe, Ill., 1956).

Internal migration and population turnover are analyzed in Peter R. Knights, *The Plain People of Boston, 1830–1860: A Study in City Growth* (New York, 1971); Stephan Thernstrom, *Poverty and Progress: Social Mobility in a Nineteenth-Century City* (Cambridge, Mass., 1964); Howard P. Chudacoff, *Mobile Americans: Residential and Social Mobility in Omaha, 1880–1920* (New York, 1972); Stephan Thernstrom, *The Other Bostonians: Poverty and Progress in the American Metropolis, 1880–1970* (Cambridge, Mass., 1973); Dean R. Esslinger, *Immigrants and the City: Ethnicity and Mobility in a Nineteenth-Century Midwestern Community* (Port Washington, N.Y., 1975); and Stephan Thernstrom and Peter R. Knights, "Men in Motion: Some Data and Speculations about Urban Population Mobility in Nineteenth-Century America," *Journal of Interdisciplinary History,* 1 (1970), pp. 7–35.

Black migration from the South to the industrial North is nicely summarized in Reynolds Farley, "The Urbanization of Negroes in the United States," *Journal of Social History,* 1 (1968), pp. 241–58, and in Daniel M. Johnson and Rex R. Campbell, *Black Migration in America: A Social Demographic History* (Durham, N.C., 1981). Black migration from the rural South to southern cities is treated in Howard N. Rabinowitz, *Race Relations in the Urban South, 1865–1890* (New York, 1978).

The most useful analysis of immigrant arrival and dispersal throughout the United States remains David Ward, *Cities and Immigrants: A Geography of Change in Nineteenth-Century America* (New York, 1971). Essays by David Ward and Richard A. Easterlin in Stephan Thernstrom, ed., *Harvard Encyclopedia of American Ethnic Groups* (Cambridge, Mass., 1980), present superb data and analysis on immigration and settlement patterns.

On urban transit and spatial development, an influential early monograph was Sam Bass Warner, Jr., *Streetcar Suburbs: The Process of Growth in Boston, 1870–1900* (Cambridge, Mass., 1962). Other important studies include Clay McShane, *Technology and Reform: Street Railways and the Growth of Milwaukee, 1887–1900* (Madison, Wis., 1974); Joel A. Tarr, *Transportation Innovation and Changing Spatial Patterns in Pittsburgh, 1850–1934* (Chicago, 1978); and Roger D. Simon, *The City-Building Process: Housing and Services in New Milwaukee Neighborhoods, 1880–1910* (Philadelphia, 1978).

On rapid transit, see Charles W. Cheape, *Moving the Masses: Urban Public Transit in New York, Boston, and Philadelphia, 1880–1912* (Cambridge, Mass., 1980). A useful European comparison can be found in John P. McKay, *Tramways and Trolleys: The Rise of Urban Mass Transport in Europe* (Princeton, N.J., 1976).

Studies of individual cities that demonstrate the impact of transportation on urban growth include Robert M. Fogelson, *The Fragmented Metropolis: Los Angeles, 1850–1930* (Cambridge, Mass., 1967); Harold M. Mayer and Richard C. Wade, *Chicago: Growth of a Metropolis* (Chicago, 1969); and Harold L. Platt, *City Building in the New South: The Growth of Public Services in Houston, Texas, 1830–1910* (Philadelphia, 1983). Key articles on various aspects of urban transit include George Rogers Taylor, "The Beginnings of Mass Transportation in Urban America," *Smithsonian Journal of History*, 1 (1966), No. 2, pp. 35–50, No. 3, pp. 31–54; and Glen E. Holt, "The Changing Perception of Urban Pathology: An Essay on the Development of Mass Transit in the United States," in Kenneth T. Jackson and Stanley K. Schultz, eds., *Cities in American History* (New York, 1972), pp. 324–43.

Several recent studies have also examined the early impact of the automobile on urban life. These include Mark S. Foster, *From Streetcar to Superhighway: American City Planners and*

Urban Transportation, 1900–1940 (Philadelphia, 1981); Howard L. Preston, *Automobile Age Atlanta: The Making of a Southern Metropolis, 1900–1935* (Athens, Ga., 1979); and Paul Barrett, *The Automobile and Urban Transit: The Formation of Public Policy in Chicago, 1900–1930* (Philadelphia, 1983).

For the relationship between urban space and new forms of architecture, see Sigfried Giedion, *Space, Time and Architecture* (Cambridge, Mass., 1949); Vincent Scully, *American Architecture and Urbanism* (New York, 1969); Carl W. Condit, *The Chicago School of Architecture: A History of Commercial and Public Building in the Chicago Area, 1875–1925* (Chicago, 1964); Carl W. Condit, *Chicago, 1910–29: Building, Planning, and Urban Technology* (Chicago, 1973). The new high-rise architecture is also discussed in Carl W. Condit, *The Rise of the Skyscraper* (Chicago, 1952) and Paul Goldberger, *The Skyscraper* (New York, 1981).

The development of the urban apartment house can be traced in Andrew Alpern, *Apartments for the Affluent* (New York, 1975); Douglass Shand Tucci, *Built in Boston: City and Suburb, 1800–1950* (Boston, 1978); John Hancock, "The Apartment House in Urban America," in Anthony D. King, ed., *Buildings and Society: Essays on the Social Development of the Built Environment* (London, 1980), pp. 151–89; and Gunther Barth, *City People: The Rise of Modern City Culture in Nineteenth-Century America* (New York, 1980), which contains a chapter on the apartment house as a new form of urban residence.

Studies of the new tenement house architecture and its social impact can be found in James Ford, *Slums and Housing,* 2 vols. (Cambridge, Mass., 1936); and Edith Abbott, *The Tenements of Chicago, 1908–1935* (Chicago, 1936).

City growth and industrial development were closely linked during the late 19th century. Important studies of American economic growth and industrialization during the 19th century include Walt W. Rostow, *The Stages of Economic Growth* (Cambridge, 1960); Harold G. Vatter, *The Drive to Industrial Maturity: The U.S. Economy, 1860–1914* (Westport, Conn., 1975); Robert L. Heilbroner, *The Economic Transformation of*

America (New York, 1977); Peter George, *The Emergence of Industrial America: Strategic Factors in American Economic Growth since 1870* (Albany, N.Y., 1982); and Allan R. Pred, *The Spatial Dynamics of U.S. Urban-Industrial Growth, 1800–1914* (Cambridge, Mass., 1966).

The corporations and the railroads were intimately linked to industrial and urban growth. The most comprehensive study of the corporation and its influence on the American economy is Alfred D. Chandler, *The Visible Hand: The Managerial Revolution in American Business* (Cambridge, Mass., 1977). On the building of the railroad system, see George Rogers Taylor and Irene D. Neu, *The American Railroad Network, 1861–1890* (Cambridge, Mass., 1956), and Alfred D. Chandler, Jr., *The Railroads: The Nation's First Big Business* (New York, 1965).

The new factory system of the industrial age is the subject of Daniel Nelson, *Managers and Workers: Origins of the New Factory System in the United States, 1880–1920* (Madison, Wis., 1975). On the influence of Frederick W. Taylor and the introduction of scientific management, see Daniel Nelson, *Frederick W. Taylor and the Rise of Scientific Management* (Madison, Wis., 1980), and Samuel Haber, *Efficiency and Uplift: Scientific Management in the Progressive Era, 1890–1920* (Chicago, 1964). The link between the scientific management of Frederick W. Taylor and the mechanization of production is emphasized in Sigfried Giedion, *Mechanization Takes Command* (New York, 1948).

Division of labor in the workplace is the subject of Harry Braverman, *Labor and Monopoly Capitalism: The Degradation of Work in the Twentieth Century* (New York, 1974). Changing perceptions of work are analyzed in Daniel T. Rodgers, *The Work Ethic in Industrial America, 1850–1920* (Chicago, 1978). The tremendous growth of consumerism during the industrial period is treated in Daniel J. Boorstin, *The Americans: The Democratic Experience* (New York, 1973). On the department store as a "palace of consumption," see Gunther Barth, *City People: The Rise of Modern City Culture in Nineteenth-Century America* (New York, 1980).

For an examination of industrial growth on the urban

periphery, see Graham Romeyn Taylor, *Satellite Cities: A Study of Industrial Suburbs* (New York, 1915), and Stanley Buder, *Pullman: An Experiment in Industrial Order and Community Planning, 1880-1930* (New York, 1967). Many satellite cities ultimately were annexed by the larger central cities. For a good analysis of this annexation process, see Jon C. Teaford, *City and Suburb: The Political Fragmentation of Metropolitan America, 1850-1970* (Baltimore, 1979).

The urban booster tradition, particularly in the American West, is discussed in Daniel J. Boorstin, *The Americans: The National Experience* (New York, 1965); Glenn C. Quiett, *They Built the West: An Epic of Rails and Cities* (New York, 1934); John W. Reps, *Cities of the American West: A History of Frontier Urban Planning* (Princeton, N.J., 1979); Lawrence H. Larsen, *The Urban West at the End of the Frontier* (Lawrence, Kan., 1978); Gunther Barth, *Instant Cities: Urbanization and the Rise of San Francisco and Denver* (New York, 1975); and Bradford Luckingham, *The Urban Southwest: A Profile History of Albuquerque, El Paso, Phoenix, and Tucson* (El Paso, Tex., 1982). On the early booster spirit in Miami, see Sidney Walter Martin, *Florida's Flagler* (Athens, Ga., 1949).

During the past decade or so, Frederick Law Olmsted has been the subject of a vast outpouring of scholarship. Interested readers might begin with Olmsted's own classic statement on the place of parks in urban society: "Public Parks and the Enlargement of Towns," *Journal of Social Science*, 3 (1871). Three volumes of *The Papers of Frederick Law Olmsted* have been published to date by Johns Hopkins University Press (Baltimore, 1977-83), the third of which deals primarily with the beginnings of Central Park in New York City. Other volumes of Olmsted writings include Albert Fein, ed., *Landscape into Cityscape: Frederick Law Olmsted's Plans for a Greater New York City* (Ithaca, N.Y., 1967) and S. B. Sutton, ed., *Civilizing American Cities: A Selection of Frederick Law Olmsted's Writings on City Landscapes* (Cambridge, Mass., 1971). Two important biographies of Olmsted have also appeared: Laura Wood Roper, *FLO: A Biography of Frederick Law Olmsted* (Baltimore, 1973), and Elizabeth Stevenson, *Park Maker: A Life of Frederick Law Olmsted* (New York, 1977).

Other important Olmsted studies include Albert Fein, *Frederick Law Olmsted and the American Environmental Tradition* (New York, 1972); and Cynthia Zaitzevsky, *Frederick Law Olmsted and the Boston Park System* (Cambridge, Mass., 1982). For a general study of the urban park movement, see Galen Cranz, *The Politics of Park Design: A History of Urban Parks in America* (Cambridge, Mass., 1982).

The best study of Daniel H. Burnham is Thomas S. Hines, *Burnham of Chicago: Architect and Planner* (New York, 1974). For the 1893 Chicago World's Fair, see David F. Burg, *Chicago's White City of 1893* (Lexington, Ky., 1976), and R. Reid Badger, *The Great American Fair: The World's Columbian Exposition and American Culture* (Chicago, 1979). Burnham's Washington plan is discussed in John W. Reps, *Monumental Washington: The Planning and Development of the Capital Center* (Princeton, N.J., 1966). Burnham's San Francisco planning is analyzed in Judd Kahn, *Imperial San Francisco: Politics and Planning in an American City, 1897–1906* (Lincoln, Neb., 1979). The best source for the Chicago plan is Daniel H. Burnham and Edward H. Bennett, *Plan of Chicago* (Chicago, 1909). A good introduction to the city beautiful movement generally can be found in Mel Scott, *American City Planning Since 1890* (Berkeley, Calif., 1969), while William H. Wilson, *The City Beautiful Movement in Kansas City* (Columbia, Mo., 1964), provides a specific case study.

URBAN GOVERNMENT AND POLITICS

A massive literature has informed our understanding of American urban government and politics. Useful studies of early American city government include Ernest Griffith, *History of American City Government: The Colonial Period* (New York, 1938), and the more recent study by Jon C. Teaford, *The Municipal Revolution in America: Origins of Modern Urban*

Government, 1650–1825 (Chicago, 1975). For early 19th-century governmental patterns, see Charles R. Adrian and Ernest S. Griffith, *A History of American City Government: The Formation of Traditions, 1775–1870* (New York, 1976); Peter R. Gluck and Richard J. Meister, *Cities in Transition: Social Changes and Institutional Responses in Urban Development* (New York, 1979); and Edward K. Spann, *The New Metropolis: New York City, 1840–1857* (New York, 1981).

The gradual provision of municipal services in response to riots, fires, epidemics, and other crises in government can be traced in such representative books as Sam Bass Warner, *The Private City: Philadelphia in Three Periods of Its Growth* (Philadelphia, 1968); Roger Lane, *Policing the City: Boston, 1822–1885* (Cambridge, Mass., 1967); James F. Richardson, *The New York Police: Colonial Times to 1901* (New York, 1970); Robert M. Fogelson, *Big-City Police* (Cambridge, Mass., 1977); Nelson M. Blake, *Water for the Cities: A History of the Urban Water Supply Problem in the United States* (Syracuse, 1956); Raymond A. Mohl, *Poverty in New York, 1783–1825* (New York, 1971); and John Duffy, *A History of Public Health in New York City, 1625–1866* (New York, 1968). Two good studies examine the development of urban schooling in the early 19th century: Carl F. Kaestle, *The Evolution of an Urban School System: New York City, 1750–1850* (Cambridge, Mass., 1973), and Stanley K. Schultz, *The Culture Factory: Boston Public Schools, 1789–1860* (New York, 1973).

The city bosses and machines are the subject of a vast literature, ranging from the attacks of contemporary reformers and journalists to the scholarly works of recent historians. Early studies of the machines include two classic books: James Bryce, *The American Commonwealth* (New York, 1888), which has a good section on the Tweed ring; and Moisei Ostrogorski, *Democracy and the Organization of Political Parties* (New York, 1902). One of the most influential reformist attacks on machine government was made by Lincoln Steffens in *The Shame of the Cities* (New York, 1904).

The reinterpretation of the urban political machine began

with Robert K. Merton, *Social Theory and Social Structure* (New York, 1957). A more recent functional analysis is John M. Allswang, *Bosses, Machines, and Urban Voters: An American Symbiosis* (Port Washington, N.Y., 1977). For a study placing the rise of the machine in the larger context of urban government, see Ernest S. Griffith, *A History of American City Government, 1870-1900: The Conspicuous Failure* (New York, 1974). A recent study which effectively challenges the conspicuous failure thesis is Jon C. Teaford, *The Unheralded Triumph: City Government in America, 1870-1900* (Baltimore, 1984).

The Tweed ring has provided an endless source of fascination for students of urban history. A straightforward account can be found in Alexander B. Callow, Jr., *The Tweed Ring* (New York, 1966). Seymour Mandelbaum, *Boss Tweed's New York* (New York, 1965), interprets the boss as a central decision maker who used multiple office holding and payoffs to control the city government. Leo Hershkowitz, *Tweed's New York: Another Look* (New York, 1977), is an outright defense of Tweed as a great city builder. For Tammany's development after Tweed, see Martin Shefter, "The Electoral Foundations of the Political Machine: New York City, 1884-1897," in Joel H. Silbey et al., eds., *The History of American Electoral Behavior* (Princeton, N.J., 1978), pp. 263-98; Nancy Weiss, *Charles Francis Murphy, 1858-1924: Respectability and Responsibility in Tammany Politics* (Northampton, Mass., 1968); and Thomas M. Henderson, *Tammany Hall and the New Immigrants: The Progressive Years* (New York, 1976).

The connection between politics and sports is elaborated in Steven A. Riess, *Touching Base: Professional Baseball and American Culture in the Progressive Era* (Westport, Conn., 1980); and Stephen Hardy, *How Boston Played: Sport, Recreation, and Community, 1865-1915* (Boston, 1982). The links between politics, sports, and crime are suggested in Mark H. Haller, "Organized Crime in Urban Society: Chicago in the Twentieth Century," *Journal of Social History*, 5 (1971-72), pp. 210-234.

Studies of machine government in other cities, some from

the functionalist perspective, include Zane L. Miller, *Boss Cox's Cincinnati: Urban Politics in the Progressive Era* (New York, 1968); Lyle W. Dorsett, *The Pendergast Machine* (New York, 1968); William M. Maury, *Alexander "Boss" Shepherd and the Board of Public Works* (Washington, D.C., 1975); William A. Bullough, *The Blind Boss and His City: Christopher A. Buckley and 19th Century San Francisco* (Berkeley, Calif., 1979); Walton Bean, *Boss Ruef's San Francisco* (Berkeley, Calif., 1952); Joel A. Tarr, *A Study in Boss Politics: William Lorimer of Chicago* (Urbana, Ill., 1971); and John M. Allswang, *A House for All Peoples: Ethnic Politics in Chicago, 1890-1936* (Lexington, Ky., 1971).

On Baltimore's boss, Isaac F. Rasin, see James B. Crooks, *Politics and Progress: The Rise of Urban Progressivism in Baltimore, 1895 to 1911* (Baton Rouge, La., 1968). The best source for material on Martin Behrman of New Orleans is John R. Kemp, ed., *Martin Behrman of New Orleans: Memoirs of a City Boss* (Baton Rouge, La., 1977). Denver's Robert W. Speer is studied in Thomas J. Noel, *The City and the Saloon: Denver, 1858-1916* (Lincoln, Neb., 1982). For a debate among historians on the machine system, see Scott Greer, ed., *Ethnics, Machines, and the American Urban Future* (Cambridge, Mass., 1981). A good collection of essays is Bruce M. Stave and Sondra Astor Stave, eds., *Urban Bosses, Machines, and Progressive Reformers,* 2d. ed. (Malabar, Fla., 1984).

The urban reformers have also attracted considerable attention from historians. Richard Hofstadter, *The Age of Reform* (New York, 1955), portrayed the progressive reformers as middle class and politically conservative. This view was also argued in George E. Mowry, *The California Progressives* (Berkeley, Calif., 1951). Several historians have described urban reform as a movement of business and professional elites: Gabriel Kolko, *The Triumph of Conservatism: A Reinterpretation of American History, 1900-1916* (New York, 1963); James Weinstein, *The Corporate Ideal in the Liberal State, 1900-1918* (Boston, 1968); and Samuel P. Hays in several essays in *American Political History as Social Analysis* (Knoxville, Tenn., 1980).

An early attack on the Hofstadter middle-class reform interpretation can be found in J. Joseph Huthmacher, "Urban Liberalism and the Age of Reform," *Mississippi Valley Historical Review,* 49 (1962), 231–41. Huthmacher found the chief sources of urban liberalism among the working class and immigrant voters and their elected representatives. A full-scale development of this interpretation is John D. Buenker, *Urban Liberalism and Progressive Reform* (New York, 1973). Melvin G. Holli, *Reform in Detroit: Hazen S. Pingree and Urban Politics* (New York, 1969), distinguishes between structural reform and social reform. David P. Thelan, *The New Citizenship: Origins of Progressivism in Wisconsin, 1885–1900* (Columbia, Mo., 1972) sees progressive reform as a radical attack on corporate power that cut across traditional class, ethnic, and interest group barriers.

The link between urban politics and spatial changes in the industrial city is argued in Richard C. Wade, "Urbanization," in C. Vann Woodward, ed., *The Comparative Approach to American History* (New York, 1968), pp. 187–205. On ethnocultural and religious divisions as the basis of urban politics, two important studies are Richard J. Jensen, *The Winning of the Midwest: Social and Political Conflict, 1888–96* (Chicago, 1971), and Paul Kleppner, *The Cross of Culture: A Social Analysis of Midwestern Politics, 1850–1900* (New York, 1970).

An excellent study of the mugwumps is Gerald W. McFarland, *Mugwumps, Morals and Politics, 1884–1920* (Amherst, Mass., 1975), which links the mugwump reformers to the later progressive movement. The good government reform efforts of the late 19th century are the subject of William H. Tolman, *Municipal Reform Movements in the United States* (New York, 1895), and Clifford W. Patton, *The Battle for Municipal Reform: Mobilization and Attack, 1875–1900* (Washington, D.C., 1940). An important study of civil service reform is Ari Hoogenboom, *Outlawing the Spoils: A History of the Civil Service Reform Movement, 1865–1883* (Urbana, Ill., 1961).

Recent scholarly works on urban structural reform include Kenneth Fox, *Better City Government: Innovation in American*

Urban Politics, 1850–1937 (Philadelphia, 1977); Martin J. Schiesl, *The Politics of Efficiency: Municipal Administration and Reform in America, 1880–1920* (Berkeley, Calif., 1977); and Bradley R. Rice, *Progressive Cities: The Commission Government Movement in America, 1901–1920* (Austin, Tex., 1977). For case studies of two structural reformers, see Gerald Kurland, *Seth Low: The Reformer in an Urban and Industrial Age* (New York, 1971), and Edwin R. Lewinson, *John Purroy Mitchel: The Boy Mayor of New York* (New York, 1965). An overview of municipal government during the entire period can be found in Ernest S. Griffith, *A History of American City Government: The Progressive Years and Their Aftermath, 1900–1920* (New York, 1974).

Socialist reform in urban America is treated in Bruce M. Stave, ed., *Socialism and the Cities* (Port Washington, N.Y., 1975), and James Weinstein, *The Decline of Socialism in America, 1912–1925* (New York, 1969). For Milwaukee socialism, see Bayrd Still, *Milwaukee: The History of a City,* rev. ed. (Madison, Wis., 1965), and Sally M. Miller, *Victor Berger and the Promise of Constructive Socialism, 1910–1920* (Westport, Conn., 1973). On Morris Hillquit and socialism in New York City, see Norma Fain Pratt, *Morris Hillquit: A Political History of an American Jewish Socialist* (Westport, Conn., 1979).

The theme of moral reform runs strongly through Paul Boyer, *Urban Masses and Moral Order in America, 1820–1920* (Cambridge, Mass., 1978); James H. Timberlake, *Prohibition and the Progressive Movement, 1900–1920* (Cambridge, Mass., 1963); David J. Pivar, *Purity Crusade: Sexual Morality and Social Control, 1868–1900* (Westport, Conn., 1973); and Mark Thomas Connelly, *The Response to Prostitution in the Progressive Era* (Chapel Hill, N.C., 1980). Two recent studies with good insights on moral reform are Perry Duis, *The Saloon: Public Drinking in Chicago and Boston, 1880–1920* (Urbana, Ill., 1983) and Roy Rosenzweig, *Eight Hours for What We Will: Workers and Leisure in an Industrial City, 1870–1920* (Cambridge, England, 1983).

Recent historians are beginning to examine the distribution

and use of political power in the industrial city. Two major studies are Carl V. Harris, *Political Power in Birmingham, 1871-1921* (Knoxville, Tenn., 1977), and David C. Hammack, *Power and Society: Greater New York at the Turn of the Century* (New York, 1982). Related studies of elites, power, and political decision-making are Eugene J. Watts, *The Social Bases of City Politics: Atlanta, 1865-1903* (Westport, Conn., 1978); and Frederic Cople Jaher, *The Urban Establishment: Upper Strata in Boston, New York, Charleston, Chicago, and Los Angeles* (Urbana, Ill., 1982).

CITY AND SOCIETY

Modernization theory provides the theoretical framework for the writings of Robert H. Wiebe and Samuel P. Hays. Among the most important of these are Robert H. Wiebe's *The Search for Order, 1877-1920* (New York, 1967) and *The Segmented Society: An Historical Preface to the Meaning of America* (New York, 1975); and Samuel P. Hays's *The Response to Industrialism, 1885-1914* (Chicago, 1957) and *American Political History as Social Analysis* (Knoxville, Tenn., 1980). Also useful is Richard D. Brown, *Modernization: The Transformation of American Life, 1600-1865* (New York, 1976). A good discussion of modernization theory and its application can be found in Thomas Bender, *Community and Social Change in America* (New Brunswick, N.J., 1978).

The economic and social dislocations of the late 19th century are the subject of an extensive literature. A good beginning is the collection of essays on the three big depressions of the period by Samuel Rezneck, *Business Depressions and Financial Panics: Essays in American Business and Economic History* (Westport, Conn., 1968). Other useful studies are Paul T. Ringenbach, *Tramps and Reformers, 1873-1916: The Discovery of Unemployment in New York* (Westport, Conn., 1973); Florence Peterson, *Strikes in the United States, 1880-1936* (Washington, D.C., 1938); and Jerry M. Cooper, *The Army and*

Civil Disorder: Federal Military Intervention in Labor Disputes, 1877-1900 (Westport, Conn., 1980). On social disorder in progressive America, representative studies include Kenneth T. Jackson, *The Ku Klux Klan in the City, 1915-1930* (New York, 1967); David Allan Levine, *Internal Combustion: The Races in Detroit, 1915-1926* (Westport, Conn., 1976); and William M. Tuttle, Jr., *Race Riot: Chicago in the Red Summer of 1919* (New York, 1970).

Two recent studies of urban crime and disorder contend that rates of murder and violent crime declined in the late 19th century, as labor violence began to supplant the interethnic conflict of midcentury, and as blacks and white ethnic groups became more separated spatially. See Roger Lane, *Violent Death in the City: Suicide, Accident, and Murder in Nineteenth-Century Philadelphia* (Cambridge, Mass., 1979), and John C. Schneider, *Detroit and the Problem of Order, 1830-1880* (Lincoln, Neb., 1980).

The best study of cataclysmic thinking is Frederic Cople Jaher, *Doubters and Dissenters: Cataclysmic Thought in America, 1885-1918* (New York, 1964). Also useful are Martin Ridge, *Ignatius Donnelly: The Portrait of a Politician* (Chicago, 1962), and Eric H. Monkkonen, *The Dangerous Class: Crime and Poverty in Columbus, Ohio, 1860-1885* (Cambridge, Mass., 1975).

Social control theories have shaped numerous recent studies of social welfare and educational history. Important books on late 19th-century social welfare which advance the idea of charity as social control include: Roy Lubove, *The Professional Altruist: The Emergence of Social Work as a Career, 1880-1930* (Cambridge, Mass., 1965); Blanche D. Coll, *Perspectives in Public Welfare: A History* (Washington, D.C., 1969); Hace Sorel Tishler, *Self-Reliance and Social Security, 1870-1917* (Port Washington, N.Y., 1971); and Nathan I. Huggins, *Protestants Against Poverty: Boston's Charities, 1870-1900* (Westport, Conn., 1971). For a debate among social welfare historians on the merits of the social control thesis, see Walter I.

Trattner, ed., *Social Welfare or Social Control?* (Knoxville, Tenn., 1983). Social welfare historiography is also discussed in Raymond A. Mohl, "Mainstream Social Welfare History and Its Problems," *Reviews in American History,* 7 (1979), pp. 469–76.

On the work of the settlement houses in the cities, begin with Allen F. Davis, *Spearheads for Reform: The Social Settlements and the Progressive Movement, 1890–1914* (New York, 1967). Other studies include Davis's biography of Jane Addams, *American Heroine: The Life and Legend of Jane Addams* (New York, 1974), and Louise C. Wade, *Graham Taylor: Pioneer for Social Justice, 1851–1938* (Chicago, 1964).

The past decade and a half has witnessed an outpouring of revisionist scholarship on the history of urban education. The most useful studies include Michael B. Katz, *Class, Bureaucracy, and Schools: The Illusion of Educational Change in America,* rev. ed. (New York, 1975); Marvin Lazerson, *Origins of the Urban School: Public Education in Massachusetts, 1870–1915* (Cambridge, Mass., 1971); Joel Spring, *Education and the Rise of the Corporate State* (Boston, 1972); David B. Tyack, *The One Best System: A History of American Urban Education* (Cambridge, Mass., 1974); Meyer Weinberg, *A Chance to Learn: A History of Race and Education in the United States* (Cambridge, England, 1977); Paul C. Violas, *The Training of the Urban Working Class* (Chicago, 1978); and Ronald D. Cohen and Raymond A. Mohl, *The Paradox of Progressive Education: The Gary Plan and Urban Schooling* (Port Washington, N.Y., 1979).

The theoretical underpinnings of the playground movement are illuminated in Dominick Cavallo, *Muscles and Morals: Organized Playgrounds and Urban Reform, 1880–1920* (Philadelphia, 1981). On various aspects of juvenile reform and child saving, see Joseph M. Hawes, *Children in Urban Society: Juvenile Delinquency in Nineteenth-Century America* (New York, 1971); Robert M. Mennel, *Thorns and Thistles: Juvenile Delinquents in the United States, 1825–1940* (Hanover, N.H., 1973);

and Stephen Schlossman, *Love and the American Delinquent: The Theory and Practice of 'Progressive' Juvenile Justice, 1825-1920* (Chicago, 1977).

A good introduction to the Social Darwinist thinking of the industrial era can be found in Richard Hofstadter, *Social Darwinism in American Thought* (Philadelphia, 1944). A recent reexamination of the subject is Robert C. Bannister, *Social Darwinism: Science and Myth in Anglo-American Social Thought* (Philadelphia, 1979). The intellectual challenge to evolutionary thought and to classical economic theory is traced in Morton White, *Social Thought in America: The Revolt Against Formalism* (New York, 1949). Eric F. Goldman, *Rendezvous with Destiny: A History of Modern American Reform* (New York, 1956), presents a broad interpretation of the crusade for social and environmental reform—for reform Darwinism.

The classic works of Henry George, Edward Bellamy, and Jacob Riis still repay careful reading. Excellent recent studies of these early environmental thinkers include John L. Thomas, *Alternative America: Henry George, Edward Bellamy, Henry Demarest Lloyd and the Adversary Tradition* (Cambridge, Mass., 1983), and James B. Lane, *Jacob A. Riis and the American City* (Port Washington, N.Y., 1974). On the muckrakers, see Louis Filler, *The Muckrakers: Crusaders for American Liberalism* (University Park, Pa., 1976), and David M. Chalmers, *The Social and Political Ideas of the Muckrakers* (New York, 1964). For the social gospel movement, begin with Robert D. Cross, ed., *The Church and the City, 1865-1910* (Indianapolis, 1967).

The best introduction to the realistic and reformist fiction of the progressive era remains the novels themselves. The best and most interesting include Upton Sinclair, *The Jungle* (New York, 1906); Stephen Crane, *Maggie: A Girl of the Streets* (New York, 1896); Frank Norris, *McTeague* (New York, 1899) and *The Pit* (New York, 1903); Theodore Dreiser, *Sister Carrie* (New York, 1900), *The Financier* (New York, 1912), and *The Titan* (New York, 1914); Ernest Poole, *The Voice of the Street* (New

York, 1906) and *The Harbor* (New York, 1915). A good analysis of the urban theme in 20th-century American fiction can be found in Blanche H. Gelfant, *The American City Novel* (Norman, Okla., 1954). Other critical studies of realism in American literature include Walter B. Rideout, *The Radical Novel in the United States, 1900–1954* Cambridge, Mass., 1956); David M. Fine, *The City, The Immigrant and American Fiction, 1880–1920* (Metuchen, N.J., 1977); and Park Dixon Goist, *From Main Street to State Street: Town, City, and Community in America* (Port Washington, N.Y., 1977). The new realism in art and illustration is analyzed in Robert H. Bremner, *From the Depths: The Discovery of Poverty in the United States* (New York, 1956).

Important studies on public health and sanitary reform include Martin V. Melosi, ed., *Pollution and Reform in American Cities, 1870–1930* (Austin, Tex., 1980); Louis P. Cain, *Sanitation Strategy for a Lakefront Metropolis: The Case of Chicago* (De Kalb, Ill., 1978); Martin V. Melosi, *Garbage in the Cities: Refuse, Reform, and the Environment, 1880–1980* (College Station, Tex., 1982); and Judith Walzer Leavitt, *The Healthiest City: Milwaukee and the Politics of Health Reform* (Princeton, N.J., 1982).

The housing movement generated a substantial contemporary literature of reform, as well as more recent historical analysis. Roy Lubove, *The Progressives and the Slums: Tenement House Reform in New York City, 1890–1917* (Pittsburgh, 1962), is an excellent piece of historical research. Other recent studies include Anthony Jackson, *A Place Called Home: A History of Low-Cost Housing in Manhattan* (Cambridge, Mass., 1976); Thomas L. Philpott, *The Slum and the Ghetto: Neighborhood Deterioration and Middle-Class Reform, Chicago, 1880–1930* (New York, 1978); and Gwendolyn Wright, *Building the Dream: A Social History of Housing in America* (New York, 1981).

On the history of planning in the United States, the following studies are especially useful: Mel Scott, *American City Planning since 1890* (Berkeley, Calif., 1969); John W. Reps, *The*

Making of Urban America: A History of City Planning in the United States (Princeton, N.J., 1965); and Donald A. Krueckeberg, ed., *Introduction to Planning History in the United States* (New Brunswick, N.J., 1983). The garden city idea is treated in Daniel Schaffer, *Garden Cities for America: The Radburn Experience* (Philadelphia, 1982). Anthony Sutcliffe, *Towards the Planned City: Germany, Britain, the United States and France, 1780-1914* (Oxford, 1981), compares American planning developments with those in Europe.

A varied and growing literature is beginning to lay out the full dimensions of the communal response to industrial America. The fullest elaboration of the antimodernism theme can be found in Jackson Lears, *No Place of Grace: Antimodernism and the Transformation of American Culture, 1880-1920* (New York, 1981). For the handicraft and decorative arts movement, see Robert J. Clark, *The Arts and Crafts Movement in America, 1876-1916* (Princeton, N.J., 1972).

The reformist critique of industrial capitalism espoused by the National Labor Union and the Knights of Labor has been discussed in several studies in late-19th-century labor history. The best of these are Gerald N. Grob, *Workers and Utopia: A Study of Ideological Conflict in the American Labor Movement, 1865-1900* (Evanston, Ill., 1961); David Montgomery, *Beyond Equality: Labor and the Radical Republicans, 1862-1872* (New York, 1967); and Milton Derber, *The American Idea of Industrial Democracy, 1865-1965* (Urbana, Ill., 1970).

New approaches to the study of working-class culture were initiated by E. P. Thompson's innovative *The Making of the English Working Class* (London, 1963). Studies of American workers pursuing this line of analysis include Herbert G. Gutman, *Work, Culture, and Society in Industrializing America* (New York, 1976); and David Montgomery, *Workers' Control in America: Studies in the History of Work, Technology, and Labor Struggles* (Cambridge, England, 1979). Two excellent collections of articles and essays from the perspective of the new working-class history are Milton Cantor, ed., *American Workingclass Culture: Explorations in American Labor and*

Social History (Westport, Conn., 1979), and Michael H. Frisch and Daniel J. Walkowitz, eds., *Working-Class America: Essays on Labor, Community, and American Society* (Urbana, Ill., 1983).

The new interest in working-class social history has resulted in a number of important case studies of industrial communities. Among the most useful are Daniel J. Walkowitz, *Worker City, Company Town: Iron and Cotton-Worker Protest in Troy and Cohoes, New York, 1855–84* (Urbana, Ill., 1978); Alan Dawley, *Class and Community: The Industrial Revolution in Lynn* (Cambridge, Mass., 1978); John T. Cumbler, *Working-Class Community in Industrial America: Work, Leisure, and Struggle in Two Industrial Cities, 1880–1930* (Westport, Conn., 1979); Theodore Hershberg, *Philadelphia: Work, Space, Family, and Group Experience in the 19th Century* (New York, 1981).

In recent years, historians of immigration and ethnicity have revised earlier interpretations about the pervasive nature of the assimilation process. The ethnic parish was particularly important in maintaining ethnic subcultures in the United States. Important studies of the religious dimension of ethnicity include Jay P. Dolan, *The Immigrant Church: New York's Irish and German Catholics, 1815–1865* (Baltimore, 1975); Victor Greene, *For God and Country: The Rise of Polish and Lithuanian Ethnic Consciousness in America* (Madison, Wis., 1975); Silvano Tomasi, *Piety and Power: The Role of Italian Parishes in the New York Metropolitan Area* (New York, 1975); and Randall M. Miller and Thomas D. Marzik, eds., *Immigrants and Religion in Urban America* (Philadelphia, 1977). On immigrants and schooling, see John Bodnar, "Materialism and Morality: Slavic-American Immigrants and Education, 1890–1940," *Journal of Ethnic Studies,* 3 (1976), pp. 1–19; James W. Sanders, *The Education of an Urban Minority: Catholics in Chicago, 1833–1965* (New York, 1977); and Selwyn K. Troen, *The Public and the Schools: Shaping the System in St. Louis, 1838–1920* (Columbia, Mo., 1975).

Some of the most exciting research in ethnic history has focused on the reconstitution of old country communities in the

American industrial city. Rudolph J. Vecoli has pioneered this research in several important articles: *"Contadini* in Chicago: A Critique of *The Uprooted,"* *Journal of American History,* 51 (1964), pp. 404–16; "Prelates and Peasants: Italian Immigrants and the Catholic Church," *Journal of Social History,* 2 (1969), pp. 217–68; "The Formation of Chicago's 'Little Italies,'" *Journal of American Ethnic History,* 2 (1983), pp. 5–20. John Bodnar's article, "Immigration and Modernization: The Case of Slavic Peasants in Industrial America," *Journal of Social History,* 4 (1976), pp. 44–71, suggests that modernization represented a synthesis between the old culture and the new.

Monographic studies of immigrant groups have proliferated in recent years. Among the best are John W. Briggs, *An Italian Passage: Immigrants to Three American Cities, 1890–1930* (New Haven, 1978); Josef J. Barton, *Peasants and Strangers: Italians, Rumanians, and Slovaks in an American City, 1890–1950* (Cambridge, Mass., 1975); John Bodnar, *Immigration and Industrialization: Ethnicity in an American Mill Town, 1870–1940* (Pittsburgh, 1977); Caroline Golab, *Immigrant Destinations* (Philadelphia, 1977); William M. DeMarco, *Ethnics and Enclaves: Boston's Italian North End* (Ann Arbor, Mich., 1981); Dino Cinel, *From Italy to San Francisco: The Immigrant Experience* (Stanford, Calif., 1982); John Bodnar et al., *Lives of Their Own: Blacks, Italians, and Poles in Pittsburgh, 1900–1960* (Urbana, Ill, 1982); and Olivier Zunz, *The Changing Face of Inequality: Urbanization, Industrial Development, and Immigrants in Detroit, 1880–1920* (Chicago, 1982).

Along with ethnic culture, the family served as a custodian of tradition in the industrial world. For a good sampling of the new family history, see Virginia Yans-McLaughlin, *Family and Community: Italian Immigrants in Buffalo 1880–1930* (Ithaca, N.Y., 1977); Tamara K. Hareven, *Family Time and Industrial Time: The Relationship between the Family and Work in a New England Industrial Community* (Cambridge, England, 1982); and Richard Sennett, *Families Against the City: Middle Class*

Homes of Industrial Chicago, 1872–1890 (Cambridge, Mass., 1970).

On the black family, the standard work is Herbert G. Gutman, *The Black Family in Slavery and Freedom, 1750–1925* (New York, 1976). Other important studies touching on black family life in the northern urban ghettoes include Gilbert Osofsky, *Harlem: The Making of a Ghetto* (New York, 1966); Allan H. Spear, *Black Chicago: The Making of a Negro Ghetto, 1890–1920* (Chicago, 1967); David M. Katzman, *Before the Ghetto: Black Detroit in the Nineteenth Century* (Urbana, Ill., 1973); Kenneth L. Kusmer, *A Ghetto Takes Shape: Black Cleveland, 1870–1930* (Urbana, Ill., 1976); James Borchert, *Alley Life in Washington: Family, Community, Religion, and Folklife in the City, 1850–1970* (Urbana, Ill., 1980); Vincent P. Franklin, *The Education of Black Philadelphia: The Social and Educational History of a Minority Community, 1900–1950* (Philadelphia, 1979); Elizabeth Hafkin Pleck, *Black Migration and Poverty: Boston, 1865–1900* (New York, 1979). Discussing both black and immigrant families is Carl N. Degler, *At Odds: Women and the Family in America from the Revolution to the Present* (New York, 1980).

THE TWENTIETH-CENTURY CITY

Good historical studies of urban America after the 1920s include Blake McKelvey, *The Emergence of Metropolitan America, 1915–1966* (New Brunswick, N.J., 1968); William H. Wilson, *Coming of Age: Urban America, 1915–1945* (New York, 1974); George E. Mowry and Blaine A. Brownell, *The Urban Nation, 1920–1980* (New York, 1981); and Mark I. Gelfand, *A Nation of Cities: The Federal Government and Urban America, 1933–1965* (New York, 1975). Placing American urban developments in a global and comparative perspective is Brian J. L. Berry, *Comparative Urbanization: Divergent Paths in the Twentieth Century* (New York, 1981).

On the growing sunbelt cities of the South and Southwest, see Carl Abbott, *The New Urban America: Growth and Politics in Sunbelt Cities* (Chapel Hill, N.C., 1981), and Richard M. Bernard and Bradley R. Rice, eds., *Sunbelt Cities: Politics and Growth since World War II* (Austin, Tex., 1983). For what the future might hold for the American city, the following are especially interesting: President's Commission for a National Agenda for the Eighties, *Urban America in the Eighties: Perspectives and Prospects* (Washington, D.C., 1980); Arthur P. Solomon, ed., *The Prospective City: Economic, Population, Energy, and Environmental Developments* (Cambridge, Mass., 1980); and Gary Gappert and Richard V. Knight, eds., *Cities in the 21st Century* (Beverly Hills, Calif., 1982).

For further guidance through the vast and still growing literature on American urban history, the following may be useful: Raymond A. Mohl., "The History of the American City," in William H. Cartwright and Richard L. Watson, eds., *The Reinterpretation of American History and Culture* (Washington, D.C., 1973), pp. 165–205; Kathleen Neils Conzen, "Community Studies, Urban History, and American Local History," in Michael Kammen, ed., *The Past Before Us: Contemporary Historical Writing in the United States* (Ithaca, N.Y., 1980), pp. 270–91; and Raymond A. Mohl, "The New Urban History and Its Alternatives," *Urban History Yearbook* (1983), pp. 19–28.

Important new reference guides to urban history bibliography include John D. Buenker et al., eds., *Urban History: A Guide to Information Sources* (Detroit, 1981); Barbara Smith Shearer and Benjamin F. Shearer, eds., *Periodical Literature on United States Cities: A Bibliography and Subject Guide* (Westport, Conn., 1983); and Neil L. Shumsky and Timothy Crimmins, eds., *Urban America: A Historical Bibliography* (Santa Barbara, Calif., 1983).

INDEX